AND STILL THEY DANCE

AND STILL THEY DANCE

Women, War, and the Struggle for Change in Mozambique

Stephanie Urdang

Monthly Review Press
New York

Photo Credits:

Map: Mozambique Information Office, London. *Introduction:* Women refugees from area recaptured by Mozambique army, Zambezia province. Mozambique Information Agency/Sergio Santinamo. *Chapter 1:* Zora traditional dance, Inhambane province. Mozambique Information Agency/ Anders Nilsson. *Chapter 2:* Women working in the cooperative fields of their communal village, Gaza province. Stephanie Urdang. *Chapter 3:* Home is underneath a box car, Moatize refugee camp, Tete province. Mozambique Information Agency/Anders Nilsson. *Chapter 4:* Gilda Mohlanga driving a tractor, Moamba state farm. Stephanie Urdang. *Chapter 5:* Mama Leia (right) with member of the People's Assembly with manioc from Mama Leia's field. Stephanie Urdang. *Chapter 6:* Green Zone cooperative, Maputo. Mozambique Information Agency/Joel Chiziane. *Chapter 7:* CIM factory worker. Stephanie Urdang. *Chapter 8:* Day care center for workers' children, Maputo. Stephanie Urdang. *Chapter 9:* An Operation Production evacuee from Maputo in Niassa province. Stephanie Urdang. *Chapter 10:* Women share a joke about polygamy at a meeting in Gaza province. Stephanie Urdang. *Chapter 11:* Literacy exam, Gaza communal village. Stephanie Urdang. *Chapter 12:* Lina Magaia (center) at Três de Fevereiro Village, Gaza. Stephanie Urdang.

Library of Congress Cataloging-in-Publication Data
Urdang, Stephanie.
  And still they dance: women, war, and the struggle
for change in Mozambique / Stephanie Urdang.
  p. cm.
  Bibliography: p.
  Includes index.
  ISBN 0-85345-772-7 : $28.00.   ISBN 0-85345-773-5 (pbk.) : $12.00
  1. Women—Mozambique—Social conditions. 2. Women—Mozambique-
-Economic conditions. 3. Women—Employment—Mozambique. 4. Women
in development—Mozambique.   I. Title.
HQ1799.U73 1989
305.4'0967'9—dc19   29068
                                                                CIP

Monthly Review Press
122 West 27th Street
New York, N.Y. 10001

Manufactured in the United States of America

10 9 8 7 6 5 4 3 2 1

For Lina's daughters, Sonyka and Saqina,
and all the children of Mozambique—
may they yet see the vision realized.

Contents

Acknowledgments   9
Map   12
Prologue   13
Introduction: Equality, Development, Peace   20

1. And Still They Dance   32
2. Village Under Siege   46
3. Harvest of Bitterness   64
4. Rural Development Policy   90
5. Transforming the Countryside   110
6. Contradiction and Change   131
7. Women in the Factories and at Home   151
8. Outside the New Family   171
9. Operation Production   186
10. Fighting Polygamy and Lobolo   200
11. Beyond the Family   220
12. A Decade in Women's Lives   235

Notes   245
Selected Reading   249
Index   253

Acknowledgments

The year of my first visit to Mozambique—1980—was the year the South African government began its first direct attacks on Mozambique. Their targets, unlike those of the rebel bandits they supported, included specific people, and two of them, both exiled white South Africans, members of the outlawed African National Congress, were my friends.

The bomb for Ruth First was sent by letter, to the Center for African Studies at the University of Eduardo Mondlane, Maputo. It exploded, killing her, when she opened her mail on August 17, 1982. I met Ruth for the first time in Mozambique, when I arrived at the center where she was research director. She warmly welcomed me, generously putting whatever material I needed at my disposal. I remember feeling very ambivalent about her offer to comment on my work. I found her intimidating, although this feeling lessened as I got to know her a little better, and I was worried that my work would not live up to her exacting standard.

The bomb for Albie Sachs exploded when he opened his car door on April 8 this year, ironically Mozambican Women's Day, a national holiday. He lost an arm but he survived, along with his determined spirit. I knew Albie in Cape Town before he went into exile, and meeting him again in Mozambique was the beginning of a good friendship. On my visit last year, he was a particularly appreciated source of information and support and we talked at length about the changes that had come about in my absence.

During the months I spent in Mozambique over a period of seven years, I made many close friends, friendships that grew out of the unique circumstances of living and working in a country with which we felt such solidarity. Most were women, women with whom I laughed, talked, discussed, obsessed, and exchanged experiences and observations. Some gave critical comments on

9

my drafts. Judith Marshall gave me a room to stay and work, and much more; the months that I lived with her helped my understanding significantly. On my most recent visit my friend Rebecca Reiss filled the same role, helping me with her mixture of humor and good judgment through the shock of returning after a break that coincided with the escalation of terrorist activities. Teresa Smart traveled with me in 1983 to the north and the south, as interpreter and co-worker, providing her own invaluable insights and impressions. Among others are Signe Arnfred, Sam Barnes, Merle Bowen, Julie Cliff, Polly Gaster, Linda Goodacre, Judith Head, Maureen Mackintosh, and Linzi Manicom. These are friends for a lifetime.

My two interpreters were Anastaçia Guimerães who works for the national office of the Organization of Mozambican Women (OMM) in their foreign affairs department, and Lina Magaia, journalist and head of the agricultural development program for Manhiça district, Gaza province. They are both special people, as the pages that follow testify. Both the OMM and OMM secretary-general Salome Moiane went to great lengths to support this long project, coming through with transport and interpreters even when their own work suffered as a result. Thank you.

In New York, Barbara Barnes inspired me to write this book soon after her return from working in Mozambique. Many others supported my work—reading chapters, providing information and analysis from their own work and perspectives. I am particularly grateful to Rob Davies, Joe Hanlon, Allen Isaacman, Barbara (Bobby) Isaacman, Bill Minter, Dan O'Meara, Otto Roesch, and John Saul.

I want to thank Brian Holmes for taking on a patently unfair share of child care, both in New York and when I traveled to Mozambique last year. He deserves extra credit for having weathered living with a writer who, when under duress and deadlines, can be less than pleasant. Karen Judd, my editor at Monthly Review, is the editor every writer should get: she was able to draw out a much stronger draft from the one I first produced with tact, patience and humor that left no room for defensiveness on my part, only sincere gratitude.

Finally, this project would have been impossible without the funding I got from a number of sources. A generous grant from the Ford Foundation covered a major portion of the research in the field and the writing of the book. Other essential grants came from

Carol and W.H. Ferry, whose support for my work from my first trip to Guinea-Bissau to my most recent trip to Mozambique always came with encouragement and personal concern for the issues I was researching. Additional funding came from the Funding Exchange, United Methodist Committee of Relief, and the United Methodist Church, Women's Division.

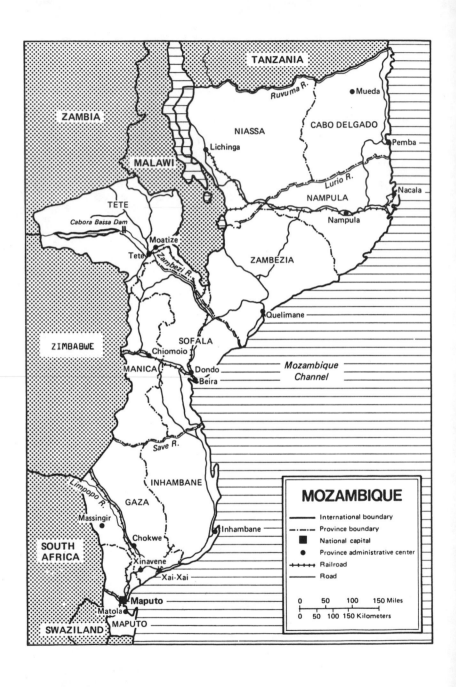

TANZANIA

Ruvuma R.

ZAMBIA

● Mueda

NIASSA

CABO DELGADO

Lichinga

● Pemba

MALAWI

Lurio R.

Nacala

TETE

NAMPULA

Cabora Bassa Dam

Moatize

Nampula

Tete

Zambezi R.

ZAMBEZIA

ZIMBABWE

Quelimane

SOFALA

Mozambique Channel

Chiomoio

MANICA

Dondo

Beira

Save R.

INHAMBANE

Limpopo R.

GAZA

Massingir

● Inhambane

Chokwe

SOUTH AFRICA

Xinavene

Xai-Xai

Maputo

MOZAMBIQUE

——————— International boundary
—·—·—·— Province boundary
■ National capital
● Province administrative center
+‍+‍+‍+‍+ Railroad
——————— Road

0   50   100   150 Miles
0 50 100 150 Kilometers

Matola

SWAZILAND

MAPUTO

Prologue

In Mueda, high up in the plateau area of northern Cabo Delgaldo province, peasants successfully organized a 3,000-member agricultural cooperative in the mid 1950s. It was a profitable co-op and gave its members, who were exempt from forced labor on the sisal plantations, unique independence and control over their work. But it did more than this; it developed political consciousness. When on June 16, 1960, the provincial governor paid a visit to the area, a large and peaceful crowd gathered outside the administrative building to protest his presence. The governor invited the leaders inside. When they emerged after four hours, the governor asked if anyone wanted to speak out. Many did. They moved to the side as told and were promptly bound and beaten by the police. When the horrified crowd began to surge forward, the would-be speakers were whisked into vans and driven off. The furor became intense. The governors ordered troops to open fire. Point-blank they trained their rifles on the crowd of unarmed civilians. When the shooting finally stopped, 600 were dead. Many more lay wounded.

It was a tough lesson, one well learned. More than any other single event, it showed that independence could not come peacefully to Mozambique. Within two years the Front for the Liberation of Mozambique (Frelimo) was founded, forging three separate organizations into one, under the leadership of Eduardo Mondlane, a key figure in the process.

"Mozambican people!" declared the Central Committee of Frelimo on September 25, 1964, four years after the Mueda massacre, "in the name of all of you, Frelimo today solemnly proclaims the General Armed Insurrection of the Mozambican people against Portuguese colonialism for the attainment of the complete independence of Mozambique."[1] The "general armed insurrection" was planned to begin in four provinces. In fact, only the one in the zone of Chai, Cabo Delgado, was successful: an attack by twelve Frelimo guerrillas on the Portuguese administration headquarters left eight Portuguese dead. The operation itself was minor, but it sparked a process that signaled the beginning of the end of colonial rule.

In Portugal's so-called African territories, the colonial era was marked by a particular brutality. Portugal looked at Mozambique and saw little more than a pliable mass of uncivilized people who could provide the cheap labor essential to building Portugal's weak economy. They imposed a tax on every family as one source of income. But cheap labor was the crux of the system, and forced labor—the dreaded *chibalo*, as it was widely known—was implemented. Men and women were forcibly recruited for periods of up to two years. Pay was a pittance when it was there at all. Any pretext was used to pull in the laborers, who found themselves ordered to work settler plantations, build roads, work as servants. No food was provided. No clothing. The roads were built primarily by women, who were ordered to bring their own tools and when they did not, dug the hard earth with their fingers at gunpoint. Rape was common. So was the whipping of men and women who did not perform as told, or whose exhaustion made them falter.

When Antonio Salazar—the man synonymous with fascism in Portugal—came to power in 1928, the metropole's essential textile industry was in trouble: of the 17,000 tons of raw cotton needed each year, only 800 tons were produced in the colonies. Importing the rest ate into profits and drained the economy. What better way to remedy this than to make those African peasants grow it for them? And so to forced labor was added forced production: families were forced to grow cotton and then sell their harvests at far below market value. It was disaster for the peasants, who had to sacrifice crop fields to cotton, and who did not have enough time left over to grow enough food for their families. Hunger and famine became widespread.

Each step of the way was regulated: when to plant, when to reseed, the number of times a field had to be weeded, the dates of the final harvest; and each step of the way was overseen by the dreaded *sipais*—the African police who worked for the Portuguese state and were particularly vicious—as well as the state-approved chiefs and local administrators. If peasants refused to cultivate cotton they were arrested, put in chains, beaten, and often exiled for a few years to São Tome, a small colonized island off the west coast of Africa. If they failed to produce the mandated minimum they were sent to work in forced-labor gangs to build railways, roads, and other state projects. If farmers were found to have sown only a portion of the demarcated area, the *sipais* whipped them, and when the farmers were women, and they often were, they regularly resorted to rape. Even after the forced production was legally brought to an end, little changed. Peasants were still forced to grow cotton.

Not all the peasants buckled under. They resisted in whatever way they could, from cooking the seeds before going through the motions of cultivation to show that cotton could not be grown on that piece of land, to burning warehouses, to fleeing, to covertly withholding labor. Cotton more than anything else probably served to mobilize the peasants behind Frelimo. Samora Machel described his own political education as beginning "not from reading Marx and Engels, but from seeing my father forced to grow cotton for the Portuguese and going with him to the market where he was forced to sell it at a low price—much lower than the white Portuguese growers."[2]

A Cabo Delgado peasant turned Frelimo activist remembered well the hardships. One time, when he lay ill in his hut, a group of *sipais* entered and beat him severely because he had not finished planting his cotton field. One of his attackers then brutally raped his wife. Unable to comfort her, he was bound and taken away to a sisal plantation where he was forced to work a strip of land each day. Still ill, he could not produce what was demanded. Again he was beaten. The laborers received food once a day and only if they had completed the day's quota. And then, hungry, they would take a spoon of the evening corn meal porridge and find themselves chewing sand and pulp. Many workers died.[3]

For the Portuguese it was an effective system. Within just seven years enough cotton was brought into Portugal from its colonies to fulfill the needs of the textile industry. So pleased were the colonialists by the results that they expanded the program to rice and then to peanuts, which could be grown on land unsuitable for cotton.

There was no relief in sight. Forced labor and forced production were a systemic part of colonial rule. The peasant farmers, some 90 percent of the Mozambican population, had little to look forward to other than back- (and mind-) breaking work to satisfy the rapacious settlers. They could not send their children to school as no schools were provided. It was the exception who made it to the missionary schools, and those were often no more than centers for exploited labor. Health services were limited and who had the money to pay for them? And what was there to eat? Cotton?

. . .Those strange times
    Which stormed existence
    And eroded
    The hopes for a new life
    Leaving behind
    The blackness of anguish

    Those strange times
    Which shrouded the Mother Earth
    Killing hope
    And sowing despair

    Those strange times
    When the whip hissed
    And tore
    A man's living flesh
    Raising a cry of rage
    —inert rage

    . . . .

    Those strange times
    Times of dense shadows
    Times of anguish
    Times of humiliation
    Times of inert rage
    Those times have vanished defeated

    This is a time of the certainty of a joyful day
    This is a time of war against rottenness
    This is a time of revolt against the whip
    This is the time of armed struggle.

                    —Armando Guebuza[4]

Those "strange times" could not last. The Portuguese rulers might have believed they could hold on to their colonies ad infinitum, but the colonized decided otherwise. Inspiration came, in part, from countries to the west and north of Mozambique, where independence groups sat down to negotiate independence with their British and French colonial masters. The masters saw the writing on the wall and decided to withdraw while the going was good. To withdraw without struggle meant that a firm hold could be kept on the economies of their former colonies, and the age of neocolonialism dawned. Mozambicans began to organize their own movements to pressure Portugal into similar negotiation.

Portugal had other ideas. The economy was so dependent on the exploitation of its colonies—most particularly Mozambique and Angola—that the Portuguese were in no position to simply withdraw. The violence with which the colonizers were willing to respond to a challenge to their authority was made more than clear at Mueda. But it was a violence that ultimately could not contain the force of Frelimo as it rallied the people of Mozambique to its side and became the embodiment of the people's will to be liberated. It kept in motion an armed struggle that liberated about one-third of the country; that set in motion the beginnings of a new society based on democratic, socialist principles; that mobilized large numbers of Mozambicans who adopted Frelimo's policies as their own cause; that built schools and health posts and child-care centers; that focused on the need for a new Mozambican whose newly developed political consciousness encompassed the liberation of women. And it was an event that set in motion an armed struggle that eleven years later ended at the negotiating table in Lusaka. But it did more than liberate Mozambique.

"The 25th of September—mark it," said Eduardo Mondlane in early 1969. "That day may well go down as one of the most important in the history of Africa—not just Mozambique. Our struggle is more than one nation. It is the beginning of the liberation of southern Africa, and who knows, it may yet lead to the liberation of Portugal itself."[5] On February 3, 1969, a few days after these prophetic words were spoken, Eduardo Mondlane was assassinated when a parcel bomb, delivered to him courtesy of Portugal's secret police, blew up. It was his successor, President Samora Machel, who ushered in Frelimo's victory, and who had

the difficult task of orchestrating Mozambique's independence—
until he too was killed in 1986.

Part of this history had already been lived by the time I left
South Africa, where I was born, in the early 1970s. As the rest of
the history unfolded, the solidarity organizations in Europe and
North America tried hard to spread the information as widely as
possible. An important element of this was the ability to report
firsthand. When in 1974 I was invited to Guinea-Bissau to visit the
liberated zones to see and report on the liberation struggle, I
jumped at the chance. What particularly grasped my imagination—spurred by my growing involvement in and commitment to
feminism—was the reported advances for women. I spent two
months in the liberated areas, talking with women about the
changes they were experiencing and how they viewed what
Amilcar Cabral—the liberation movement leader assassinated a
year earlier—had termed "fighting two colonialisms." Independence came quicker than anybody had hoped, and I went back in
1976 to complete the interviews for my book on the subject.

Reports on the situation in the liberated zones of Mozambique
mirrored what I found in Guinea-Bissau. Women indeed had been
moving ahead, changing the roles imposed on them by the peasant
society and the colonial system. But war is a special case. Every
oppressed Mozambican or Guinean knew to the core of her or his
being what it meant to live under the brutality of Portuguese
colonialism. Mobilizing people to take up arms to rid the country
of an easily identified external enemy needed skill but could get
dramatic and visible results. While the ideology of the movement
provided a basis for women's involvement to flower into something far more profound, policy and programs were required to
push ahead after independence when expectations were raised—
often unrealistically—in the course of the independence struggle
itself. As Cabral was wont to say, "When we are independent, that
is when our struggle *really* begins." How to provide the understanding that independence does not bring with it instant relief
from poverty and underdevelopment? How to continue the process of building political consciousness without the spur of a
visible enemy or of dramatic victories? How to foster awareness

that the second phase of the revolution continues to require great sacrifice and hard work? And how to continue to mobilize women once they are not as "necessary" to development as they were to armed struggle?

It was to Mozambique that I went to try and answer some of these questions. My first visit came just after the fifth anniversary of independence. My most recent coincided with the thirteenth anniversary. I went to record what I hoped to be a further unfolding of history, this time a reaffirmation of the potential of women to involve themselves with strength in the development of their country. It was not all I recorded. In the end I had to record the violent attempt to destroy this nation and what the women had tried to achieve.

By my most recent visit in mid-1987 the pervasive presence of South Africa through that government's policies of destabilization could be felt everywhere. The struggle has come full circle. Mozambican women are once again fighting a brutal, external force—this time in the guise of fellow Mozambicans. But it is the regime of South Africa, that country that I left twenty years ago now, the country I still tend to think of as "home," that is the cause of the atrocities that have become a daily reality for millions of Mozambicans and that affect women even more bitterly.

◈Introduction◈

Equality, Development, Peace

In 1975 the United Nations Decade for Women was declared in Mexico City. Women gathered from every continent to discuss goals and strategy for nationally based women's liberation. For many, it seemed like a new beginning: in the West, discussion was moving from purely feminist circles to take on a more global dimension, while women in the Third World who were struggling for national independence and development were beginning to demand substantive changes in the role of women in society. Together they generated an energy that was encouraging and a belief that an international understanding of the diverse but convergent needs of women would somehow help achieve the necessary changes.

But no one had any clear models. Hopes that the decade would encourage a surge of demands for emancipation to reverberate throughout the world and force governments to put this more firmly on their agendas were greeted with a mix of enthusiasm and skepticism. By the time of the end-decade conference in Nairobi in 1985 it was clear that in important, quantifiable respects little progress had been made in most of the world. Women were still the poorest members of society, were still at the bottom of the heap when it came to political participation and a share in power, had made little progress in shifting the statistics in their favor on such fundamental concerns as literacy, education, earning power, health. While women in some countries were slightly better off, those in others had lost ground over the ten years. The watchwords of the decade—equality, development, and peace—were in general no closer and, particularly in terms of peace, the women of the world were a lot worse off.

Coinciding with the Declaration of the Women's Decade in Mexico City was another beginning: on June 25, 1975, after more than ten years of armed struggle, Mozambique had won independence from centuries of Portuguese colonialism. Perhaps Mozambique might provide an effective model: Would this small, impoverished country be able to show, by its progress, what could be achieved in this symbolic decade?

The signs were good. The war for national independence had succeeded, under the leadership of Frelimo, in liberating portions of the territory and beginning to transform society in these areas. The movement clearly articulated the importance of the liberation of women. The word "liberation" when applied to women is often relegated to the terminology of Western feminists. Not so in Mozambique. It is integrated into the ideological perspective on the need for building a new society, encapsulated in the oft-quoted statement of Frelimo's past president, Samora Machel, and found among the slogans inscribed on the walls of buildings: "The liberation of women is the fundamental necessity for the revolution, a guarantee of its continuity and a precondition for victory."

These words were first spoken in an address that Samora Machel gave at the founding conference of the Organization of Mozambican Women (OMM) in 1973, when the thought of victory seemed still something for the distant future. Emphasizing that the "emancipation of women is not an act of charity, the result of a humanitarian or compassionate attitude," Machel went on to say that "the main objective of the revolution is to destroy the system of exploitation and build a new society which releases the potential of human beings, reconciling them with labor and with nature. This is the context within which the question of women's emancipation arises."[1]

Frelimo had already built a reputation for taking these words seriously: efforts to translate them into practice were underway in the liberated zones years prior to independence. Countless women were working in Frelimo as political mobilizers, some rising to the ranks of leadership. Many more were bearing arms and taking their place among the ranks of the women's detachment. Women had been given the chance, and they had risen to the challenge.

Five years later, in 1980, I went to Mozambique to see how well the new government in turn was able to respond to the needs of women. I returned twice again by the end of the Decade for Women in 1985. The theme of the decade—Equality, Development, and Peace—could have been the motto of the first decade of Mozambique's independence. While I did not expect to find true equality by the end of the decade, I did hope to find significant inroads, and a policy moving ahead, pushed by the women themselves.

The period from 1980 to the end of 1983, the time of my second to last visit, can be viewed to a large extent as the period of hope. Nineteen eighty was the year of Zimbabwe's independence and the end of Mozambique's war with Rhodesia: with independence, the country could turn its resources and human energies to development. From the end of 1983 to the time of my most recent visit, in June 1987, and onward to the present, is a time of devastation, if not defeat. The war-ravaged country I found made me wonder if the assessment I had undertaken had become an academic exercise. The war had wrought so many changes. It had interfered with the program of development, and affected close to a third of the population—fleeing from their homes, living in refugee camps—if not the bush, suffering constant attacks by the South Africa-backed Mozambique National Resistance (known as the MNR or Renamo), seeing their children killed or kidnapped, or watching them die from hunger when they could no longer feed them. How many women could struggle for their liberation when they were fighting for survival? It was almost as if Mozambique had been on one track after independence, and I was following the progress along that track—with a good spattering of stoppages, blocks, and side-tracking—and suddenly Mozambique had switched to a totally different track, trying to keep its people alive in the face of this onslaught.

Yet given the nature of Mozambique's revolution and the example it could set for the region, it was perhaps inevitable that South Africa, the overbearing giant on its borders, would try to destroy its achievements. Thus Mozambique and its struggle for the liberation of women remains a cogent case study for the decade. But it also becomes a case study for the impact of destabilization on women.

Equality. Development. Peace. In Mozambique I understood more than ever why the links between these goals were stressed during the United Nations Decade, as they were, over and over. Equality requires support mechanisms, mechanisms such as legal protections; literacy, education, and training programs; day-care and health programs—all necessary to women's labor and hence the sexual division of labor. But the ability to provide such support demands development, which in turn requires peace. As a book prepared for the decade argues: "Only by sharpening the links between equality, development and peace, can we show that the 'basic rights' of the poor and the transformation of the institutions that subordinate women are inextricably linked. They can be achieved together through the self-empowerment of women."[2]

Self-empowerment: this critical word goes a long way toward underscoring both the successes and the failures of the efforts to liberate women in Mozambique. While the lack of peace has been a major obstacle to economic development that both benefits and involves women, blame for the lack of progress in certain crucial areas cannot be placed on external factors alone. Patriarchal attitudes are alive and well in Mozambique: empowerment, where it exists, is still something bestowed on women by men, and the "self," for women, remains somewhat stifled. The very fact that the leadership—albeit male—has tried to empower women through laws, provision of resources, policy definition, and general, strong support is a vital contribution that should not be minimized. Yet the commitment to "women's concerns"—an increasingly imprecise array of items that affect women more particularly than men—too often takes the place of a genuine belief in and call for gender struggle. Women's concerns are for the most part—though not exclusively—synonymous with women's problems. And problems are regularly taken to mean those that concern women in relation to the family.

Women are encouraged to take on men's roles in every sphere. They are made equal in law and in the constitution, and are engaged in diverse tasks that were previously regarded as men's domain. But when it comes to perhaps the most fundamental issue—the sexual division of labor within the household—little change can be perceived. This is no surprise given the deeply rooted nature of the sexual division of labor and the relatively few years since independence. What is more disturbing is that it has not been taken up, except tangentially, as an issue to be addressed. Although it is evident that gender struggle is based as much in the family as in the workplace and wider community, it is shied away from, even to the point of discouraging women from engaging in a struggle for equality within that household.

While the sexual division of labor as it affects women is acknowledged as one of the areas of women's subordination, the idea that the way to alter the status quo should be associated with conflict—with gender struggle—seems to threaten the male leadership more than a little. As a result women are actively called upon to leave aside such struggle, not to use women's liberation as a "weapon," and to wait. In time, it is argued, men themselves will become more politicized and realize that women are overburdened in the domestic sphere; they will respond by offering help and ultimately taking on more work and responsibility in the household.

The sexual division of labor allocates to women specific domestic tasks, which place an excruciatingly heavy burden on women's daily lives. Half the battle for women's liberation and equality lies in the need to ensure the full participation of women in production outside the home as well as their equal access to and appropriation of society's resources resulting from such production. The other half is the need for both men and women to share domestic labor and responsibilities within the household, so that women *can* participate in outside production. Despite official efforts to defuse the process of gender struggle, however, sharp contradictions are apparent. Women are not only encouraged to take on men's roles and to work outside the home—if not in the wage labor force, then in cooperatives or in political work—but also to do extra tasks to help build a new society. Sufficient hours there are not. Women, especially younger women, are therefore making demands of men, ignoring the exhortation to play down any conflict. Some of the younger women I interviewed were adamant that they would not accept a relationship that was not based on greater equality.

The very stress on women entering production, moreover, is a contradiction. In Mozambique, as indeed in sub-Saharan Africa as a whole, this is not simply synonymous with entering the wage labor force. Women are already heavily engaged in production— agricultural production; it is the women who are, to a vast degree, the family farmers. Moreover, unemployment is rife, and has been since independence; it is not simply a result of the war. For women to play their part in production (aside from family farming) and development, the basis for their production needs to be transformed. Clearly such transformation can be achieved only if women participate fully in the planning process. Although this point has been acknowledged in Mozambique, particularly in the earlier years, no concrete plans have been proffered detailing how women's participation can be realized. The gap between theory and practice is seen most acutely in the absence of such proposals in the plans of action worked out each year by the women's organization, OMM. In keeping with OMM's perception of its role as a mass organization of the party, it follows party direction of women's issues rather than initiating, intervening, and pushing the party in its formulation of policy toward women. This failing was most keenly felt after 1983 when the program for rural development—the nation's priority—shifted away from state farms to family farming and private farming.

The state farms, despite the fact they received priority in allocation of resources, were badly conceived and never viable. In 1983, at the Fourth Party Congress, they were acknowledged to be a grave, far-reaching failure of the development strategy. The party at that time put forward a new program of agricultural reform that gave priority to family farming and private farming. Given women's prominent role in family farming, this shift augured well: it presented a unique chance to work out a policy that would support women's productive roles. As such, OMM could have had a critical input, insisting on the need to involve women in production decisions for both the household and the nation. But the organization did nothing. As a result, national policy has focused much more directly on cash cropping and surplus than on ensuring food for daily consumption. The likelihood is that the gap between women (as family farmers) and men (as cash croppers) will grow rather than shrink, and women will be increasingly marginalized from national production.

OMM's failure to take a position on the direction of the new policy contrasts markedly with its own and party statements from the early years. Indeed, in the initial years of independence these made it seem unlikely that Mozambique would fall into the pattern repeated throughout neocolonial Africa, where state-sponsored development programs left women progressively marginal roles in family farming while men took on the task of cash cropping. Development agents inevitably favored male farmers when it came to the introduction of appropriate technology, extension services, funding and loans, access to seeds, training. Men accordingly brought in the cash, while women continued to produce food for the table, and the gap in equality between men and women widened as a result. Frelimo seemed determined to avoid this trap. I read with excitement one particular position statement in a text prepared for the 1976 conference of OMM. Speaking of the need to transform subsistence agriculture, it concluded:

Mozambican women not only cannot remain outside this process, but they must be its principal agents and beneficiaries. The Mozambican peasant woman has to be assured equal opportunities to learn new techniques, to have access to the use of machines, to the acquisition of theoretical knowledge and above all to participating in the political organs, in the direction and management to the same extent as her participation in the work.[3]

But words such as these appear to have been relegated to rhetoric, as the ideas were never incorporated in the development plans. Thus, for instance, state farms were given priority in the agrarian reform program—in terms of allocation of resources if not in official policy statements. The state farms are the only employer of wage labor in the rural areas, and this labor is essentially male.

It is possible that the rhetoric should have been foreseen. Despite the clarity of the goals of the early statement by OMM, no provision was made to include women in the planning process itself. One of the worldwide obstacles to the achievement of the goals of the Women's Decade was the failure to consult women, especially on policy that affected them. In Mozambique, one must ask whether the outcome could have been different, at least to some degree, if government had gone to the women themselves before embarking on their program of rural transformation. It is fairly certain that they would have insisted on strong state support for family production rather than pumping limited resources into state farms. Eight years earlier, then, Mozambique could have shifted to family farming, better managing to feed the population. Just possibly it might have been better able to withstand the enemy onslaught when it came.

Such consultations are not something new to Frelimo. They were the core component of mass participation during the war and the central element in Frelimo's emerging popular democracy. There is a more recent and striking example of how the party and the women's organization went to the masses: preparations for an OMM conference in 1984 on the social issues concerning women used this method, sending out brigades to hold meetings with women in all walks of life, from one end of the country to the other. Judging by the enthusiasm generated, the heated debate, and concrete suggestions that came out of these meetings, some of which I witnessed, the involvement of women and men in grappling with issues so fundamental to their daily lives is not impossible to achieve.

Mozambique's failure to avoid the neocolonial development pattern raises troubling questions for the ability of a postrevolutionary society to fully liberate women. Patriarchal attitudes apparently cross all boundaries, uniting all men in their continuing exploitative practices. Can any society succeed in changing women's lives without recognizing this and confronting it directly?

Certainly patriarchal attitudes have not vanished with the coming of a new society in Mozambique. One just has to look at the makeup of the top levels of leadership and who makes the decisions—regarding both women and men—to see it in operation and to see some of the reasons for the continuation of women's inequality. But in Mozambique and other postrevolutionary societies, there are real gains that have been made by women. To ignore these and the kind of support—economic and political— that women get from their governments and political party is to ignore some real, tangible advances. In Mozambique, for instance, resources are taken out of the tight budget to ensure the running of the women's organization and the government guarantees that women get a share of development aid. Economic support especially is generally far greater than women get from official channels in Western societies—at least without bitter struggle—and this with chronically and painfully less access to resources.

It is hard to appreciate the extent of either the gains or official support without understanding the position of women under colonialism and the legacy of crippling underdevelopment that came with its overthrow: the absence of skills for the vast majority of the population is matched by an absence of social and legal struggle for economic and political rights. Despite a shortage of skilled party and government personnel, however, the commitment to economic development and accompanying social emancipation was often put into practice in imaginative ways. The change in agricultural policy in 1983 is an example. The shift to family farms at least provided women with an important platform for gender struggle. Without the escalation of MNR activities soon after the Fourth Congress, Mozambique's economy would have had more of a chance to recuperate—and perhaps with it, women might have been able to put gender struggle on the agenda themselves.

MNR's deliberate targets were the services that Frelimo had provided the people as part of its development program: communal villages, the health service, the schools, the water pumps, the irrigation schemes. Without denying the role of the government in the collapse of the economy, the program for independent development was not given a chance. It was within this context that specific gender interests were pushed to a back burner. When priorities have to be reset, it is seldom that the priorities for women remain in the forefront. This inability to push ahead a development policy that would benefit women as much as it does men has meant that total equality remains a hope for the future, not an achievement of the present.

Yet it is possible that this too must be anticipated. Destabilization—and with it, often war—seems to be becoming a permanent fixture of anti-imperialist revolutionary societies, located in regions that are regarded as the sphere of interest of the industrialized Western nations. One must wonder whether any development planning, including the role of women, should integrate the prospect of ongoing war. In this context, the Mozambican slogan "A Luta Continua!" (the struggle continues) takes on new meaning. Mozambique set out to achieve something new and inspiring in Africa. That Frelimo has not been able to achieve the goals it set itself does not detract from this attempt and leaves at least some hope that it might yet come through. In the final analysis, it has provided a fundamental contribution to an understanding of the complex and protracted process of emancipating women. The difficulties and obstacles it has confronted lay to rest romantic notions that good intentions are sufficient to ensure profound social transformation.

At the end of the United Nations Decade, and after four trips to Mozambique, I had many questions about the interlocking goals of equality, development, and peace, and whether one is possible without the other two. But I have no clear answers. The chapters that follow, built around my interviews with women in urban and rural areas, are organized to draw out the tensions and contradictions between these goals and the reality of famine and war. Chapters 1 through 3, based on my most recent visit, show a Mozambique independent but at war. Visiting a village in the south, where clinics, wells, and schools are constantly under attack, I wonder if Mozambique is simply building targets for the MNR. Later on, touring the war-ravaged Tete province, the most fertile in the country, where the harvest this year is zero, I understand the cruel contradiction for women: hard as their lives may be as producers for the family subsistence as well as keepers of the household, it is harder still when they cannot even work the land, and are unable to keep their children alive.

With Chapters 4 and 5 the focus shifts to the period of my first visits, before the war, and looks at the impact on women of the state's development policy, particularly with regard to rural transformation. Chapter 4 examines the state farm policy and the effort to try to integrate women into the wage labor force in the rural areas; Chapter 5 looks at communal villages, once so promising, but stalled by 1982 due to the continued priority given to state farms in terms of allocation of resources. The expectation that women's lives would be transformed with their integration into production was reexamined in 1983, with the breakdown of state farms and redistribution of land to family farms, both within and outside the communal villages. I returned in 1987 to see the impact of the new agricultural policies on a village in the south. Chapter 6 describes my visit. The village was thriving—as ironically were agricultural cooperatives in the green zones, in part due to the war itself. Yet with the all-too-typical emphasis on cash-crop production the inherent danger is that women's production for the table will quickly be regarded as less crucial than men's production of cash crops.

These chapters focus on what is perhaps the central contradiction for Mozambican women today: the failure of the government to involve them in planning for rural development. Given that women remain the primary producers of food, is not rural transformation a woman's concern?

Chapters 7, 8, and 9 look at what is viewed as the major realm of women's concerns: the family. Chapter 7 shows the tensions felt by women who are now working in factories, but still must run the household, and the differences for single and married women. As war and underdevelopment have left the state unable to free women from responsibility for family subsistence and provide the child care necessary to let them join the labor force, the struggle for equality shifts to the family, as it has in other postrevolutionary societies. In Mozambique, however, the nuclear family is now held out as an ideal for the new society; it is seen as an aid to change, rather than an obstacle to equality. Thus "gender struggle" is discouraged, and women are urged to "speak with kind words" and to work even harder so that men will be shown up by their example and change their ways. The contradictions inherent in this policy have forced many women to take up the gender struggle, both at work and at home.

Chapters 8 and 9 look at the difficulties the ideal of the "new family" presents for those outside—single and divorced women, most of them with children. Chapter 8 presents the new, angry voices of single women in factories, women experiencing the joys and hardships of a new independence. Chapter 9 presents the darker side, the appalling consequences for urban women who were judged "nonproductive" and relocated to the countryside to work, alone, on state farms or communal villages.

The ideal of the new family, however, arises out of the circumstances of Mozambique's history: in the rural areas of the south especially, the peasant household was sustained by the interrelated customs of polygamy and *lobolo* (brideprice), which recognized women's important role in production while reinforcing the patriarchal family. Efforts to eliminate these practices create new contradictions, however, as Chapter 10 makes clear: interviews with women who defend the practices as necessary to family survival even though they suffer from them reveal the impossibility of piecemeal social change.

Taking women's concerns beyond the family, Chapter 11 presents a close look at the literacy program and its impact on women, stressing how much more women have to gain from literacy, and how much harder they have to fight for it. As a result of the difficulties, more women than men give up the struggle for literacy, even though they have so much more to gain.

Finally, in chapter 12, the stories of three women sum up these contradictions; the realization that despite the problems, they have come so far, can perhaps let us understand why in the face of everything they still go on dancing.

◈ 1 ◈
And Still They Dance

It is a clear winter Sunday in June, when I set out for a long walk around Maputo, basking in the feel of the air, the smell of the earth, the soft winds that play on my arms. It all seems so familiar that it is hard to believe that I landed just twenty-four hours earlier. My eagerness to get back to this country that I have grown so attached to is muted by layered emotions. The very attachment causes anxiety. I know I am not returning to the land of hope that I first visited in 1980, five years after independence. It is 1987 and when I disembarked from the Mozambican airline's jumbo jet, I entered times of hardship, of war and hunger, of devastation. Still apprehensive of the enormity of what I might find on this fourth visit after a break of three and a half years, I go in search, this quiet Sunday, of signs of change.

I walk first along Avenida Friedrich Engels with its glistening vista of the sea beyond the trees that border the avenue. It is a scene of utter tranquility. Overlooking this expansive view are rows of mansions that once housed Mozambique's wealthy settlers and administrators. Now the flags of various African nations move softly with the breeze. Beyond lie the beaches of Maputo, brown rather than golden sanded, edged by palm trees, the sea sparkling invitingly. This beach does not match others I have basked on along the country's coastline, but it holds a special attraction, with the flat sea that changes with the moods of the weather. I was drawn often to take long walks in the early morning or to ride my borrowed bicycle to where the beach ended in a narrow river and a small fishing village. I think of the last time I was there, though, on a hot summer's day. We were having a farewell picnic for a *cooperante,* a volunteer who was returning to Europe. All of us had made an effort to bring a special dish of food to share. As we ate our feast a group of African children stood silently nearby, dressed is threads, watching us eat. We shared our food, but I could not enjoy the picnic. It was too harsh a reminder of the hardship and inequities.

There was a period too, between my last visit and this, when the beach remained empty for weeks. A father and a son had gone for a walk, stepped on a landmine planted by the MNR, and lost their legs.

And yet these thoughts do not linger long, for Maputo seems so incredibly normal. Ominously normal somehow because even though I can't yet sense it, I know that a very different reality lies a hairbreadth beneath the surface. It's just that on this first day back it's hard to find. Children play in the streets as they have always done, in that universal game, hopscotch, the "court" scratched with a stone on the uneven and broken cement sidewalk. Hop, hop, jump the go, calling encouragement to each other in Portuguese and giggling in their fun. They have no shoes. Younger children run up and down, playing tag, or playing with stones or other objects that their imaginations fashioned into something other.

In a small park overlooking the river two young women braid each other's hair into intricate styles. Their faces are so relaxed, their bodies so at ease, that they seem to communicate an added peacefulness to the scene. A man's voice reaches me, in slow recitation. I follow the sound and find a middle-aged guard of a mansion-turned-day-care-center on a straight-backed chair in the middle of the driveway. He sits so correctly, as if in the presence of his teacher, as he concentrates hard on his new literacy manual, his right index finger moving under each word, which he intones aloud. Each person I pass greets me with a friendly *bom dia* or *boa tarde* depending on whether it's still morning or already afternoon. Children come up to me and stare with open curiosity and then smile back with the equally friendly openness of their elders.

I look into the windows of stores looking for clues. A few are far better stocked than I remember, but the prices are way out of reach for the majority of the city's population. Most display but a paltry few items sitting on faded paper. As I scribble in my notebook, recording the absence of goods, people pass by and stare at me, puzzled. I feel self-conscious as if I am examining inner secrets of their lives, for these stores say so much about the economic collapse that I almost feel uncomfortable peering into this poverty. Because of the lack of foreign exchange, virtually no consumer goods can be imported for sale in these stores. What is produced domestically, such as shoes or cloth, has to be carefully rationed. The factories that are producing do so well below potential because of the lack of spare parts, raw materials, component parts, most of which must be imported when the scarce foreign currency permits.

I set off for the *Baixa*—downtown Maputo—past the large, now virtually empty department stores, and the shops sporting for the most part inferior quality clothes at superior prices. I walk through the grand arches and into the high-ceilinged marketplace. I remember it well from previous visits: women sitting hunched and listless behind the large cement ledge that serves as the stall. A bunch of greens here. A pile of small hot chilies there. A few lettuces. Perhaps every week or ten days the word would get out that the market had onions, or carrots, or eggplants, and people would stand patiently in long *bishas*, the lines that were as much a part of Maputo life as the absence of consumer goods.

I was therefore unprepared for what I saw. A market alive and packed from one end to the other with fruits and vegetables of every description. Bright red cabbages. Large bunches of fresh "couve" leaves—a member of the cabbage family used in the preparation of a local dish. Mounds of onions, of tomatoes. Oranges, papaya, avocados. Carrots and eggplants, yellow squash and green peppers. There was fish, eggs, ice cream. Sometimes, I was told, there were even chickens. It smelled like a market, rich and tempting. But there was a catch: the prices. The government had deregulated prices with the intention of encouraging producers. This had indeed happened. But the prices were so steep that this market full of vegetables had no *bishas* and was uncrowded with customers. Onions were $4.00 per kilo, for instance. Tomatoes slightly less. When I shopped another day for vegetables for three or four days for four people, I spent more than half the average worker's monthly pay. But as a friend who had worked in Mozambique for many years commented: "The prices are no higher than they were on the black market. And now at least things are available to everyone."

The scene in the *Baixa* market symbolizes in part what has happened to the Mozambican economy. It certainly highlights the problems that the government faces in trying to get the economy back on track. For the casual visitor the produce in the market would indicate prosperity. And in fact this new abundance is used as an example by those agencies and governments wishing to push Mozambique into adopting a capitalist economy. The mass of produce is the antithesis of the stories of famine and starvation that come from all parts of the country.

Frelimo inherited a country without foreign exchange. The Portuguese colonialists had systematically and lucratively robbed Mozambique of its resources. After the tea, cotton, cashews, and any other exports were sold on the European market, the profits went straight to Portugal, or rather into the bank accounts of those few families that controlled the economy, and were never reinvested in Mozambique. The new Mozambican government took over a country in 1975 that was impoverished to the extreme, a population with an illiteracy rate of over 90 percent, and virtually no one with the skills to step into the void left by 250,000 fleeing Portuguese settlers and white Mozambicans who deserted the country when they no longer could control it. Today, of every dollar spent inside the country, 90 cents comes from the outside in the form of loans and aid, and 10 cents is internally generated. But even this Ministry of Finance figure is disputed by some Mozambique analysts as being far too optimistic. Mozambique has the highest debt-service ratio in the world—between 160 and 190 percent of the *planned* 1987 exports. Real exports are closer to 10 percent of the planned.

If the prices in the market had not been decontrolled, there would still be no food in the market. It is not worth a farmer's while to produce food, transport it to Maputo, and sell it at low prices determined by the government. Their profits are meager. And little in the way of consumer goods is available to provide any measure of incentive. But if it is worthwhile for the farmers to produce then they will bring their crops to the market, with the potential for buying the limited high-priced goods that would otherwise be totally out of reach. And so the expatriates with their large salaries, and the small number of Mozambicans with money, can shop in volume at the market. Other Maputo residents buy small amounts of absolute necessities, while the increase in food production means that those living in the rural areas around Maputo have more to eat.

I walk through the streets of "cement city"—so dubbed by the African shanty dwellers who were not allowed to live there. Caught in a web of tight restrictions, Africans had to live in their *caniço* (reed) houses cheek by jowl, one after another, crammed together as if oblivous to the vast open space beyond. In contrast this cement city was graced with wide if now eroded boulevards, flowering jacaranda trees, frangipani and bougainvillea, red-tiled roofs and apartment buildings with pastel-washed cement walls. The signs of disrepair are so evident. The worn-away and broken sidewalks, the pitted tarmac roads, the houses lost behind overgrown foliage, the tiles slipping down the side of the roofs, gates that swing on broken hinges, cracks in the plaster of buildings. It all deteriorates more year by year. Interspersed are spruced-up houses and buildings taken over by aid agencies and expanding embassies that brought in their own paint and equipment.

The Lisbon that I walked through just three days earlier is only a better-kept version of this city. I appreciate why Lourenço Marques, the name given by the Portuguese to the capital, was called the Lisbon of Africa. This is a faded version of a Lisbon transplant. During the colonial period they were both beautiful cement cities. Except the one was under occupation and the gateway through which wealth was extracted in order to maintain the other.

In the pleasant cafes of Bissua, Luanda, and Lourenço Marques, and in the cafes of Lisbon as well as clandestine settings, disgruntled officers of the Portuguese army were making their plans to bring this colonial life to an end. Perhaps at the very table I sat at in a cafe in central Lisbon, making notes and waiting for my plane to leave late that night for Maputo, officers had been deep in conspiracy in the early 1970s.

It is thirteen years and one month after I first heard the announcement over radio in the liberated zones of Guinea-Bissau that the fascist government of Marcello Caetano had toppled in a coup, April 1974. Independence for the colonies—Guinea-Bissau and Cape Verde first, then Mozambique and Angola—followed in succession. On June 25, 1975, in a grand midnight ceremony, the new Mozambican flag replaced that of Portugal. Twelve years later to the month, I sit in a cafe in a city where white, Portuguese propagandists for the South Africa–supported Mozambique National Resistance (MNR) invent and distort reality to try and convince the world to look at Mozambique through warped lenses. Their lies attempt to mask the atrocities that caused the death of at least 100,000 Mozambicans, and left 5.9 million—over one-third of the population—to face starvation. The famine sweeping over rural Mozambique is "man"-made—and the man in questions is P. W. Botha, South Africa's president.

Botha, previously South Africa's hard-line minister of defense, took over as prime minister in 1978, and signaled the ascendancy of the South African military and a new hard-line policy toward its neighbors. He redirected the regime's policy toward the region, from one that was inward-looking, defensive, and intransigent to one that was aggressive, outward looking, and intransigent. With regard to Mozambique, the policy was designed to render the new state so fragile and dependent that it would have neither the will nor the capacity to fight back. The sharp shifts in policy were dictated to a large extent by events at home that were making life increasingly uncomfortable for Botha and his gang.

The liberation of their neighbors, Mozambique and Angola, from a seemingly invincible Portuguese colonial force sparked a new wave of resistance in South Africa. "If the Mozambicans and Angolans can do it, then we can do it," was a refrain reflected in the outpouring of demonstrations. Then began an extended period of uprisings. It was not only the "how" of independence that provided a model, but the potential of such liberation giving birth to socialist states so close to home that troubled those in power. Further, Mozambique was in an ideal geographical position to support the South African liberation struggle.

Botha's concerns were more than political. Mozambique's deep, natural harbors make it well suited to replace South Africa as the gateway for the exports of landlocked Zambia, Zimbabwe, and Malawi. Because of the bad state of repair of Mozambique's harbors and because of roads that were incapable of handling the heavy traffic, these landlocked nations continued to pay more than double in road transport and tariffs than would be the case if they could send their goods out of Maputo or Beira. A stronger, more developed region was needed to counter South Africa's economic stranglehold on the region, and for this reason the Southern African Development and Coordination Conference—SADDC—

was formed in 1980. South Africa greeted this development with considerable wariness.

The South African Defense Force moved quickly to begin the destabilization of the region. Because Mozambique posed the strongest threat, it became the main target. A major help in the destabilization campaign fell into South Africa's lap with the independence of Zimbabwe: when the remains of the MNR were hastily evacuated from Rhodesia at the eve of independence, recruits were easily netted from the remnants. MNR had been established by Rhodesian intelligence—with South African collusion—in 1976 as a tool to gather intelligence information on freedom-fighter activities in Mozambique. MNR would not exist but for South Africa's heavy backing. It is because Machel and Frelimo realized this that the Mozambican government was compelled in March 1984 to sit down with its arch enemies to sign the nonaggression pact, known as the Nkomati Accords, after the town just across the border where P. W. Botha and President Samora Machel met.

I remember how disturbed I first felt when hearing of the pact, how distressed many of my Mozambique-supporter friends were, and how it troubled us to see photos of President Machel and his wife, Graça Machel, shaking hands with Botha and his wife. The accords called for the expulsion of the African National Congress (ANC) from Mozambique, except for a small diplomatic representation, and the Machel government made quite a show of fulfilling the accords. Said a friend to me caustically, "When you sup with the devil, you need a lo-oo-ng spoon." Could there be a spoon long enough, I wondered. But when the dust settled and emotions subsided it was clear that the Machel government had no option. They were being squeezed by the terrorism of the MNR and directly attacked by South Africa. South Africa's destabilization strategy was beginning to have a crippling effect on Mozambique.

Direct attacks began within days of Ronald Reagan's inauguration as U.S. president, on January 30, 1981. Truckloads of South African commandos drove into Matola, seventy kilometers from the South African border, destroyed three houses, killed thirteen ANC members and a Portuguese passer-by. Two South Africans were killed by return fire from ANC members. Other raids followed, including railway and port sabotage and attacks on civilians, mostly Mozambicans, and the assassination of Ruth First in

August 1982. Ruth, the wife of Joe Slovo, top ANC military commander, was the research director of the Maputo University's Center of African Studies.

The president who signed the accord to try and stop such attacks is now dead. On his way back from a meeting in Lusaka his plane crashed on South African soil on October 18, 1986. The unexplained events surrounding the crash leave many certain of South Africa's implication in his death. For a number of months, awaiting the outcome of the inquiry, the Mozambican government declined to point a direct finger at its neighbor. But while I was in Mozambique, President Chissano made a speech at Mueda commemorating the massacre. "Our enemies, who are colonialism, are still colonialism," he said. "Our enemies, who are still racism, decided to resort once more to violence and murdered our president, Samora Machel."

As I walked on, I wondered where the most recent of the open South African attacks—after a lull since the signing of Nkomati—had occurred. It would be another two days before I would hear a fuller account, and write in my journal:

Small hours of the morning, May 29, in Maputo. An attack on three buildings. One is an warehouse used by the ANC. Only three people are there. Two manage to escape, one by hiding in a barrel. The young Mozambican guard is killed. He had brushed off ANC concerns that he remain at the warehouse at night because of the potential for attack. He wanted to remain at his post. The second is a house, now empty. The third is the flat across the hall from some South African exiles. A young Mozambican couple are asleep in their beds. With them is their eighteen-month-old daughter. With their domestic workers, in a separate room, is their seven-year-old son. At two in the morning the attackers burst into the flat. Some are black. They speak Portuguese. Some are white. They speak an unrecognizable language that is identified as Afrikaans. They tie the young couples' hands behind their backs. Their son comes to investigate, in terror. He tries to go to his bound mother and father. He is forced back into the bedroom. The little girl tries incessantly to reach her mother. She is pushed aside. The parents make a dash to the balcony to scream for help.

"We're Mozambicans!" they shout. "Help us! Help us!" The attackers take aim and let loose a volley of bullets into their backs.

They toss the toddler onto her mother's body, and later, when the Mozambican police come to the apartment, they have to peel the little girl away from where she is still clinging. Four weeks later she still doesn't sleep. She still cries out for her Mama. When the phone rings she rushes eagerly to pick it up first. "Mama?" she asks, her voice rising in hopeful expectation. "Mama?"

I walk toward my last destination before turning back, straight up the hill from the *Baixa* to the Praca da Independencia. I always remembered it as an imposing square, made grandiose by the high columns and ornate moldings and archway doors, an outsize monument to a city that the Portuguese fancifully built to conjure up an era quite out of place in Africa. When I enter the square and looked up at the building, I stop dead in my tracks. The giant portrait of Samora Machel, which was a special symbol of new times, has vanished. In a rush, I relive the same stab of anguish I felt when I first heard of the plane crash that killed the president. But his vanished face makes his death all the more real. The square seemed to shrink a bit, to have lost some of its imposing aura. I thought of all the places I had seen Machel's picture, hanging from homemade frames in villages, from well-used, often rickety frames in post offices, from newer, neat frames in government buildings. In that gaping emptiness I understand the strange Sunday silence in the square: it is not just the escalation of enemy activities, the famine, the starving children. Machel has been killed and there is a new government, a new president. President Joaquim Chissano's earnest face looks down on Mozambique from those frames now.

I first met President Chissano in New York in September 1975. Mozambique was just three months independent and he, as the first foreign minister, led the Mozambican delegation to the flag-raising ceremony when the fledgling nation became the newest member of the United Nations. The Southern African Committee threw a party and six or seven members of the delegation came, many young and still new to life beyond the war zones.

With them was Shafudine Khan, the well-loved Frelimo representative to the United Nations and the United States who had lived frugally in New York while petitioning the United Nations, talking on campuses, to church groups, to sympathetic and unsympathetic people in Congress and the government, to supportive and unsupportive Americans, explaining and reexplaining the justice of their cause. Over the years he attended the New York parties of the many friends he made here. When we tried to cajole him onto a dance floor his reply was stock: "I am a Muslim. I don't dance. But when we are victorious, then I will dance." That night, Khan danced. And he danced many years earlier than either Frelimo or its supporters had thought possible.

While Khan took to the floor, Chissano stood on the sidelines, engaged in serious conversation. One of the more forthright members of our committee, a very tall and elegant Afro-American, broke in and took the hand of this slight man, gaunt from over a decade of harsh life in the liberated zones. They began to dance, quite sedately at first. And then, in a flash, as if Chissano remembered that there was something that must be celebrated, he unleashed his energy. He began to really dance. His legs moved so fast to the energetic rhythms they seemed to blur. He danced as if he was wiping out the memory of the years of Portuguese oppression, or the brutality visited upon his people. He danced as if he was forgetting the long years of war and sacrifice and loss of life. He danced as if, yes, Mozambique was finally independent. He danced with abandon. He danced from the sheer high of victory.

Dance is deeply embedded in Mozambican culture. As part of building cultural and hence political understanding during the war, southerners learned the dances and the songs from the north. Those from central Mozambique learned the songs of the south. In the schools and in the localities, girls and boys, women and men, learned the culture of their neighbors, people they might have regarded as threatening or alien. While they moved to the rhythms of each other's dances, Frelimo hoped that through better exchanging the varied and rich cultures of Mozambique, unity could be forged.

In the south I visited factories and agricultural cooperatives and watched the almost sedate song and dance act, the *xicombela*, where the lead would recite the main refrain, which recalled an event in history, pronounced a goal of the revolution, told of a recent happening, while the chorus would, with agile movements worthy of acrobats, dance and mime the emphasis. I heard songs that women sang in chorus, raising hoes or sticks above their heads, and proclaiming their gratitude to Frelimo or vowing to work hard for the new country. In central Mozamique the women danced in the middle of a large circle, rattles made from seeds tied to their ankles, men and women drumming with vitality to provide the background. In the north I watched women, faces covered with broad white markings, dance while others sang in high-pitched tones exhorting the dancers to more and more intricate movements of the body, which were mimicked by the young girls and children who joined them.

Yet others danced. In 1980 I visited the *caniço bairro*—a neighborhood of reed houses—of Mavalane, and met one of the oldest members of the women's organization, Maria Masinga. Her hair was completely white and her old, wrinkled face and callused hands told of the many years she had lived on the margin in poverty, years to which she could attach no number as she could neither read nor write and had no birth certificate. "The women's organization saved my life," she said simply. She meant it. Maria Masinga had been abandoned by her husband because she was infertile. Her only means of survival over the years was by cultivating a small plot of land some five hours' walk from her shack outside of Maputo. Then, around the time of independence, her legs could no longer take her those miles. She feared she would suffer the fate of many elderly women she had known who died from hunger, alone in their little houses. Soon after independence OMM began organizing in Mavalane and she began to work with them. When she had nothing to eat, they brought her food. She is never hungry now, she says. And she slowly coaxed her old, frozen joints to permit her to stand. She raised her arms above her head and gingerly swayed from side to side in an imitation of the dancing she must have done with energy in her youth. "Ai," she said, "If I could dance I would be dancing my thanks all the time. All the time."

I remembered Mama Leia. As secretary of the women's organization at Três de Fevereiro communal village she was my host during the days at a time I spent in her village. When I told her my grandmother's name was Leah, spelled differently but pronounced the same, she smiled appreciatively: "Then you are my granddaughter," she said. And she always responded to my protestations when she insisted that I eat more when I had eaten my fill, rest when I wasn't tired, sleep more comfortably when I didn't expect privilege, with, "But you are my granddaughter." Her face, when unsmiling, could look serious with the weight of her responsibilities. But when she smiled, her grin was wide and exuberant and catching. And she smiled often, particularly when she danced. I have images that will be with me many years, of my "grandmother" dancing with joy when I arrived at her village, and dancing her appreciation and fond farewell when I left. My efforts to dance with her and her co-workers were a great source of laughter. Later we drove away, looking back on the group of exuberant women rhythmically swaying to the strains of one of her favorite songs, "Kanimambo, Macheli"—Thank You, Machel!

Dance found its way into other settings. I remembered Lina Magaia. One of my interpreters for a number of trips, Lina had become a friend. She was an unending source of deeper insights, an enjoyable comrade, and someone with the ability not just to interpret language but to translate cultures. One visit was to a women's agricultural cooperative outside of Maputo in early 1982. After the guided tour, looking at poorly cultivated fields, mangy rabbits, a few little ducklings, and limited other livestock, we sat in a circle with twenty or so workers and I asked questions about their work and their lives. I looked at the women sitting straight-backed and serious, and wondered what motivated them to work with such commitment three days a week although they had not yet been able to reap any profits. I knew I would get a stock answer if I asked whether they felt discouraged.

Lina grasped my problem. "Tell me," she asked them, "if a man comes here tomorrow and says to you, 'I will buy your cooperative and I will pay you a regular salary each week,' will you sell?" There was an emphatic murmur of nos and nevers. This is our cooperative, they said. Every day we see progress even though it is slow. You have just seen our new little ducklings. We believe we will make it and the cooperative will look after us well. One young woman disagreed. She would definitely sell. Lina asked her why. She stood up and looked straight at Lina. "You are pregnant," she said to Lina, "You *believe* that the baby inside you will grow up healthy and look after you in your old age. But you don't *know*. I must feed my children. I must feed them now."

Sitting with us were two officials, one from the district Frelimo headquarters, the other from the district women's organization, who happened to be visiting the same day. They whipped out their notebooks, and asked officiously, pencils poised, "What is your name?" There was silence. The women looked down, very uncomfortable. Lina was up in a flash. Clapping her hands, and swinging her large, flexible body she began to dance as she pulled one woman after another to her feet and led them in a rousing Frelimo song. They all joined in the vigorous dance. When the tension had cleared the women sat down and we continued our questions. At one point I was randomly asking women for some of their background, including their names. I avoided asking the "dissenter." Lina nudged me. "Ask her. It is important that she realizes she can say her name without repercussions." So I did. No notebooks came out. And when we left and the workers danced their good-bye, they were joined by the two officials.

Dance is a vibrant expression of Mozambican zest for life. Mozambicans danced even as they suffered brutality under the Portuguese colonialists; they danced even as they struggled to win their war of liberation; they danced in victory when this war was won; they danced even as they fought a second war with their racist neighbor Rhodesia; but once more they danced in victory and with hope when this war came to an end with Zimbabwean independence in 1980. And now, in my most recent travels I saw Mozambicans dance again, even as the atrocities of the MNR mount up and they struggle to keep their economy going. This time though they do not sing in praise and with purpose to build a new nation. They sing their determination to rid the country of the "armed bandits." Their high hopes for an immediate end to their suffering after Frelimo came to power have been dashed. And still they dance.

◈❥ 2 ◈❥
Village Under Siege

The Landrover heads out of the hectic drive-where-you-can traffic of early morning Maputo, past old battered cars that chug along with trucks and a few jeeps, new buses filled with workers heading to the factories that skirt Maputo, and the inevitable fancier cars of the *cooperantes*, embassies, and aid agencies. An American friend, Rebecca, and I reach the large traffic circle at the edge of the city and make our way onto the open "highway" going south toward the South African border, and pick up some speed. Our destination is the district of Boane along the road to Namaacha, a town close to the Swazi border. A visit has been arranged to the communal village of Eduardo Mondlane, the first communal village established in Maputo province, now deeply hurt by the MNR raids.

We begin to leave the traffic behind. We pass Matola, the pretty suburb built by the Portuguese, with tree-lined streets, neat houses, and its own *caniço* slums. Matola residents now live in fear of MNR attacks, which have been many. At night. We travel during the day, on through the flat African veld, small hills in the distance, miles of scrub and bush, clumps of trees and the occasional river. My heart soars with a particular intensity, as it always does when I first head into the African countryside after leaving New York. I relax. Feel calm. Look forward to getting away from the city. I glance back toward Maputo as we drive. The buildings so tall and white, gleaming in the morning sun like obelisks. It seems so abnormal somehow from this distance, yet it has its own beauty too, rising off the banks of the Maputo River and the shore of the protective curved bay.

Our destination is not far, about thirty kilometers. It wouldn't be safe to drive much further. I have been on this road often before, either to Namaacha, or on my few visits across the border to Swaziland. As we drive I consider the irony of it all. In 1983 the most frantic part of setting up my program was finding transport: transport provided by the women's organization on earlier visits was no longer available due to hard times. Now I have transport. I can borrow a friend's Landrover any time for my work. I have dollars to buy as much gas as I need at the *Loja Franca*—the foreign-exchange store—gas station. But I cannot travel more than thirty kilometers out of Maputo in any direction. Those that go further must travel in military-escorted convoys or at great risk alone.

After about forty-five minutes we pass a small sign announcing the district of Boane. We reach the "town," a few low, dilapidated brick buildings, one-story high on each side of the road. We turn right onto a sandy road, past a deserted cement building with a solitary gas pump. It looks as if it has not been used forever. A few yards down and we reach a T-junction. Beyond are fields being tended by women and a few tin and reed houses. On our right is the "sede." We park our Landrover and enter the building. It is empty, with only a few pieces of furniture standing on the painted cement floor. It is still cool from the night air. There is little to suggest that this is an office of the district administration. A few young women, reserved and attentive, greet us and bring out two wooden chairs.

The district secretary of defense is sent for and arrives elegant in his new, well-pressed camouflage pants with the brown and green splotches familiar the world over, topped by a camouflage jacket of uneven green and brown stripes. His beard and mustache are small and thin, accentuating his distinct youth. He can be little over twenty years old. He has a revolver in a leather holster, also new, strapped to his belt. Only his boots are worn. High above the ankles, black and showing signs of many hours of marching. Perhaps someone has used them before him. Or they are signs of the military training he went through.

Ruis Rafael offers his hand in a friendly greeting, the left hand touching the right elbow as he shakes my hand, a polite custom of the region. His face is gentle and he is very considerate. I felt an immediate empathy for this young man with his many respon-sibilities. His district is under constant, if random, attack. And its proximity to South Africa must lead to some sleepless nights. But his demeanor suggests ease and I wonder how busy he is on a day-to-day basis.

We retrace our route back onto the main road and then turn off onto another tarred road that crosses a sturdy new bridge over the Umbeluzi River. Next to it lies the old bridge, in ruins, victim of a recent cyclone. I think of other collapsed bridges I saw in 1980, but those were victims of Rhodesian army incursions across the border. Below us on the banks of the Umbeluzi is spread out a colorful array of clothing as women and children wash their laundry in the river and beat the garments out on the rocks. On the opposite bank, cattle—surprisingly fleshy, considering the drought—drink from the river. The tar road ends abruptly and I am thankful that it is a Landrover that we are driving as we bump and shake our way around and over potholes of the pitted dirt track. A mansion sits on the rise of a hill overlooking vast and irrigated green fields. It is a private farm now owned by a Mozambican. Doesn't he worry about being attacked? I ask. No, he has his own private and well-trained militia to protect the farm. No one feels safe from the MNR. Not even the wealthy.

A few miles further we are stopped at the control post. The soldier on duty asks us quite sternly where we are going. The secretary of defense answers politely from the back seat. The soldier smiles and waves us on. Ruis Rafael did not pull rank. A few miles on and we enter the small village. The village of Eduardo Mondlane looks as if it has been established in the middle of nowhere. The veld stretches far and wide on all sides. Browned earth looking scorched from the drought.

We stop the car in a clearing and a member of the village assembly comes to greet us. After explanations in Ronga that we would like to talk to residents about the attacks—particularly women—he sets off to find the secretary general of the women's organization. He returns shortly followed by a slight older woman, readjusting her *capulana* (traditional length of cloth) around her waist. Her *capulana* is new, one that she would keep for special occasions such as our unexpected visit. Her clothes underneath show signs of extensive wear. Her cream sweater covers a blouse that is very frayed around the edges. She has one blue cotton terrycloth sock, and one beige orlon one, both covered by canvas shoes, backs folded under the heels because they don't fit. Her gray hair shows under her broad striped maroon and yellow woollen hat. She is very thin.

Mavis Gideon greets us with a friendly smile and listens and nods as we ask again to interview villagers. She tells us to follow her and the man who first greeted us goes off in the opposite direction. She is now our host. As we walk she explains that it is hard to find women to interview as most are busy working in the fields. It is not yet 10 o'clock, the prime time of the day for farming. I ask if they have an agricultural cooperative at the village, one of the goals of the communal village program. Yes, but as it is a little distance away from the village it's unsafe to farm now.

We begin our tour of the small village of two hundred families, walking along a sandy and stony "roadway" that separates rows of small houses and the small plot of land that surrounds each one. Washing hangs on lines next to the mud-and-reed houses, which for the most part look shabby but well kept. The earth is brown, the grass is brown, the houses are brown. There is little vegetation. The few people we pass and the children who come to stare show the signs of severe poverty. Their clothes are torn and very old. The children are thin. Some have distended bellies, the telltale sign of malnutrition and kwashiorkor. There is a sense of desolation.

The people offer friendly *bom dias* and the children giggle. But they are people into whose lives fear has become an everyday affair. Five times the bandits came at night, creeping up silently for the attack. Sixteen villagers were killed in all, mostly members of the militia—*milicianos*—trying to defend their people. Some bandits were killed too. How many the villagers couldn't tell. One was left in the village, and two wounded dead were found nearby. The worst attack occurred the previous November. When another came soon after, everyone fled. They slept where they could, camping out with relatives, on verandas of buildings, even in the bush. Three months passed before it seemed quiet enough to return. The bandits have not come at night again. Not yet.

"That house was attacked," says Mavis Gideon pointing to an empty plot with the charred remains of a house. A rusted enamel basin and a large cracked clay water jug lie among the rubble. The bandits forced the family out of the house and then burned it to the ground, all their belonging still inside. The family rebuilt their house in another part of the village.

Many of the houses look as if they could do with some rethatching, and latrines stand without roofs and with skimpy walls. "The river has run out of reeds," she explains. I take it at face value, thinking it must be the drought. "How can a river run out of reeds?" exclaims the more knowledgable Rebecca. Rivers always have reeds as long as there is water and the Umbeluzi is still deep. Mavis explains patiently that there is only one place in the river that is safe to go for reeds. Everyone from the district goes there. Now it is stripped bare. The river *has* run out of reeds.

We ask if anyone was ever taken by the bandits. Yes, says Mavis Gideon; her daughter, for instance. She goes off to find the younger woman so I can talk with her. She returns with Elena Samuel, who has a young baby tied to her back. Her *capulana* too is fairly new. She has no shoes.

Elena was taken captive seven months ago when she went to fetch water. The village had no water and women must go a long, long way to get water from a spring. Elena points to the distant hills. This time, her husband and another man from the village went too because they were taking an ox and cart to carry back barrels full for a number of families. Four bandits, armed with guns and bayonets, were waiting in ambush. They had already taken other captives. They asked many questions. "Are there troops in the village?" "Who are you taking the water to? Troops?" "Are there vehicles in the village?" "Where is the food stored?" Elena and her companions didn't answer. While they were being interrogated one of the men with Elena managed to escape and run back to the village. Some militia members came and there was a battle. When one of them was killed, the others returned to the village.

The bandits forced everyone to strip. The clothes that were too worn were put in a pile and burned. The rest they kept. Elena Samuel was eight months pregnant so they let her keep her clothes. I think of the umpteen stories I have heard about bandits slitting open pregnant bellies. Usually in attacks on villages. Elena was "lucky."

When night came they told her husband to lie down and go to sleep. He didn't trust them and kept on the alert. They came and tried to strike his neck with a bayonet. As it came down, he dodged. It came again. He dodged. He managed to fight off the bandits and escaped with a gun. But it had no ammunition so he threw it away.

The bandits beat all the others harshly with sticks and then told them to go, all but three women. Elena Samuel was one of these. The bandits by then numbered fifteen. They camped with their captives overnight near the spring and at dawn the next day told the women they had to carry water. With a large, heavy can on her head Elena began to walk. All day she walked, without a stop, to dusk—eight months pregnant, carrying a heavy load. The bandits had guns. She walked. At nighttime they finally stopped near the outskirts of Namaacha. The women were given manioc porridge to eat, made from stolen manioc. The water was taken from them and they were told to go. Elena walked a whole other day until she finally reached home. No one in the village has gone to that spring again, Mavis explains as we walk on. The cart may still be there for all they know. The ox made its own way home. Two months after the attack the village got its own water pump. All they have to do is to turn a central tap and water from the Umbeluzi River—purified by riverbank filtration—flows into their containers.

Now they have water, but they have little food. There should have been two harvests this year but the rains never came. Villagers get some food supplies from the state, and some from the district. But it isn't enough. The small stores from previous harvests are being used up fast. And widows, those women without husbands, have nothing. Their neighbors have no surplus to give them. People don't eat very much. They try to hang onto their seeds for when the rains finally do come. Sometime they must come. But meanwhile when their children are hungry what can they do? Some families eat their seeds.

We walk on in silence after Mavis Gideon stops talking. Then I ask if there have been other attacks. She shows no change of expression when she says yes, a few days earlier the bandits stole some cattle from the kraal a little way outside the village that held forty head of cattle belonging to three families. The families decided to wait twenty-four hours before sending the ten-year-old herders to bring the cattle to the safety of the village. The bandits always come, make their attack or steal cattle, and then are gone. A full day has always been enough of a precaution. Two days before our visit in mid-afternoon the boys left. They haven't returned. Their relatives went to look for them. All they found were fresh boot prints. They got scared and returned to the village. Now the families wait. "Why do you think they took the children?" I ask. Don't know. *Não Sei.* Shrugs. Contemplative silence. Then: "Probably to get information about the village from them. About the militia. About village defense. *Não sei.*" I think of the children that have been kidnapped in the thousands, forced to fight and kill and never return.

Rebecca and I look at each other. A little nervously. There are bandits right in the vicinity, in the midst of the open veld. It wasn't quite what I had bargained for when I asked to interview *affectados*. I begin to understand what the villagers must feel behind their seeming calmness. But the calmness is infectious. We walk

on, turning to the right and up another village "street." We meet
the old grandfather of one of the boys. He recounts the story for us
again. He is also calm. He has not quite finished his story when we
hear a commotion back down the road. People are running, talking
loudly, gesticulating. Someone comes to tell us what had happened. Elena's husband was out of the village, maybe a kilometer
or two, chopping logs for firewood when some bandits shot at him.
He managed to flee unharmed. He called to the others he passed
on the way, and they joined his flight. People are agitated: the
bandits are near our village!

Rebecca and I once more exchange looks. We think of the long
open road we still must travel back to the district capital and the
one solitary control post manned by a few soldiers. Rebecca thinks
of the Landrover and how this might attract attention. She has
been in situations before when villagers or district leaders have
asked her to leave the area because her presence will single out the
village as special and jeopardize the safety of the village as well as
her own. I think of the fact that foreigners have been kidnapped.
Foreigners have been killed. "Shouldn't we leave?" she asks the
secretary of defense. "No, no. No problem," he says. "Let's go and
look at the pump and the water pump and the new school that is
being built. Later we can interview the husband and find out what
happened." "What about the open road we have to drive on?" He
gives a dismissive wave of the hand. "The bandits are out there,"
he points casually in one direction. "We will be going that way,"
he points casually in the other direction. We continue our visit.

Rafael is proud of the new services in the village and is eager to
show us. We visit the pumps where women are standing in line to
collect water. They laugh and rearrange their capulanas in a flurry
when I raise my camera to eye level. We go to look at the new
school building that will house an elementary school for the three
villages in the district. Nearby is the new health post. Antonio
Dumende, the health agent, is a young man, looking neat in his
white uniform and glasses. The clinic is quite well stocked with
basic medicines for fevers, malaria, dehydration. Some penicillin,
antiseptics. Antonio Dumende is from the village and his parents
still live there. The villagers elected him to go and study in
Maputo for two years to be a health agent. He is recently back to
look after the village's health needs. He lives in the district capital
and every morning he sets off early to ride the long dirt road on his
bicycle and then returns to Boane each evening before dark. An-

tonio says he would prefer to live in the village but he can't. It is too dangerous. The health workers and teachers are the first targets of the NMR. We leave the small clinic and go out into the clearing again near our parked Landrover. There seems no point to staying longer. I cannot ignore a flutter of nervousness. "Let's go," I say firmly so that no more "no problems" will shift my resolve. We walk to the car. We just get up and go, aware of how this privileges us from the villagers who wave good-bye to us.

Rebecca drives fast. I look toward the distant hills and wonder which bush, which tree, which hill, protects the groups of bandits. In the silence I reflect on the village we are leaving behind. It is like a garrison without an army. They have their militia to be sure. Fifty for two hundred families is not a bad ratio. But they have limited matériel to defend the village in a serious attack. Many have already been killed. Even Elena Samuel's husband, who belongs to the militia, was almost killed by the bandits. When he goes to chop wood alone he knows *not* to take his rifle. Without it, if ambushed, he can argue that he is just a simple peasant and maybe he will be left alone. With it, he is immediately identified as a *miliciano* and will be killed. No hesitation. The villagers cannot work in their collective fields. They cannot herd their cattle. They could not, when they needed it, go and collect water. They have run out of reeds for their houses. And they are hungry. They stay in the confines of the small village in the middle of the vast dry veld and hope that they won't be attacked. The attacks used to only come at night. And even though they have not been attacked directly in over six months, they cannot relax. One old peasant says to us, shaking his head: "Night is turning into day."

We pass the control post. The secretary of defense says nothing to the soldiers and seems so unperturbed by the event that I begin to think maybe I was worrying unduly. And indeed we get back to Boane and then to Maputo without hitch. No problem. But all the while I was nervous. The incident, insignificant in the scale of things, brought the war a smidgeon closer to me.

Later we hear from a Canadian water engineer who was also in the village the same day that shortly after we left someone from the village went on a bicycle to tell the control about the bandits. The control soldiers didn't dally. They grabbed their rifles and were off. But they did not find the bandits. Not that day. The *cooperante* and his organization decided that he should no longer go to that village on a regular basis. The area has become far too dangerous. I was not worrying unduly. "Night is turning into day."

Não há problema. No problem. How many times did I hear that phrase? The expression was not used as frequently on earlier visits, certainly not in terms of potential disaster. It is a way of believing one can ward off danger. One has to go on living, to treat life day by day as if this were the norm. The line between what can be accepted as normal and what is too dangerous simply shifts as the war escalates. There is only a problem when you are actually caught in an ambush, actually attacked in a convoy, actually kidnapped. Otherwise, it's a matter of continuing to work as usual. But it can lead to taking bigger risks than necessary.

I spoke to a friend who was visiting Mozambique at the same time as I, who had lived there a number of years previously. He decided on arrival that he would not travel in a convoy. Too perilous. But after being in Mozambique a few weeks he began to absorb this new perception of "no problem." So when in central Mozambique he was told that there was no problem, he could safely travel in the convoy, it had been safe for a few months, he did. Later he found that an Italian *cooperante* had been attacked in that convoy a few weeks earlier. He had only been slightly injured; he hadn't been killed. So "no problem." Another friend, having little option, had traveled down the Beira corridor, from Harare to Beira, at night without military escort. He had been worried, but his traveling companions were at ease. Many people now traveled unescorted at night. The reasoning was that the more people that traveled at night the better. It spread the odds. As there is only one attack every three or four weeks, and there are many cars traveling at night, the chance of any one car being attacked is very small. No problem. A foreign doctor I met told me that she had been surprised by the large number of people who traveled long distances by road to attend a conference in Maputo. "Weren't you worried?" she asked one health worker. "No, there was no problem," he replied with an indifferent tone of voice. Then he added as if an afterthought, "The car behind me was attacked. But I had no problem."

So this is what the communal village program has come to, I thought as we drove back to Maputo from Eduardo Mondlane village. The goal of bringing a better life to village peasants has been replaced by the basic struggle to survive the constant attacks and the subsequent devastation by the MNR. The villages have seen firsthand the destruction, have been attacked so often they have fled, cannot carry out their regular daily activities. But despite this, the promises of the communal village program are still being implemented here. New school. Water pump. Health clinic.

These material improvements were part of Frelimo's early vision. It is a vision that the government continues to try to implement where it can, despite the possibility that the resources might be wasted. Between 1982 and 1985 alone, UNICEF estimates, 40 percent of the schools were destroyed or had to be abandoned and over 340,000 children were left without schools.[1] By the time of my visit, two years after these statistics were recorded, the estimated number is well over 500,000. The clinic in Eduardo Mondlane still operates, although their "barefoot doctor" must ride his bicycle over sandy dirt tracks each morning and evening, and at times he must feel very frightened. By 1987, 42 percent of the rural clinics had been destroyed or forced to close down. Health workers and teachers are routinely singled out for murder by the bandits. A Ministry of Health report on the impact of destabilization on health quotes the official figures—twenty-one health workers killed, forty-four kidnapped—but cautions that these are absurdly low because they do not include village health workers, or the numbers forced to leave their posts because of attacks or because the clinic had to be closed down for fear of attack. Neither do—or can—the figures take into account the effect on the morale of health workers of living in an isolated and dangerous situation, or the reluctance of many newly graduated health workers to be posted to rural areas. These are among the reasons that make it impossible to give a full picture of the situation in quantifiable statistics.[2]

The statistics on the number of facilities forced to close down or destroyed are easier to compile. But these also cannot give the whole picture. A total of 213 have been destroyed, another 382 looted and/or forced to close. This is 31 percent of the total primary health care network. By the end of 1986 there were 1,326 peripheral health units instead of the projected minimum of 1,921. The provision of primary health care is a particular success story for Mozambique, as at independence, after a year of transitional government, there were only 426 such clinics.[3]

What seems amazing to the visitor, but actually is simply another instance of Mozambique's refusal to give up in face of constant attack, is the way that clinics continue to be constructed, or to be reopened. Dr. Julie Cliff, head of the epidemiology section for the Ministry of Health, who has been for me a source of information and insights since I first began visiting Mozambique, was the co-author of the report. I was moved by her stories of the young men and women who continue to train and continue to try to serve their people in this critical area. One young woman district health worker was kidnapped twice and managed to escape twice. At the time of her first kidnapping those who knew her—and the situation—feared the worst. She would be killed at worst, raped and brutalized at best. But she was kidnapped along with a group of patients who all through their ordeal never revealed her role and led the bandits to believe that she was a patient like them. Still, they were suspicious because of the way she dressed. She told her captors that she had recently had a miscarriage. It is taboo to touch a woman for a period after a miscarriage. This did protect her, but they constantly assured her that when this time was over they would abuse her freely. The first time she tried to escape they found her. A gun was placed alongside her head and fired. "Next time you try, we won't fool around." She tried again and made it.

Julie told me, too, how those in the outlying areas will go to great lengths to try to get to seminars and courses for retraining and updating. One district health director in Zambezia province drove his car along a dangerous road to Pebane and then walked the 200 kilometers to Quelimane to attend a seminar. At the end of a training course for traditional birth attendants, Julie asked whether they had any last questions. As a doctor she felt sure she could give them the benefit of her knowledge for any question that might come up. One young woman raised her hand. In the tone of someone asking the best way to apply a bandage, she asked what could be done about the fact that their wells were polluted by dead bodies. "I couldn't answer," she told me. "I still can't."

In Eduardo Mondlane, the water engineer still went ahead and put in the water pumps although the long pipeline from the river is an open invitation to sabotage. The construction of the school has not been suspended because it might yet be burned down. How long will they be able to live there? Now that "night has turned into day" will these symbols of continued rural transformation not be the next targets, adding numbers to the already grim statistics?

If the war continues there is little hope for development that integrates women or the emancipation it should foster. Without peace, this village might be one of the next to be abandoned, its houses collapsing and disintegrating one by one as the bush, grass, and weeds of the open veld, left untamed, encroach bit by bit, to eventually cover over what was once a symbol of the process of change.

The setting up of communal villages throughout the country was envisioned as a major mechanism for ensuring the liberation of women. Collective living, combined with the provision of new technology, services, and other resources, could transform women's heavy workload. Because of women's predominant role within the household and in family production, they potentially stand to reap greater benefits from the communal village program than the men. One of the most challenging problems confronting the program is the realization of the commitment of the party, the state and the women's organization to the emancipation of women—how to effect the transformation of the sexual division of labor and ensure that women are as prominent as men in all facets of the village life, not only economic, but political and social.

Women are the focus of the household, the main producers, the ones solely responsible for domestic labor, and the reproducers of this labor power through their role as bearers and rearers of children. Men's labor, on the other hand, is peripheral to this essential task. Their critical input comes from the infusion of cash into the family economy and the way in which their authority defines the relationship between the family and the wider community. In other words, they have the political power within the family. The women have little political power, despite their fundamental role in the family economy. Their work does not, alas, bring with it commensurate rights to decision making, although it can bring with it a certain status.

The unequal relationship between men and women is a relationship that has been well articulated in official documents expressing concern for women's role in the rural sector and the oppression it gives rise to. A text from the Second Conference of the Organization of Mozambican Women describes the woman peasant as the "most oppressed and exploited woman in Mozambique." It continues:

> Reduced to an object of pleasure, a reproducer of children, a producer of food for the family's subsistence, an unsalaried worker in the service of the "head of the family," the woman peasant at the same time has a very great revolutionary potential from which the Mozambican revolution cannot be cut off. This observation is based on the objective reality that our principal activity is agriculture and that most agriculture is for subsistence and is done by women.
>
> The revolution must aim at transforming this agriculture into organized, planned, collective agriculture. Mozambican women not only cannot remain outside this process, but they must be its principal agents and beneficiaries. The Mozambican peasant woman has to be assured equal opportunities to learn new techniques, to have access to the use of machines, to the acquisition of theoretical knowledge and above all to participation in the political organs, in the direction and management to the same extent as her participation in the work.[4]

"Most agriculture is for subsistence and is done by women." According to the 1980 census, 70 percent of the economically active population works in family agriculture. Ninety-three percent of these workers are women. Family production goes beyond the concept of subsistence, although the terms are often used interchangeably. The hope is for a surplus that can be sold to buy basic necessities that cannot be harvested from the fields—soap, cooking oil, *capulanas*, hoes. The most vivid image of women in Mozambique is that of a woman in her *machamba*, or family plot, legs straight, her body forming a V as hour after hour she is bent over double, hoeing, sowing, weeding, day in and day out, under clear skies and hot sun. Sometimes this work is done with a baby on her back and the only rest might be when the infant cries in hunger and the mother finds a place at the edge of the field to nurse her child. She can be in her field as early as 5:30 A.M., and she will work until midday when the sun, high in the sky and burning hot, is too harsh to work under. Men will help with seasonal tasks—clearing the land, for example. Plowing the fields, particularly if the plow is drawn by cattle, by tradition is strictly the man's domain. The image of women producers is repeated millions of times throughout the vast terrain of sub-Saharan Africa, where women are responsible for some 80 percent of family production.

But when she returns home from the fields, the woman's work is only partially done. The food has to be processed—hours of pounding with a large pestle into a mortar, both fashioned from tree trunks, removing the husks from rice, pounding maize into flour for the staple porridge, grinding peanuts to a fine meal. The sound of pounding fills the air at all times of the day, a rhythmic thumping that is carried across the African veld. So is the smell of wood smoke from each family's cooking fire. The lighting of the fire comes only after hours of searching for fuel, often traveling long distances as the supplies nearer home are depleted. Water for cooking, for washing dishes, for ablutions, must also be collected. In some dry areas of Mozambique where water sources are few and far between, a journey of two hours in each direction is not uncommon and the return journey is made with a twenty-litre container of water carried on the head, so heavy that it takes two to lift it there. Laundry is often done at a river's edge or other water source, again a journey of greater or lesser distance. The house and living area must be swept and cleaned. Food must be cooked. Leaves must be gathered from wild plants to be used as supplements in cooking. And throughout the day, as a backdrop to all the other work, is the never-ending responsibility for child care. All these tasks are performed with little if any access to technology that could shorten the time involved and reduce physical strain. And all the while, unless a woman is infertile or past child-bearing age, she is virtually constantly pregnant or breast feeding.

Given this unrelenting reality of the productive labor of the African peasant woman, it is sobering that Mozambique is one of a handful—if that—of African countries that gives it any weight in economic planning or social policymaking. Fewer still are leaders who are as articulate and emphatic in describing the need to integrate women into a development process that takes this into account so that they may play an equal role in society. A prime way of achieving this, according to the plans for developing Mozambique, is through involving women in the communal villages and the setting up of cooperatives in the villages to form the economic basis for the villages. There were high hopes for these villages. A report from the Third Party Congress in 1977 reads:

The organization of peasants into rural communities is essential for the development of collective life in the countryside and for the creation of necessary conditions for socialized agriculture. . . . It is in these, through collective production, that the workers' ideological battle grows stronger. The villages permit a rapid growth of revolutionary class consciousness and the consequent freeing of the workers' immense creative capacity. The organization of people into communal villages makes it possible for us to achieve self-sufficiency in food relatively quickly and also enable us to satisfy health, education, and cultural needs.[5]

Picture the Mozambican landscape: dispersed homesteads, each with its own family *machamba*, dot the length and breadth of the country. Each family works in isolation, far from water sources. No health services. No schools. A sense of community is hard to develop when your nearest neighbor is at best half a mile away, maybe a number of miles. Then picture the ideal communal village. Water on tap at a centrally located pump. A school for the children with attendance compulsory. Literacy and adult education classes for their parents. A diminished workload with time to learn to read and write, to participate in the political life of the village. A small health clinic serviced by a health agent trained in the capital. An agricultural cooperative provides a surplus for the villages, in lieu of taxes, so that more services can be provided. Electricity one day? Transport? Tractor? Radios, even television? A village where anachronistic traditions, particularly those that women find oppressive, no longer find a place. A village where women are outspoken and where their demands are heard. Where they are considered equals. Where development projects benefit women, are designed to benefit women who have equal say in how they are carried out. Without peace, this remains theoretical.

Looking at the small, impoverished village-under-seige in Boane, the three watchwords of the Decade for Women jolt into my mind: Equality. Development. Peace. It was here, almost more than anywhere else in Mozambique, that I really appreciated in my gut the interconnection of these three words. But it almost hurt, as such realizations can do, when I walked around Eduardo Mondlane, talked to the women, looked at their faces, felt the encroachment of the bandits, and found myself making that switch from intellectual sense to emotional sense. This village was set up within a few years of the beginning of the United Nations Decade for Women, in that time of great hope for previously unimagined possibilities. Women such as Mavis Gideon, out-spoken leader, had achieved a degree of equality, although real equality was something she could perhaps hope for for her grand-daughters. Development was concrete: it meant water, school, clinic, democratic processes that led to the election of the local government, of which she is a member. To her the communal village meant neighborliness and concern for each other, which translates into help. It meant the beginning, at the very least, of the "transformation of the structures of subordination."

What is absent is peace. The absence of peace makes the potential for equality and development elusive. The war could put an end to this process, not only for this village in the district of Boane, but for most of the communal village program in Mozambique and, with it, the improvements for women.

Driving back to Maputo I think of Mavis Gideon. I had met many like her in the communal villages I visited when I traveled in the provinces, in Gaza, Cabo Delgado, Zambezia, Maputo, Nampula, Niassa. Women who took on or were urged into leadership roles that were inconceivable in colonial times. Mavis is a member of the secretariat for the village *bairro* she lives in, responsible for health. She is secretary-general of the village unit of OMM. She is on the OMM coordinating council for the province. I think of her, as we drive away. "Mavis Gideon, an English name!" I said to her. "Yes, I was born in Natal," she responds, in English, and she looks down, her hand rubbing at her mouth as if to erase her shyness. Her eyes still on the ground, she said again in English, haltingly, almost with surprise that she remembered even these words: "I have forgotten my English." She has probably not spoken it since she left South Africa as a young bride. Her husband worked in a cigarette factory in Natal province where she was living and he brought her with him to Boane when he returned. She has lived there ever since. How lonely she must have been at first, coming from the semi-urban areas of Natal and her childhood to rural areas of impoverished Mozambique and Portuguese colonialism, far from her own family, where no Zulu and no English were spoken. She had to learn a new language and join a new family. She never learned Portuguese, but then the rural woman who does is the exception. Now her children and her grandchildren are Mozambican. So is she. She is also a militant.

The new life promised her and her family is illusory right now. When she talks about the village, she does not speak first about the new services as her counterparts did back in 1980. She talks of the attacks. Her voice was even, matter-of-fact. She might be describing the state of the crops in a more favorable year or the size of the village. No fear is conveyed. But it's her eyes that tell all. There is a tiredness that tells of the longing for peace.

◈3◈
Harvest of Bitterness

Claudina José grew up in Chipera, a very small town in one of the more fertile areas of Mozambique, the northern province of Tete. Like the majority of people living in Tete, her family are peasants. For generation after generation women have worked the land while the men lent a hand with the critical seasonal tasks. Considering the lack of health services in the past the families are quite healthy: the corn meal porridge is supplemented by fish from the surrounding rivers, which together with an agricultural surplus supply enough cash to purchase whatever limited goods might be available. Claudina was raised to work the land like her mother and her grandmother before her. According to custom, she was married young to a man chosen by her family. Her husband was a good deal older than she, and already had one wife and a number of children. By the age of eighteen Claudina had two children herself.

But Claudina's life has not been just like her mother's. She was seven when her country won its independence and the right age to begin taking advantage of the schools provided by the state. She had passed fifth grade and could speak Portuguese. Free from Portuguese colonialism and with the armed struggle that liberated two-thirds of Tete now in the past, she could expect to play a fuller role in the life of her country than the older generation could ever have imagined. She could look forward to a better life for her children than her grandmother and mother could have dreamed of.

But these expectations soon died. Tete, the western "prong" of the crooked Y that the map of Mozambique mimics, borders on three countries—Zimbabwe, Zambia, and Malawi. In Malawi, for reasons that include that country's friendly relations with South Africa and President Banda's own designs on northern Mozambique, the MNR has found a safe haven and a border across which supplies can be sent. The MNR today operates over large areas of Tete. Chipera was first attacked in 1984. The bandits came at night in small bands, killed the secretary general of the village, stole food from their fields, and then came back again, kidnapping villagers and killing others, targetting teachers. In 1985 they attacked more brazenly during the day. With their sharp knives, they slit the throats of women they found working in the fields. Terrified, the villagers fled to the surrounding bush, returning during the day to work their *machambas* whenever it seemed safe. For a few months they managed to live like this until the bandits came after them in the bush.

With nothing more than the clothes on their backs, the villagers fled the area that had been their home for generations. Chipera, surrounded in all directions by rivers, was virtually an island. The only way they could escape was in the small dugout canoes that the fishermen used for their livelihood. The fishermen began transporting the villagers, small group by small group, across the river to safety. But when the bandits discovered their route, they came at night and burned the boats to cinders. For six months Claudina and her family lived in the bush, always accompanied by the fear of being found by the bandits. They scavenged food and were always hungry.

They lived like this until they were able to cross the river. But beyond this river lay the broad Zambezi, an even greater obstacle. They headed for a point on the river where the government was trying to arrange transportation to the southern bank. At this place, which Claudina called "emboké"—an embarcation point—they had no food. Her older child, aged two-and-a-half, weakened by months of sporadic eating, got sick. Within a few days he died. Her younger, still breast-fed, was not yet affected by the lack of food. They were at the *emboké* for two months before the bandits reached them. An emergency evacuation was organized by the government and the villagers were taken to a place where a refugee camp was planned. But day after day nothing came. They were not allowed to leave. Provisions would be arriving, they were told. But they didn't come.

Then her baby began to show the effects of malnutrition. She felt her only hope was to get to Estima, which she heard was more secure and had food available. But her husband forbade her to go. He said that he had his other wife and their four children to care for. How could he go with her? With rising panic she watched her nine-month-old child, getting thinner and thinner. One night, after she made sure her husband was asleep, she tied the ailing infant to her back and set off for Estima. Already 5,000 people had been resettled at Estima, but for newcomers there was little to offer beyond a walled-in yard around the only cement building in the area, a very dilapidated ex-administrative center of the Portuguese. She was given a place to sleep on the open ground, sharing the yard with two hundred others. Every day food was handed out, which she cooked with the other women over the fires they made. But it was too late to save her baby. He died two days after she got to Estima.

The drive to Estima from Tete City, the provincial capital, took over two hours through some of the most barren and dry countryside I have seen in Mozambique. Everything was brown, a pale, dusty brown: the earth, the trees, the dried grass, the mud-and-thatch houses of the occasional village close to the road that broke the endless flat landscape. But it was not the brown of rich earth or the brown of a dry season after the wet. It was the brown of the absence of color, sucked dry so that every last trace of moisture had been drawn into the hot air and never replaced. It was brown as far as the eyes could see on the open, never-ending veld. The white clouds, high in the African sky, were light and wispy, denying any possibility of rain. The people we occasionally passed looked thin, their clothes were ragged, and I wondered how they coped under the perpetual sun waiting for the rains that never came. The whole of the south of Tete province is stricken by drought—nothing new for that area, which is as likely as not to be bypassed by the rains from one season to the next. It is the north of Tete, in contrast, in districts such as Angonia and smaller settlements such as Chipera where the rains can be relied on and where the vegetation and forests are thick and green and the mountains glorious.

As we neared Cabora Bassa the road became steep and winding, leading to the site of the dam that was built with Portuguese and South African capital during the colonial era to sell South Africa much-needed hydroelectric power. We made a brief obligatory stop at Songo, the district capital, to be greeted and welcomed, and returned to the road, driving away from flower-decked roadsides and roundabouts, and neat brick houses and shabby tennis courts and swimming pools—signs of the time when the Portuguese were there in relative splendor. Despite the massive dam, there is no local irrigation. And the landscape soon reassumed its uniform brown.

We turned off the road to Estima and the driver stopped in front of a building that is now home for two hundred people who have recently found refuge here. Most are women. Some were preparing food. Some were pounding grain, others were stoking fires and cooking the staple corn meal. A few small pots of beans were boiling in plain unsalted water. Here and there three or four women sat together over branches of trees, pulling off the small, dark green leaves and stacking them in a pile for cooking into a sauce for the corn meal. They were the only greens available. *Leaves.*

Lina Magaia, who was accompanying me as interpreter, was off, my tape recorder in hand, to find women to interview. Lina's combination of direct but sympathetic questions and her special personality had people eager to tell their stories. She was soon reclining on the reed mat brought out for her, surrounded by a group of young women, including Claudina. The baby Claudina was holding began to cry. "You can feed your baby," she said, thinking the young woman might be holding back because of our presence. "She's not mine," Claudina answered. "Mine are dead."

Claudina's story translated into life the statistics published by UNICEF: the infant mortality rate is 200 per thousand. Only one other country in the world—Angola—has rates as high. One third of Mozambique's children are dead before their fifth birthday— 325 to 375 per thousand.[1] However, health officials think even these figures are too low. The 1987 Ministry of Health report estimates for the displaced in Tete are shockingly grim: the under-five mortality rate here is between 443 and 552 per thousand. UNICEF estimates that between 1981 and 1986, 320,00 children had died as an indirect result of the war, 84,000 in 1986 alone. Most died from diseases that in more normal times could be prevented or be cured by simple treatment.[2]

I walked around the small encampment. There were very few men. Most of those that slept there were out looking for material to build houses or wood to use for the fires. There were children of all ages playing in the yard and outside in front of the building. Some had come with their parents. Some were there alone. "See that girl?" said Claudina pointing to a twelve-year-old helping to cook. "She is here alone." Her mother had fled with her and her infant brother from Chipera to the *emboké*, the point on the Zambezi River. But there was not enough food to eat. So tying her baby to her back, the young girl's mother went to scavenge food. In the bush they encountered bandits, and both mother and baby were killed. Against the wall sat an old woman, who had been brought to the emboké by her daughter. The daughter also went to look for food, leaving her two young children in the care of their grandmother. She never returned. The grandmother brought them to the center and tries to look after them although she is very old.

Other statistics came to mind: in just one year—1986—the Ministry of Health estimated that 200,000 children lost or were separated from one or both parents.[3] Children were often found wandering in the bush, totally lost, knowing little but their own or their parents' first names. Their parents had been killed or separated from them during the panic of fleeing. The chance of ever being reunited with family was small. It was hard to know where to begin to look among the hundreds of thousands of refugees.

"Do you want your own *machamba*?" Lina asked Claudina. "Hai!" she exclaimed, "and go back to Chipera? No! If I can, I want my *machamba* here. No one wants to go back. But if only the war would stop, then I would go back. Now, I would like the chance to build a house here. Life is not easy," she said in understatement. "We have no place to sleep. We live in the fresh air. We want a new life. During the war the soldiers of Frelimo were good to us. We lived well with them. Not like the bandits who come to kill us. They don't like our independence. What do these bandits want? First they came to ask for food. If people refused to give the food, they killed them. Even those that gave them food, they killed. And yet they say they will bring us independence. What kind of independence is this? I'd like the government to kill all these bandits."

The center had little to offer besides security and minimal provisions—corn, soap, sometimes dried milk. No meat or fish, no vegetables, no oil to cook with. Estima was the furthest distance that vehicles could travel without military escort and the Mozambican authorities had high hopes for the area. They planned to resettle 70,000 refugees who had fled the Malawi. They would develop agricultural projects including irrigation schemes, build villages, and give the peasants land to cultivate. I looked over the flat, dry land that stretched in all directions and wondered, in the midst of a drought, how this could be achieved on such a large scale. When I raised my reservations with others in Tete City, I realized the scheme had its critics, who questioned the sense in planning such a large project and pumping massive resources— aid—into it, not knowing whether it could work.

Soon after I left Mozambique the road to Estima and its sole control post was attacked a number of times. Travel became risky. When I was there I queried some old Tete hands about the advisability of traveling so far from the city. I was wary of the easy *não há problema* and thought it prudent to double-check. "It's OK," I was assured. "There have been no attacks on that road for many months." And then my friend added with a cautionary smile, "Well, not as of today."

Attacks began on the road from Tete to Estima. For a time it looked as though it would be necessary to halt the transportation from Tete City of the masses of material needed for water pumps, housing, and schools, the hoes and other agricultural equipment, the food and clothing, the medical supplies for 70,000 people. But the region was resecured, and the attacks have stopped. Estima itself though, had not been attacked. Well, not as of today.

During the war of liberation, Tete was the third front to be opened by Frelimo. First came Niassa and Cabo Delgado provinces, both bordering on Tanzania, which provided a secure rear base for the guerrilla army. Of the three countries that share borders with Tete, two—white-ruled Rhodesia and Malawi— would have been happy to see Frelimo fail. Zambia was sympathetic though, and as Frelimo clocked up successes in the first two provinces, Frelimo decided to open Tete to the war, using Zambia as the rear base. Tete in itself had little strategic importance. But with Frelimo firmly entrenched in the liberated zones of Cabo Delgado and Niassa, it could hope to move down into the vital central provinces of Zambezia and Sofala and Manica. For this it needed Tete. The people of Tete were quick to respond. In 1972, four years after the front was opened, Frelimo controlled over half the province and new fronts to the south were ready to be opened. Key to their success was the way in which the peasants worked together with Frelimo guerrillas to attack Portuguese army bases, mine roads, and disrupt transport. When Claudina related that Frelimo soldiers were good to her people she was not being glib. And the people were good to Frelimo. They became one.

Then suddenly the war was over. What looked like the beginning of the fulfillment of their dreams for a new society turned out to be a short breathing space. Within three years they were at war again, this time across the border against the forces of Ian Smith's Rhodesia and the newly established MNR. Considerable effort went into fending off these new aggressors. Finally, in 1980, this war ended too, when the independent nation of Zimbabwe came into being. Mozambicans hoped to forget about the MNR, which would no longer have a base from which to operate, and to develop the province's economy in earnest.

Northern Tete is particularly fertile. Districts such as Angonia are renowned for their lush vegetation, ample rainfall, and family farming that was seldom without a surplus. The farmers of northern Tete provided enough food to feed themselves while also feeding the south of Tete, an area plagued by frequent drought. The private farms and the state farms produced enough so that Tete could export food to Beira, the second largest city, and Maputo, trucking the produce south over the road through Manica province to the port.

Dan O'Meara, who worked for the Center for African Studies at the university in Maputo, visited Angonia for two weeks in 1981. He remembers the beauty of the place, the richness of the agriculture. Fields were well planted and the harvests were good. People had enough clothes and they had enough to eat. With the surplus that family farmers could rely on year after year in this fertile area, they had access to the extras that made life easier, either purchased in Tete or traded for across the border in Malawi, when they were not available in Mozambique. Dan found that many Malawian women sought Mozambican husbands, because these men had land, and land meant security. Some 10 to 20 percent of men in the district were married to Malawian women.

Signs of Tete's recovery from the war of liberation and the war with Rhodesia were evident early on. By 1978 the government had nationalized the Moatize coal mine, twenty-five kilometers from Tete City. As part of the development plan, goals were set for the various industries. The debilitating mix of lack of foreign exchange for spare parts and raw materials, mismanagement, lack of personnel with the requisite technical or management skills, and inadequate agricultural development meant that few industries could even meet, let alone exceed, the projected goals. Nevertheless by 1980 the coal miners at Moatize had exceeded their production target of 400,000 tons. Coal traveled out along the railroad that had been built by the colonial administration to carry out coal and carry in cement for the Cabora Bassa dam. Today, the railroad no longer functions. The terminal at Moatize has been put to other use.

From Tete City we drove quickly over the good tarred road out of the city, across the bridge over the Zambezi River, toward Moatize. The open landscape, backed by hills and mountains, is broken by the eight giant storage tanks behind the fences that surround the railroad terminal. At their base are the rows of railway carriages that for many months have provided shelter to displaced peasants. Now families are sardine-packed, three to four families per boxcar, which has become home. Laundry hangs out of the windows, while children play in the dry sand under and in front of the carriages. A sad-faced women stares out of the window of one boxcar and surveys the scene. Other women lean out of adjacent windows, in a shouted conversation with each other and with women standing below. Groups of people stand together between the two long rows of carriages. At the one end people line up next to two large sacks of peanuts and rice, waiting their turn to have a scoop poured into the containers they bring. This is part of their food rations.

Whole populations of some districts now live in the camp. The district leaders are still working, but under rather different circumstances than they did at home in the north. The health workers—those who survived the attacks—work with expatriate volunteer doctors and nurses to run the clinic. A large new tent with a red cross painted on it serves as a hospital for the very sick and wounded. I had been cautioned by an aid worker in Tete City that I would not find malnourished children to photograph in Moatize. Nothing dramatic here, he said, no women and men with slashed-off ears and noses. I had had my fill of the grim stories that constantly reverberated in my head as I wondered again and again just how women ever recover from watching their children cry and then die of hunger while they can do nothing but hold them and watch helplessly. Television news photographers have captured famine-depleted Mozambicans well enough. A CBS news reporter who visited refugee camps and showed viewers wrenching photos of famine victims said that he never saw anything as bad in Ethiopia when he was covering the drought there.

All I felt was relief when I was given the results of a recent health survey of Moatize, which found that an unusually low percentage of the Moatize population is suffering from malnutrition, and most of those are the newcomers. Elsewhere, malnutrition in the refugee camps was estimated as high as 50 percent. The rations make the difference. These, though very basic, prevent malnutrition. Some supplies are handed out weekly, others monthly; they include peanuts, sugar, milk, beans, oil, maize, salt, dried fish. No meat. No fresh vegetables. But nobody goes to bed hungry. Besides the food, the refugees are given clothes and other essentials such as plates and cutlery. Most arrived in the clothes they had fled in, carrying nothing. Not like the pictures one associates with refugees elsewhere, who have somehow crammed as much as possible onto their heads and backs, pushing carts, wearing layers of clothes. No changes of clothes, no plates or utensils. Often no documents. The loss of documents has troubled many of the refugees. Documents are guarded under normal conditions with great care. Sometimes they are buried in the fields so they won't get stolen, sometimes kept in special hiding places. Under the Portuguese documents were used to oppress. Now they are used to gain access to education and health care, to register vaccinations of children, to get food from the consumer cooperatives. They have been treasured. But fleeing in a hurry often meant leaving them behind, or an attack could mean watching them burn with all one's belongings in a house set on fire.

People fled to the camp without clothes, after being forced by the bandits to strip. From one end of Mozambique to the other, bandits carried off clothes in good condition and burned those they decided were not worth keeping. People who escaped with the clothes they were wearing were left with shreds after months in the bush, and refugees would arrive at the camps wearing little more than frayed strips of material, or coarse sacks that they had managed to salvage from food centers, wound around women's waists like *capulanas*. Some were so ashamed of their nakedness that they opted to scavenge food in the bush rather than seek help. Some painted clothes onto their bodies, so that their nakedness would not be immediately noticed. Ruth Brandon Minter, who was gathering information for a report for the U.S. National Coun-

cil of Churches, recalled a conversation she had with a transport
official on a visit to Mozambique shortly before mine. He had just
returned from the refugee camp at Gorongoza near the center of
the country and spoke of the tremendous influx of peasants fleeing
the countryside to escape the bandits. The previous week had
brought 3,500 new arrivals to that single site. "There was one
group of persons," he said, "who approached our camp very
slowly, seeming to want to stay their distance. Only as they finally
came close did we realize that they were entirely nude. What we
had taken for clothes at a distance was painted on to cover their
shame."[4]

Like those at Estima, many of the residents of Moatize had lived
in the bush for months. They can now survive in the camps. But to
regain their lives will be a longer story. I wondered about the
psychological effects as I looked at women sitting listlessly under
trees or near carriages in Moatize, or against the cement wall in
Estima.

While I was interviewing Claudina in Estima, my glance was
repeatedly drawn in the direction of a number of women who were
sitting with their babies under the tree and near the wall. I was
affected by the stillness of their bodies and the total absence of
expression on their faces. It seemed that for the few hours I was
there talking to the refugees, these women did not move one
millimeter. "Normal family and community life in Mozambique is
being destroyed" states a recent report of the Ministry of Health.
"The stress caused by uprooting and insecurity, the lack of essential goods, the overcrowding in the urban areas, also contribute to
the breaking up of the family structure. The vast majority of families in Mozambique are unable to meet their children's basic
needs, not just for food and shelter but for stimulation, love and
stability. The consequence of this situation will have to be dealt
with over a long period of time."[5]

As Claudina unfolded her story, eager to share her hardship so
that those outside her country would better understand the plight
of her people, I wondered how long it would take her to recover.
She had watched her two children die, the younger just a few days
earlier. Meanwhile, pained by her own loss, she helped another
young woman care for her baby. She had left her husband against
his wishes to try to save her baby and so could not return. She
does not know where the rest of her family is. She is alone in the
camp. She is nineteen.

The boxcars at Moatize cannot accommodate the thousands that have flocked to the camp. Houses are being built on the open land across the road, and some tents have been erected. But tents wear out quickly, while the houses cannot be built fast enough. Many live out in the open, under the storage tanks or under boabab trees in the settlement on the other side of the main road. The trees offer little more than comfort. Despite the powerful sinewy trunks, the branches of the boabab tree are spikey and leafless and hence provide no shelter. Moatize is supposed to be a transit camp. But the problem of where to settle the transitory population is as yet unsolved. Benga, about twenty kilometers away, was scheduled for development for Moatize's refugees, until—shortly before my visit—the vicinity was repeatedly attacked. With Benga unsafe, Moatize continues to expand. Boabab tree or boxcar, at least it is safe.

Atanasio Andre was living under one such tree. There were 200 hundred others—men, women, and children. He had been living there only two weeks, since the day he had arrived in the camp. Atanasio Andre is a teacher. For many years, he taught in a school in Angonia district, northern Mozambique. Then in 1985, the bandits began to systematically destroy the schools in the area. He had to stop teaching. In 1986 four teachers from the district were killed. Atanasio Andre lived on in the village of Donwe, and helped cultivate the land with his wife and three children. His oldest is ten years, his youngest is three. But the attacks in the area and then on his village were stepped up and he and his family, together with the whole village, fled the area in 1987. They crossed the border to Malawi.

In Malawi they were safe, but they had little to eat and no money to buy food. Every so often a group of Donwe men and women returned to their village to pick the crops they had so carefully cultivated in the rich soil. On one of these sorties they were discovered by bandits and captured. The women were allowed to go. "You are not 'people,'" the bandits said disparagingly. "You don't count. Women are not important."

The bandits took them to a point to join up with over 250 others, who were tied together with rope in a long human chain. The bandits forced their new captives to empty their pockets, and took watches, knives, documents, money, everything. Forced to carry beans, chairs, and other goods on their heads, they were marched for hours a day, from dawn to dusk, over many miles. The food they portered was not for them; every three days or so, the captives were handed a handful of dry, roasted corn. This is all they had to eat. They were seldom given any water.

When they began their march, a cross was shaved on their heads. "So don't try and escape. We'll know who you are and we'll kill you," the bandits warned, brandishing their weapons, "And don't look back. Just walk." For the twenty-eight days they walked they were never untied. Not to sleep. Not to eat. Not to go to the toilet. Those who dared looked back were beaten. When any got tired and their pace slackened, they were beaten. A bandit would take his rifle and fire it into the ground around anyone who collapsed. "Get up, get up, get up!" Three who collapsed and could not continue were shot dead.

But, said Atanasio, it was not only the captives who got tired. The bandits did too. One night the bandits all fell into a deep sleep, and slowly, carefully, with as little movement as possible so as not to attract attention, the captives began to cut the rope. Each captive had to wait his turn, exercising supreme self-discipline. If he tried to rush he would jeopardize his and everyone else's life. One by one they cut themselves loose and fled stealthily into the night. And then the bandits woke up. Seventeen captives managed to make it to Moatize. More had escaped—over forty—but Atanasio doesn't know who was recaptured and who managed to flee to other areas. For sure, though, anyone who was recaptured was a dead man now.

While Atanasio Andre told his story, prompted by some of the seventeen who had escaped with him and were now living under the same tree, I looked around. A group of young boys had built small toy trucks out of wire with meticulous precision, which they pushed around with a rod, the wheels turning in the dry dust. The boys giggled and pushed their treasured creations and their faces into view of my camera to make sure that they would get photographed. It was a game and they were fascinated by my interest in them. In contrast, mothers sat straight-backed and straight-legged with infants on their laps. They stared out into open space, seldom turning their heads.

I carried my camera throughout the camp but found it hard to take photos. When I raised it to my eye, zoom lens protruding, I felt as if I were intruding on the lives of these refugees in some gross way: peering into and exposing their vulnerability, their lack of privacy, their loss of hope, their pain. Thinking that somehow, as a journalist, I should be recording what I saw, I took a few, but none came out very well. I could not distance myself. How different are my photos from previous visits, reel after reel, capturing women at work in their new roles, women enamored with the hope of that time.

I spent a number of hours at Moatize, walking through the camp, talking to refugees. One young woman, standing outside a small reed house, was holding a very slight infant on her hip. I was drawn to the baby's big trusting eyes and sweet face, as she clung to the shoulder and chest of what I presumed to be her mother. The baby, it turned out, was her niece. Her experiences had made her face much older than her twelve years. "How old is the baby?" I asked. "One year," the aunt replied. I was startled. She could not have weighed more than ten pounds. "Are you sure?" "One year old," she insisted. Another statistic made me wonder about this little girl's future. Surveys done between 1985 and 1987 found that 46.9 percent of children under five are stunted in growth, the effect of malnutrition.[6]

The twelve-year-old told me her family had all lived in Matenge until it was attacked. Her sister was killed in the attack, but she had been lucky, and had escaped with her mother and the infant. Another sister could not get away and was still in Matenge, which the bandits had taken over that day and still occupied. For four months the three had lived in the bush and had no milk to feed their little charge. The baby drank water. They had finally reached Moatize a month earlier. Finally, the baby has regular milk and food. I looked at the little child, and she stared back at me, her cheek resting trustingly against her aunt's shoulder. Very quiet, very beautiful, very delicate for a one-year-old. Could she come through this acute malnutrition without any damage? I wondered.

Standing nearby was Pedro Aleixo. He was twelve. He too had experienced more than one could ever dread for a child of that age. When he talked about his experiences, about fleeing his village,

about seeing people killed, he talked with the calmness of an
adult. He was born in Angonia district and lived there until his
village was attacked. Many people were killed that day, he said.
He managed to escape and travel the ninety kilometers to the
Zambian border. He does not know what happened to his parents
or where they are—if they are alive. He has a brother in Cuba who
used to write. How will his brother ever find him now? When he
was in Zambia the Mozambican government arranged for him to
come to Moatize. He is alone in the camp. He is back in school, in
fourth grade. "What do you want to do when you grow up?" asked
Lina. His voice was steady: "I want to be a soldier and kill all the
bandits."

I interviewed the head of Tete's "Calamities"—the Department
of Natural Disasters and Calamities (DPCCN)—in his office. The
picture that the director painted was a somber one. The prospects
are not good, he said. "We can only do what is possible, not what
is *needed.*"

Not that much is possible. The ultimate objective is to return the
refugees and the displaced to their homes. But as more and more
people flee, this is not an option right now. In the meanwhile a
number of resettlement schemes have been planned, to set up new
communal villages and agricultural projects so that people can
begin to rebuild their lives. Plans have had to be continually
shifted or shelved when a previously safe area is attacked and has
to be ruled out. At the same time large areas—such as in Zambezia
and Sofala—have been rendered safe again by army action.

Meanwhile the refugee camps swell. For Mozambique as a
whole, 5.96 million are dependent on food aid, including 3.31
million displaced or severely affected, while 2.65 face famine. Of a
total Tete population of 980,000, almost two-thirds—620,000—are
so-called *affectados,* a word that has entered everyday speech to
refer to those touched in one way or other by the war. The story of
Claudina or the story of Atanasio times *620,000?* Many have
stories even more brutal. And the murdered and massacred cannot
tell the way they were brutalized. The director explains that it is
hard to break down the figures. For instance, they cannot calculate
how many people have actually been killed. The number of those

affected by drought is put at 199,000, but one cannot place these in a separate category, as if somehow separate from the war. In more normal times, the drought would not necessarily mean famine because the north could provide food for the south, which has seen no rain since 1984. The war has turned survivable hardship into starvation. The number of those who have fled across the borders from Tete into Malawi, Zimbabwe, or Zambia is estimated at 300,000—out of a total population of 700,000. However, not all have stayed. Many have returned to Tete—and can be found in Moatize for example—while others have returned to neighboring provinces.

"What was the harvest in Tete this past year?" I asked. The DPCCN director gave a one-word answer: "Zero." At my silence he added: "All the crops of the people died. *All.*" And this is a province that regularly exported crops. Virtually every ounce of food had to be imported, and most of it came in the form of aid through the Calamities Department. When trade in agriculture came to a halt, Tete province lost that source of revenue. In Angonia alone, for example, 26,000 tons of maize grown on private farms and state farms were commercialized in 1982. Five years later: nothing. The whole area, except for a narrow belt around Ulongwe (the district capital), has been abandoned. The countryside still looks lush and fertile. But no crops grow.

At the time of my visit it was safe to travel by car along the road to Cabora Bassa and Estima, about 130 kilometers from Tete; to Magoe district and the central southern part of the province; and by convoy across Tete from the Zimbabwe border to the Malawi border. It was no longer possible to travel from the port of Beira into Tete to bring in the needed goods and to take out whatever exports there were. These must now be sent through Zimbabwe. A glance at a map of the area illustrates the problem well. Instead of branching off north toward Tete, trucks go all the way up the Beira corridor in convoy, make a detour through Zimbabwe, and double back into Mozambique to rejoin a military convoy at the border for protected travel to Tete City. This route almost doubles the journey, adding costs in extra fuel, extra wear and tear on the vehicles and on the convoy itself, which is also supported by the Zimbabwean army. The cost is staggering. Standing in the fields of the green zones of Tete City I watched the Zimbabwe military tanks roll by on the elevated road, followed by civilian and government trucks and some cars hurrying to the assembly point for escort to Malawi.

Tete City—midway between the borders of Zimbabwe and Malawi—is a changeover point for the convoy. Since my visit, the area
that can be safely traveled has shrunk still further. The road to
Estima has been attacked, and so has the district of Magoe. Only
the convoy route is untouched: "as of today."

DPCCN has become one of the main agencies at work in Mozambique. Initially set up to cope with the severe droughts of 1982–
1983, now, as the national director bemoaned when I interviewed
him in Maputo, it is not natural disasters that concern them, but
war. The word *calamidades*—calamities—the one word used to
refer to DPCCN by all, has taken on new meaning in Mozambican
Portuguese and was freely translated into English and other foreign languages spoken in Maputo. It is not long before the word
rolls off our tongues in the regular daily encounters with Mozambique's dire situation. *Xicalamidades* is an Africanized version
that has its own derived meaning: second-hand clothes, collected
in Europe and to a lesser extent the United States, that have
arrived by the shipload to replace the clothes that Mozambicans
have lost in the war. A poignant poem by Jose Augusto Lace, a
fourteen-year-old boy at school in Maputo, reads:

A Mozambican boy
Is very handsome
And very lively indeed
But he wears "calamities."[7]

I found myself quickly learning a number of new words, and
readopting words I had absorbed into my speech on previous
visits, but now used with more urgency. *Arranjar,* for example,
which literally means to arrange. The process of *arranjada* can be
very complex in Mozambique. Nearly everyone has access to
something, either by their own right or through their families.
Fish, maybe, or vegetables from a *machamba* outside Maputo.
Perhaps it is a service, or a car that can take someone on an errand.
This informal marketing and trading of services and goods is an
essential aspect of Mozambican life. One *cooperante* came back
from the north in a small plane crammed with sacks of rice and
beans and two skinned goats wrapped up in sacking and plastic,

hooves and tails sticking out, which her Mozambican companion had "arranged." The Mozambican generously insisted she have a small goat. It stayed in her freezer for a long time, until she gave it to someone to deal with. She ate some good goat stew as a result and no doubt the rest of the goat was used to start another series of *arranjada*. Meat seldom if ever reaches the stores, and when it does it is beyond the means of even relatively well paid Mozambicans. But whenever I was invited to eat in local homes I would be treated to meat and shrimp. I felt honored and appreciative. I had some sense of—but could never really know—what went into providing the feast at the dining table.

Candonga, an African word for black market, is just a step away from *arranjada*. Before deregulation of food prices, *candonga* was practically the only way to procure many foods—fish, meat, chicken, some vegetables. It became an everyday word, even among those who refused to participate because the government was trying hard to stop the practice. Petty *candonga* was frowned on but largely ignored—such as the buying of fish or vegetables outside the controlled market. Because of the pervasiveness of this practice, a gentler term has emerged: parallel market. Extreme *candonga*, done on a large scale for profit and not for family consumption, could result in heavy punishment. People caught selling state coal on the black market—a practice considered in a category with sabotage—were publicly flogged, for instance.

Foreign currency—*divisas*—most notably the South African rand and the U.S. dollar—can be exchanged on the black market. At the time of my 1983 visit, the dollar-to-meticais exchange rate was 1 to 40. On the black market the dollar could fetch, conservatively, forty times as much. During my last visit the meticais was devalued from the 200 to a dollar set in early 1987 to 400 per dollar. The black market rates shrank in step. The figures, though, don't mean that much. Certain goods, including critical ones, are simply not available unless one has access to *divisas*. At times these are commodities as basic as soap or milk.

With *divisas* one can shop in the *Loja Franca*, the foreign-exchange store, which has grown from a fairly small concern frequented mostly by expatriates (*cooperantes*, diplomats, and aid agency people) to a two-story department store where Africans far outnumber the white shoppers. The line for check cashers in the supermarket was always short, while the line for cash (rands and dollars) squeezed from the registers to the other side of the store and doubled back again. The basic foods find a home between rows and rows of South African preserves, huge jars of olives, rows of bottled franks, and one wonders who actually buys the canary seed, the parrot food, and even the cat food. But the African shoppers bought the staples—rice, oil, beans, peanuts, soap, for instance—as well as the "essential" nonessentials such as coke and beer.

Mozambicans who work in South Africa are able to bring home all manner of goods, and in addition bring in rands to either exchange on the black market or use to purchase food at the *Loja Franca*. The only state employees to get *divisas* as part of their salary are doctors, who earn between $75 and $150 per month in meticais, a good salary in Mozambique. In addition, they receive about $30 in *divisas*. This is a source of resentment among other workers, but the government clearly thinks that its medical services are at stake without this perk. With the proliferation of aid agencies and U.N. projects, the number of Mozambicans in Maputo who earn part or all of their salaries in foreign currency has risen sharply, with the inevitable division between those with *divisas* and those without. In the end, very few Mozambicans have access to *divisas*, and it is a word that is used much more in the context of urban life and among those already having some privileged status.

But the term by far the most pervasive, by far the most intrinsic to life throughout Mozambique, urban and rural, is *bandidos armados*. Its usage has been adopted into English, not in its Portuguese form like others, but as "bandits" or "armed bandits," signaling its seriousness. The term conveys the profoundly outlaw nature of those who are destroying Mozambique, and is used from top government level down. Together with *bandidos*, they are called *matsanga* in every local language from the south to the north, after the first insurgent leader, Andre Matsangaiza. The words of many a song I heard, whether in Gaza or in Tete, expresses the need to get rid of the *matsanga*, much as the people sang about the need to fight the Portuguese during the liberation struggle.

The name by which the movement knows itself is "Resistencia Nacional Mozambicana"—[Mozambique National Resistance.] "MNR" was used widely as a acronym. "Renamo" seems to have entered usage in late 1983, adopted first by the South Africans and then the western media. Perhaps they thought Renamo sounds more competitive with Frelimo. Both terms lend a credibility these people don't deserve, a name chosen for a movement that essentially grew out of a fiction. I carry Lina's words around with me: ". . . what kind of war is this? Isn't it terrorism they carry out? Isn't it terrorism [the South Africans] promote by sheltering, arming, and encouraging the armed bandits? Isn't it terrorism to assert that there is a civil war in Mozambique?"[8] What else to call them but bandits? Nothing made this more real to me than my visit to Tete.

"Hey, this war is very important. It has been written in the books." Lina could not suppress a chuckle when Atanasio told us how the bandits had said this when they wanted to stress that they were serious. In all likelihood they were referring to her own book, *Dumba Nenque,* which Africa World Press has recently published in the United States with the English subtitle "Run for Your Life: Peasant Tales of Tragedy in Mozambique." Her book is a compilation of stories of bandit attacks that she collected while working in Manhiça in Gaza Province and that she movingly and skillfully retells. Besides her work in the state agricultural sector developing agricultural projects for the district of Manhiça, Lina Magaia is an accomplished journalist who has published regularly in Maputo's weekly magazine, *Tempo.* The book got wide publicity in Mozambique, and the bandits could have heard about it any number of times on the radio.

With a second book planned, Lina was happy to have the opportunity to travel with me in Tete, an area she had not visited since shortly after independence. The stories we heard in the far north echoed the ones she had heard in Manhiça, way south. It is hard to read her book without tears, without the sense of the horrors reverberating over and over again from one end of the country to the other, from the Rovuma to the Maputo, as the Mozambicans like to say, referring to the two rivers that border the north and the south of their country. There is the account of a little girl, for instance:

> It happened at night, as it always does. Like owls or hyenas, the bandits swooped down on a village in the area of Taninga. . . . Among the kidnapped were pregnant women and little children. Among the little

ones was a small girl of nearly eight. . . . They put down their loads and
the bandits selected who could return home and who had to carry on.
Of those who had to keep going, many were boys between twelve and
fifteen. . . . Others were girls between ten and fourteen, who would
become women after being raped by the bandits. . . . To demonstrate
the fate of the girls to those who were going back, the bandit chief of the
group picked out one, the small girl who was less than eight. In front of
everyone, he tried to rape her. The child's vagina was small and he
could not penetrate. On a whim, he took a whetted pocketknife and
opened her with a violent stroke. He took her in blood. The child died.[9]

The fate of the young kidnapped boys is to learn to kill. The
young brother of Julieta, Lina recorded, was forced to kill Julieta's
husband, who had already been critically wounded by the bandits. "Now you're one of us." he was told. "You've been baptized.
You can come with us." Lina wrote of one small, weak-looking
bandit who stepped out from his a group and said, "Chief, I want
to kill someone. Let me choose." The bandit chief's reply was,
"No, I don't want any blood today." "Chief, chief, let me kill
someone. I want to. I want to kill one of them, let me." And he
trembled as if possessed, or drugged. He was crying. "I can't stop
thinking about the woman who gave birth to that bandit," said one
of the women who had witnessed the incident. "What would she
think if she saw her son now? What did the bandits do to him to
make him end up like that?"[10]

When I asked the people I interviewed in Tete who had been
attacked by MNR groups what the bandits were like, I was unprepared for their answers. I could not become hardened to the
stories I heard, and I felt the tingling of shock. The reply invariably
put the ages of the majority of the bandits in any one group as
fourteen or fifteen years, often as young as twelve. The commander
or chief of the group was older, perhaps in his late twenties or
early thirties. I heard, as Lina had many more times than I, how
young boys were kidnapped and soon forced to kill, sometimes
members of their own family. They were then considered inducted
and were terrorized into believing that they could now never
return home. The extent of the use of children is a source of major

concern for the Mozambican government and has been gaining international media attention.

Government sources put the number of children being used as soldiers by the bandits in the thousands. A *Washington Post* story of January 5, 1988, relates experiences of some of these kids who have been forced into the guerrilla army. José Chaque was wounded in an attack on a civilian convoy twenty miles north of Maputo in which seventy-two people died, at the end of November. He was interviewed from his hospital bed in Maputo: "I saw children—they looked like ten or twelve-year-olds—shooting people," he said.

A Mozambican News Agency reporter, Sergio Ngoça, spent several weeks traveling in Gaza province. He talked to many children who had either managed to escape or who had been freed during army operations. A twelve-year-old boy told him: "The bandits ordered us to choose somebody from among the civilians they had kidnapped and kill him. The bandits gave us an axe or a machete to strike at the person until he died."[11]

Children told Ngoça how they had been given marijuana before being sent out with assault groups. They were given military training of up to three weeks before they had to join killing raids. Said one thirteen-year-old, "If we didn't carry out the order to kill, then the bandits would kill us."

A Frelimo document reports:

> For most of the victims the traumatic experiences began on the forced march to the bandit bases. An 11-year-old recalls seeing other kidnap victims shot dead on the march by their bandit captors. Another child of the same age saw the kidnappers knife a woman to death. A child of ten whose home was attacked witnessed his mother being shot dead by the bandits before he was taken away. Another child whose mother was kidnapped with him was made to watch when the mother was sexually abused by the bandits.[12]

The psychological effects of these kinds of experiences must go very deep. Thirty-one of these child victims are being cared for by the Health Ministry's Social Welfare Department in Maputo under the treatment of doctors, a psychologist, and a social worker. They are part of a pilot study to try to help the children who have been psychologically traumatized by the experience. Their ages range from ten to sixteen and they were kidnapped in the rural areas

where they were school pupils or cattle herders. One such child is
José.

> The torments for José, aged 12, were of long duration. They began at his
> village in Inhambane when bandits appeared at his home and de-
> manded to know if his father was a militiaman. In apprehension, José
> denied this and the bandits burst into the hut and found José's father,
> who was indeed a village militiaman (José believes a neighbor had been
> coerced into identifying the father). The bandits took the father away
> and killed him; as a "punishment" to the small boy for concealing the
> truth, they mutilated him by cutting off part of an ear and chopping off
> the upper part of three fingers of his left hand. The mutilated child was
> left to recover as best he could. Months later another group of bandits
> came to his home and this time they carried off José to their camp as a
> "recruit."
>
> For the first weeks he was kept under observation and bound by one
> arm to a tree. Then, when he was thought to be sufficiently cowed, he
> was released from the bonds to begin military training. On about the
> tenth day of training he was sent out of base to fetch water, and took the
> opportunity to escape. José, who has no formal schooling, has difficulty
> in estimating the passage of time, but was able to explain that from one
> new moon to another is a month, and believes he was at the bandit base
> for about a month.[13]

I thought about Ngoça's report, which said the kidnapped include cattle herders. I remembered asking the grandfather of one
of the young cattle herders captured from Eduardo Mondlane
village why he thought the boys were taken. He said that perhaps
they were wanted to give information about the village. Then his
voice trailed off—thinking of other possibilities? He must gain
small comfort from the stories of children forced into the army as
killers.

At Estima I looked at faces of women peasants and saw despair. I
saw faces of women exhausted, emotionally and physically, by the
havoc of their lives and all that they had lost. I looked and I
thought about the perpetrators of this war.

Back in South Africa, away from the reality of this devastation,
the famine, the deaths, the brutal killings, the extensive disloca-
tion, there are those government officials and advisers who coolly

analyze the situation as though they are trying to solve some problematic but abstract equation. One such person is Professor Deon Geldenhuys of the Rand Afrikaans University, considered a major theoretician of destabilization. In a paper published in September 1982 he set out his theories, which are significant as they reflect the thinking of the apartheid regime. On the one hand, he argues:

> The destabilizer's primary objective is an avowedly political one. Essentially, he wishes to promote (or force) profound political changes in the target state. They may or may not involve structural changes—in effect toppling the regime in power—but certainly would involve major changes in the target's behavior. . . . At the very least, the destabilizer demands a fundamental shift or reorientation in the target state's policy vis-á-vis the destabilizer.[14]

This course is legitimate, he goes on, because the Republic of South Africa's neighbors are engaged in destabilization themselves.

> The provision of sanctuary to SWAPO and the ANC, together with the presence of Cuban and other communist forces in neighboring states, represents attempts to destabilize the Republic. Similarly, black states' political and moral support for the so-called liberation movements, and their clamor for sanctions against South Africa and for its international isolation, are part of a concerted campaign to destabilize the country.[15]

Geldenhuys' prescriptions are to prevent food supplies from reaching the population so that people will blame the "target regime" to support "disaffected groups in the target state", and wage what is tantamount to psychological warfare, aided by establishing radio stations to broadcast propaganda across their borders.

This was no academic exercise on the part of this political scientist. His views and recommendations have been taken up for one or a combination of frontline states by the Botha regime. In cold blood. In 1983, even before the current crisis, these recommendations were being carried out, with famine leading to the death of over 100,000 people and with the escalation of MNR activities. In the small encampment in Estima I looked at what Geldenhuys would be pleased to chalk up as a "success" for his policy.

I didn't witness children dying. I didn't see the MNR committing their atrocities. I didn't see many fleshless arms, or distended bellies. I didn't see the deadened, yellowed eyes of famine victims. But I saw and heard enough: in Boane a communal village that is under siege; in Tete a whole province that has been destroyed, with two-thirds of the population displaced, maybe more. Who can count accurately?

I had witnessed devastation in South Africa too. In 1984 I visited areas that were under threat of forced removal, people who had lived for generations in an area that was now declared "white" and who would be moved away from all possibility of livelihood and subsistence to barren, desolate "resettlement" areas where passive genocide was the order of the day. In contrast, the resettlement areas in Mozambique, which had none of South Africa's resources on tap, would attempt to provide its residents with the basis for survival. People in both rural areas were dying as a result of apartheid. But there is a difference. As bad as South Africa is, there is a strong resistance. And it is that very resistance that has given impetus to the policy of destabilization. One is horrified in South Africa by the suffering, but one knows all the while that the majority will win. The people I talked to under threat in Driefontein were battling the government's policies. Ultimately they won their battle, if not the wider war. The government had to back down and they were permitted to remain. The Mozambican peasants cannot rise up and resist the South African government directly. All they can do is hope for the day that the apartheid regime, like Smith's Rhodesian regime, will be overthrown. In the meanwhile some join the militias to defend their communities. The majority try, with their government's help, to patch up their lives.

It is impossible to be a dispassionate observer in either South Africa or Mozambique. In Estima, where I saw the direct impact of apartheid destabilization policies, there was nothing to mute the despair. Hopes have been destroyed and lives wasted—all to "destabilize" the "target regime." On previous visits to Mozambique I had spent the major part of my time in the rural areas talking to women. This meant traveling to communal villages to record how government policy had resulted in changing their lives. In 1987, it was the refugee camps that I went to, to speak to women. In Tete for example, this is where most of the women are. *Deslocadas.* Refugees from war. Here, in the refugee camps, in story after story of tragedy, it became clear: it is the women who bear the brunt of the consequences.

Women are responsible for providing food for the entire family. They do the endless domestic chores. They produce the food. It is a long day's work that keeps the family going, nurtures the children, supports every member. Maybe this work has not been sufficiently valued, but there are probably few women who do not understand its importance, which has given them some status and respect. It is something women recognize in the core of their being and that has become as organic a part of their lives as the physical nurturing, such as breast feeding, or the contact they have with the babies fastened to their backs, who are soothed by the rhythmic motions of their mothers busy with the daily tasks.

Two-thirds of one province's population have been dislocated. The majority are women. The majority of the population in Mozambique rural areas are women because the men migrate to work in the cities or across the border. The women, the farmers, remain. But now they can no longer grow their food, nurse the seedlings to full-grown plants, harvest the crops and prepare them for food and then watch their children eat. They can no longer be the protector, the one that the family looks to for security and nurturing. They listen to their children crying in hunger and cannot feed them. They watch their children die. Fathers are not exempt from this pain. But they have not been organically linked for millennia to this productive and reproductive labor that at the same time has been the source of the subordination of women.

There were women like Claudina José, who had lost her second child within days of my visit, but who talked with vivacity that flowed from a well of inner strength. They could laugh and still dream about a resettlement camp that would give them a new home away from the bandits, dream about the day they would return to their own homes. There were women who looked pained and exhausted. There were women who looked defeated. The women whose pain reached me the most, though, were those who sat, not moving, their faces reflecting an absence of expression. They stared at visitors and into cameras as if their lives were empty of existence.

◆◆4◆◆
Rural Development Policy

It was January 1982. Four heavy tractors, dwarfing their drivers, maintained a steady pace as they traversed the vast open fields, leaving neat rows behind them, ready for sowing the corn. The leader of the team wore a dust-empregnated floppy hat and perky yellow sneakers. Only when the tractors reached the edge of the field did the *capulana* wound around her waist come into view. When the third driver made a U-turn, it became clear that this tractor, too, was driven by a woman.

Five of the sixteen tractor drivers for "block one" of Moamba State Farm were women, a ratio repeated for the other four units of one of the largest state farms in Mozambique, about eighty kilometers from Maputo. The owner had abandoned the land at independence, leaving behind his already poorly paid workers without income and a farm that was run down. Vast areas were left uncultivated and machinery was eroding and broken. As the government's state farm program got underway in 1977, the land was taken over and the workers kept on. Working conditions improved immediately. Shifts were shortened and wages increased. Relationships among administrators, supervisors, and workers were transformed. And for the first time women were employed. To try to encourage women to apply, a two-week period was set aside during which applications for women only were accepted. Now almost one-fifth of the workforce is made up of women.

Rosalina Ndimande, one of the field workers hired at the time, remembered those earlier days well. "The men kept telling us we wouldn't be able to do the same work as they. When we all went to collect our wages and the men found out we were earning the same, they got very angry. When we began to work, they left the worst jobs for us—like spreading the manure. They were sure we shouldn't earn the same salary. We ignored them and went about the work as if nothing was the matter. We showed them that we could do the work just as well as they. They gradually learned to accept us and now we have no problems with the men."

No sooner had the men adjusted to working alongside women doing fieldwork—scarcely harder than the work they have been doing for millennia on their family plots—than their resentments were fueled once again. Women were trained to drive tractors. How can women possibly learn to do such a thing? Even Gilda Mohlanga's husband, who works on the farm as well, could not believe his wife capable of handling a tractor. The deepest resentment focused on salaries. In 1977 tractor drivers earned 2900 meticais per month, almost double what the agricultural workers earned. Men were furious that women were promoted, over their heads, to higher wage categories. Even the women who were chosen for the training greeted the decision with apprehension. "When Adelia from the office called me into the office one day," recalled Gilda Mohlanga, "and told me that I was going to learn to drive a tractor, I wanted to refuse. I was absolutely sure I could not do it. I had always been afraid of it, it was so big. But then I saw it wasn't so frightening up close. I walked out of the office with my instructor and he told me to get up on this thing right away. At first I couldn't keep the tractor going in a straight line. But each day I got a bit better and two weeks later I was able to begin work plowing the field. I got very excited and I would think: 'Goodness, I can drive a tractor! We women can do this kind of work!' I felt very proud. All the men—and women too——were very surprised that we could drive the tractors just like the men."

Back in the days of colonial rule, when Gilda Mohlanga was growing up, women's lives were very different. Gilda Mohlanga worked as a washerwoman for a Portuguese family in Maputo. The man of the house was a commander in the army. He and his wife had seven children and his parents were living with them as well. She did all the laundry for the family, and had to iron the clothes with a very heavy coal-filled iron. His mistress treated her very badly. She would scream at her when she did something incorrectly, telling her she was doing it wrong but never showing her how to do it right, and then beat her. When Gilda hung the washing on the line, and her employer didn't like the way she did it, she was beaten. She was given stale corn porridge to eat. There was never any meat or any vegetables, just the dry *papa*. How could they give her *papa* with nothing? *Nobody* ate it like that. But she kept her mouth closed. She didn't dare lose her job. Neither did the other workers—the nanny, who also cleaned the house, and the cook. Gilda worked every day, Sundays too, although on Sunday she was allowed to leave at noon. For this she received 500 escudos a month. The bus journey to and from work alone cost her over 200 escudos a month. When she was given her wages, they were always short. Money was deducted for any damage she did to the laundry. And worried that she or the other workers would not return, the employers always withheld a portion of their pay. She couldn't consider leaving. She needed the job and although she had tried to find other work she never could. Every day she got up before dawn to get ready and travel from her shanty home in Infulene just outside of Maputo. She had to get to work by 7:00 A.M. and worked solidly until five, when she caught a bus back home. There was so much work to do that she never even had time to stop for lunch. She and her husband have lived together in a common-law relationship for years. They have one child.

Then came independence. Her employers went off with the whole family—on a holiday, so they said. They never returned. Gilda left Maputo to stay with her aunt, who lived near Moamba. While she was there, she heard that the new state farm was accepting applications that month. She applied and never returned to Maputo. Her husband took a training course at the Umbeluzi Agricultural School, also in Maputo province, and got a job in the seed production department at Moamba State Farm when he finished. "I am proud of this new work I have," Mohlanga said. "I never thought that in my life I could work for wages on a farm. Never. Only because of Frelimo am I doing what I do today."

Gilda Mohlanga is unusual among the women who work on the state farms: few are married, even in common-law relationships. Most are single women with children to support, who have either never married or have been abandoned by their husbands. The state farms provide one of the few opportunities in the rural areas for these women to enter the wage labor force.

Maria Madonsela is another tractor driver, and single. At a very young age, her parents arranged for her to marry a man she did not know. He paid them the requisite brideprice—lobolo, as its known. From the beginning he beat her. Her two children died the same month when the older was six and the younger four. The abuses increased until she finally left him. She fell in love with another man whom her parents accepted and once more lobolo was paid. At first everything seemed fine. They were happy together and she soon had a child. But however much she wanted another child, she could never get pregnant again. The pattern repeated itself: her second husband became abusive. Both he and his mother used to shout at her and they treated her like an outcast. Her husband refused to provide food for her. "Why should I feed you if you don't have children?" he would yell. "It's like living with another man." Then one day he simply came home with a new wife, a young woman who was already pregnant, and told Maria to get out, shouting again that two "men" cannot live in the same house. She had no choice. She left.

She went to live with her parents and built her own house alongside theirs. She fell in love again, but this time she was cautious. "He has his house. I have mine. Sometimes he visits me, sometimes I visit him. I am tired of suffering. If I leave my own home to go and live with him how do I know he won't get tired of me because I don't get pregnant and beat me just like the others did? He can get tired of me if he wants and he can leave me. I can continue living in my own home." So during the day she drives a tractor and at night she goes to her own home. "Before, I was just doing the work of women in the fields and in the home. I was always crying. I cried because I had no husband. I cried because I lost my children. I cried because I had no money. But now I can support myself. I'm so happy. I have put an end to my tears."

The personal independence and the new life that the tractor drivers found at Moamba was a direct result of the policies of Frelimo and the women's organization that filtered down to the district of Moamba and was integrated into the employment practices at the farm. A basic principle of Frelimo's ideology was an emphasis on the fundamental interconnection between the total process of transformation and the liberation of women. At its founding conference in Tanzania in 1962, Frelimo committed itself to promoting the involvement of women in the armed struggle and to the establishment of a women's organization. But it took another five years before any form of women's organization emerged.

Josina Machel, Samora Machel's wife, who died in 1971 at the young age of twenty-five, is credited for being the driving force and vision behind the establishment of the women's detachment in 1967. "At first this was merely an experiment," she explained in an interview, "to discover just what contribution women could make to the revolution—how they would use their initiative, whether they were in fact capable of fulfilling certain tasks. The 'experiment' proved highly successful and this first group of women became the founder-members of the Women's Detachment, and were scattered throughout the interior, each with her specific assignment. It was soon discovered that they could play a very important role in both the military and political fields but especially in the latter."[1]

Nonetheless, not everyone welcomed the new move, the men in particular. "When we started to work there was strong opposition to our participation," remembered an early member of the Women's Detachment, "because that was against our tradition. We then started a big campaign explaining why we also had to fight, that the Frelimo war was a people's war in which the whole population must participate, that we women were even more oppressed than men, and that we therefore had the right as well as the will and the strength to fight. We insisted on our having military training and being given weapons."[2]

Given weapons they were. Many a photo taken by visitors to the liberated zones during the war show the unusual sight of a young woman with an AK47 rifle slung across her back. Nevertheless, it was the rare woman who actually saw combat. They were found to be particularly good political mobilizers. In the army their role was generally one of porterage, transporting the much-needed medical supplies and ammunition on their heads over long distances. As soldiers they were limited to defense, as part of local militias rather than the actual army. But for the most part, their work was centered around "social services"—setting up health and education programs, running the small orphanages that took in children who had lost parents to the war.

Some of the women were very young. Pauline Mateos, for instance, was seventeen when she was named a commander for the Women's Detachment, having gone through the same grueling military training inside the war zones as the men. One of the early tactics was to mobilize the wife, she said, who in turn pressured the husband to join. "Some men have no heart for fighting. They are afraid or they don't want to leave their families and fields. But

once a woman tells her man to go and fight he feels more inclined."[3] Both men and women soldiers, carrying their weapons,
would go to villages to recruit members for the army. The tactic
worked. The sight of women armed would be enough encouragement for the men. As Josina Machel said, "The presence of emancipated women bearing arms often shames them into taking more
positive actions."

The Women's Detachment remained small. It was more successful in mobilizing young women, particularly women without
children, than the general population of women. Older women
had no organization that they could see as theirs. Many were
intimidated by the sight of militant young women, and some even
hostile to the idea of women joining an army. The majority were
certainly not ready to join. It was the acknowledgment of this gap
that led to the founding of the Organization of Mozambican
Women (OMM) in March 1973 in Tunduru, Tanzania. Some eighty
women, old and young, the majority traveling on foot out of the
liberated areas, attended the conference.

President Samora Machel's opening address to the conference
provided an occasion for a statement of Frelimo's analysis of the
situation of women in Mozambique and the importance of the
liberation of women to the revolution. "Why bother with the
emancipation of women?" Machel asked rhetorically. Answering
himself: "The emancipation of women is not an act of charity, the
result of a humanitarian or compassionate attitude. The liberation
of women is a fundamental necessity for the revolution, the guarantee of its continuity and the precondition for its victory. Generally speaking, women are the most oppressed, humiliated, and
exploited beings in society," Machel continued, pointing to a fact
that is often acknowledged only begrudgingly—if at all—in other
countries of Africa. This condition arose from the time when early
humans began to produce more than they could consume, giving
rise to a stratum "which would appropriate the fruits of the majority's labor. This appropriation . . . is the crux of the antagonistic
contradiction which has divided society for centuries."[4]

Machel acknowledged that while men along with women were
subjected to the domination of the privileged stratum, there is a
special dimension to the nature of women's oppression: as posses-
sions of men they provide unpaid labor power without resistance,
as well as reproducing more workers as new sources of wealth.
Society has sustained their oppression, he argued, through ide-

ology, culture, and education. Hence women have not been involved in the planning and decision-making processes in society.

The main theme of this speech is that socialist transformation is the only basis for the liberation of women: it is the capitalist system that oppresses, and it is that system that therefore must be changed. Machel emphasized that the primary antagonism is not between men and women, therefore, but "between all exploited people, both women and men, and the social order." Thus the emancipation of women can only come about within the total revolutionary process.

Most of the women listening to this speech—many were illiterate—must have been quite baffled by the words. It was the discussions later that would translate these ideas into a sense of where to go from here and how to build a women's organization in the liberated zones. As it turned out there was barely time to begin. Just thirteen months later a coup in Portugal led to a period of transitional government in Mozambique, and within another thirteen months, independence.

It was three and a half years after that first conference that OMM called its second conference, in Maputo in November 1976, a year into the United Nations Decade for Women. Those of us looking for signs that the decade would be taken seriously pointed eagerly to the statements coming out of Mozambique. Here at least was a government, a party, and a women's organization willing to provide an analysis of the situation of women as a precursor to devising policy to influence and change it.

Again delivering the opening address, Samora Machel declared that since "the decisive factor for the emancipation of woman is her involvement in the principal task—the task of transforming the society," and since "the principal task is production," women must be involved in production.[5] Specifically, they must be more fully integrated into the process of *transforming* production. To engage in production is relatively straightforward. It requires little beyond work, although it can lead to changes in other spheres of a worker's life. Participating in the actual process of transforming production, however, affects many aspects of people's lives, both productive and personal. It can lead to the generation of new ideas, to participation in decision making, ultimately to workers' control over their role in the labor process and to a stake in the distribution of resources that are the fruits of their labor.

A main goal of the conference was to breathe new life into the women's organization. Many of the delegates complained that they were being forced back into their traditional African cultural roles. They were regarded as rear-guard support for the revolution rather than an essential part of it. They blamed in part the "machismo" attitudes of men who retreated from any serious consideration of the role of women, and to the willing acceptance by many women that their role was merely to cook and sew for the male revolutionaries. It was true that as more and more urban women joined the OMM after independence, the organization began to lean toward the aspirations of more educated urban dwellers who had not come out of the struggle and had little understanding of the political viewpoint it gave rise to.

Criticism of the leadership was one of the central points of Machel's speech. In particular, he chided the OMM leadership for adopting and pushing values that were present under colonialism. The women who were formed in this mold saw their social activities as basically charitable: "[OMM] developed courses in sewing, lessons in cooking, charity parties for poor children. . . . But what is the point of learning all this if the working woman and the peasant woman don't even own sewing machines or gas stoves? Where would they put the embroidered napkin in the empty house?" He leveled criticism against others, mainly the youth, for another misconception, which identified men as the main enemy.[6] Noticeably absent from his criticism was any recognition that as a mass organization of the party, OMM has largely been guided by the party and its goals articulated in speeches such as these by top members of the party, all male. There was no criticism of the party's role in not supporting what Machel outlined as the true contradiction in the society, which leads to the need for class struggle and a legitimate place for the liberation of women within this struggle. OMM has never been conceived of as an autonomous women's movement. It always has followed and been expected to follow the lead of Frelimo. However valid the criticisms directed at OMM, they are criticisms that could well have been directed at Frelimo at the same time.

In fact, if the old leadership was somewhat removed from the problems of working women, the new leadership seems to see itself more as an organization that interprets rather than influences party policy regarding women. Salomé Moiane, secretary general, whom I interviewed for the first time in 1981, seemed to suggest that OMM's role was not to push for policy changes or to criticize

Frelimo policy regarding women. By 1984, with OMM's Extraordinary Conference on social problems affecting women, criticism of party policy was a little more up front, but not sufficient to influence any real turnaround.

A statement that came out of OMM's second conference in 1976 was "Women can do what men can do." It was taken up by OMM organizers and leaders at all levels—regional, district, local, workplace. Simple words that could catch the imagination of the women at the conference in a way that long speeches and lengthy resolution could not; something of a rallying cry, a handle that women could latch onto and translate into their lives as a fuel for social transformation. It was a set of words that could be used to challenge men who preferred to remain attached to their own patriarchal view of their world.

Not only Maria Madonsela and Gilda Mohlanga but women in different parts of the country had their lives transformed because of these words. How widespread such changes were often depended on the quality of local and district OMM leadership, and on the persistence and drive of the women workers. It was seldom something initiated by the managers or the men.

Rosalina Ndimande is the secretary of OMM at Moamba state farm. She was one of the women first hired when the farm set aside a period for hiring women workers only. She was chosen to be the leader of her twelve-person brigade, and a few months later, when OMM was organized at the farm, she was chosen to be the secretary. Her life had been hard. She had been married for quite a while and had lived in the area. She and her husband had four children and then when the oldest was seven and the youngest just eight months they all died of sudden illness in the space of a month. She and her husband did not get on well after that. He kept picking quarrels with her and she was very unhappy. She left him and went to live with an uncle who lived in Maputo. There she tried to make a living by buying pineapples in bulk and reselling them to women who used them for making a local beer. It didn't work out too well as she couldn't make very much money, so she went to live with a sister in Moamba. Just then she heard that women were being hired at the farm. She had not been secretary long when the delegates from the district to the Second OMM Conference came back with the report and held meetings, telling the women that they must show that they can do what men can do. They all discussed how they could try to implement this in their work. The district OMM leaders went to the state farm administration and the farmworkers agreed to try it out.

The message from the OMM conference seems to have reached far corners of Mozambique. In my travels through the country in those earlier years, during that time still of hope, I saw evidence of a new determination to involve women—on state farms, in factories, at agricultural cooperatives in communal villages, in government ministries. Not only tractor drivers, but welders, local political leaders, auto mechanics. I heard too of women stoking engines, driving trains, of women carpenters and miners. There were special training courses set up to help women sidestep their lack of education and get technical training nonetheless. And no doubt, like Maria Madonsela, many of these women have had their lives transformed. But I heard too of a large state farm on a palm plantation in the district of Zambezia where over 18,000 are employed. Only three of the workers are women and all three work in the office. Or Imala State Farm in Nampula Province, which employed about 900 men and 70 women to produce cotton, beans, and millet. All the tractors and cotton seeders are handled by men. The women are seasonal workers only. According to the administration, they had not received any guidelines or directions about integrating women on a more equal basis.[7]

Take Gurue, which I visited soon after the new year of 1981. It took us a few days to reach Gurue by road from the coastal capital of Zambezia in the south, to the central northern part of the province. We had stopped on the way to visit communal villages and health centers. The road cut across central Zambezia and for hours at a time we would pass no other vehicle. I got a sense of the expansiveness of Mozambique and the underpopulation. This was fertile land we drove through, although being summer it was dry—this time the brown of earth that is resting after the rains—and it was very underpopulated. Toward the end the journey the road climbed steeply, into the highlands and to the mountains, mountains that were rich and green and towering, with a beauty that was spectacular. Here in the gentler climate, on the slopes of these mountains, the Portuguese found a perfect place to grow tea. They established thirteen tea plantations, exported the good-quality tea to Europe, and sent the profits to Portugal. For the workers on the tea plantation it was the same story over again: poverty, forced labor, terrible working conditions, no medical services, no schooling for their children, long absences from their own family farms. One of the plantations was still privately owned, but the remaining twelve were taken over by the state when the Portuguese owners abandoned their land in that hurried exodus, and was consolidated into Emocha.

We arrived at the small town of Gurue in the late afternoon, dusk drawing in over the plateau, softening the vistas of mountains across the valleys that dropped away below. I walked around the town as we waited for the local leaders to come greet us at the guest house and I breathed in the fresh, pure, and cooler air. Its beauty touched me all the more because it was so unexpected after the long ride through the more rugged landscape.

The district Frelimo leader responsible for ideological work came to greet us. A young, earnest man, he was full of apologies for keeping us waiting. Advance warning of our visit had not reached him but he was willing to arrange whatever I wished to see. Anastaçia Guimerães, my interpreter and traveling companion, explained that I was there to talk to the women of Emocha. A look of consternation flickered across his face. "This is not a good place to visit if you are interested in meeting women," he said. And then went on to bemoan the lack of OMM leadership and interest in Gurue. One woman after another had taken on the responsibility but no one was very committed. Clearly there was much ideological work that still needed doing among Gurue's women. But undaunted, we said that I would be happy to interview women working at Emocha and did not mind the lack of an OMM committee to receive me and organize my trip. He still seemed nervous, worried no doubt that I would be critical of what I saw. And he was responsible for my visit. But his friendliness never diminished and the next day, after breakfast, we got into our jeep and drove up yet steeper roads toward Emocha's plantation and tea-processing factory.

To the side of the factory was a large shed, with a number of beat-up vehicles—buses, tractors a Volkswagen beetle. Among the twenty auto mechanics were four women apprentices, while another woman was in charge of the tools. Eager for the photo opportunity, one of the young apprentices grabbed a wrench out of the hands of a mechanic who was working on the engine of the Volkswagen and buried arms in the engine so that I could record her "work." The mechanic was clearly irritated. I wondered how seriously the male mechanics, all considerably older than the youthful apprentices, took this attempt to show that "women can do what men can do." The answers to my questions were inconclusive: the men didn't mind, was all I could get in response. What was evident was that the women were proud of their new positions. The initiative had come from the women after they heard about the resolutions at the second conference. They went to the party asking for support and they got it. The party went to the administration and also got support. It took a while to get going, but finally, six months before my visit, the first apprentices were hired. They had up until then been tea packers in the factory, among the small number of women on the assembly line. Two new female apprentices had recently been added. So it was a continuing practice. But the efforts to carry out the goals of the women's conference stopped short in the garage.

We were shown over the tea-processing plant by the manager and a representative of the workers' committee. I saw the baskets being brought in from the fields, large wicker baskets that were carried on the back, heavy with the damp tea leaves, and emptied into bins ready for sorting and drying. An acrid smell of drying tea filled the air. The tea pickers coming off the fields were all men. "Is there a particular reason for this?" I inquired. The men at managerial level gave a number. Women cannot carry the large tea-baskets while picking tea because they would have to work with their babies on their backs; women are unreliable and there is a higher absentee rate among women than men; they are not really committed to work, implying that it's done just for pocket money; women cannot work on the factory floor because the bags of tea are too heavy for them to carry. One of the state farm's directors, a Sri Lankan who is on contract from his government to provide expertise, said that women prefer to do nothing at home and let their husbands bring in the money. "There is always trouble with women as they don't stay at work. They go and have babies." No one contradicted him. I thought of Sri Lanka, where tea picking is

women's work. What about their babies? What about their re-
liability? What about their strength?

Later when I met the OMM secretary for Emocha she spoke
bitterly about the difficulty they are experiencing in getting
women hired. She pointed to a group of women whose worn
clothes pronounced their poverty, who had sat patiently for hours
outside the management office. "Women come and apply for work
in rags. They need the money as much as the men, and still they
are seldom hired. The men don't care. But as women, we feel it."
She swept aside the objections to hiring women that had been
raised by the men. They were out of line. Without a strong district
OMM to draw on for support, and given the attitudes of the men,
there was little she could do to push for change.

Attempts to hire women after OMM's Second Conference had
petered out by the early 1980s. Judith Head visited Gurue a year
before my visit as part of a project she was involved in for the
Center for African Studies at the University of Eduardo Mondlane.
She found that there were some women tea pickers who had been
hired in response to the conference resolutions, but not more than
a few. The four women she interviewed were unmarried and had
gone to work because they had children to support. In order to
work, they had to cope with conditions more severe than those of
their male counterparts. All had been abandoned by husbands.
One of these women lived with her younger child in the house of
her brother, who worked for Emocha. They slept on the kitchen
floor. She had applied for a house on the plantation but wasn't
sure if she would take it even if allocated. She was scared, as a single
woman, of being molested. The second, twenty-eight years old,
went to live with her parents when her husband took a second
wife and abandoned her and her five children. She walked one
hour each way to get to work and back. She worked every month
except November and December, the peak season for her own
machamba where she grew potatoes, then in great demand. She
could sell a kilo for 100 meticais, quite a significant addition to
her income. A third woman, forty years old, had divorced her
husband ten years earlier when he left her for another woman. She
walked two hours in each direction from home to work and back.
The fourth was twenty-two, had been abandoned a year earlier and
without means of survival had applied for a job on the suggestion
of an uncle.

At Emocha, the tea pickers made 62.50 meticais a week—not enough to survive, so after hours of strenuous work in the fields during the week, the women put in hours of work in their *machambas* on the weekends and before setting off for the tea fields. Scarcely a picture of fickle workers. The men who criticized women's work habits were looking at the symptoms and describing them as the cause, instead of trying to solve the underlying problems—such as lack of day care, the need to work their own *machambas*, and the great distances from home.

There was probably a far more significant factor contributing to the lack of women in the workforce even at a time when there was something of a labor crisis at the tea plantation in general. Dr. Head saw the unmistakable signs of an escalating problem that spun like a whirlpool at the core of the accelerating economic problems of Mozambique: lack of consumer goods. With no industrial base and no foreign exchange, there is no money to import consumer goods, nothing in the stores to buy, not even such basic items as *capulanas*, soap, hoes. Without goods to buy, there is no necessity to earn a cash income. Women can better spend their time cultivating their own *machambas* to provide a surplus for barter and for the limited cash they might need. Women are the subsistence producers, and have no reason to grow more than their families can consume themselves plus a small surplus that would realize cash for other needs. As this is minimal, the nation's surplus diminishes. Foreign currency then must be used to import food, and none can be spared for consumer goods. The lack of incentives over longer and longer periods draws the vicious circle tighter.

Work on the state farms, while providing virtually the only access to a pay packet at the end of each week or month for rural women, is not sought by the vast majority engaged in family production. Most feed their families from their fields and tend to look askance at women who earn wages. But for women who have been abandoned or for other reasons have no access to land, employment on the state farms was a lifesaver, which, they discovered, did more than provide them with a means of livelihood. It provided self-respect. It provided an opportunity to "put an end to their tears." It provided economic and hence personal independence. Or potentially it could. I kept looking for the equivalent of Maria Madonsela and Gilda Mohlanga when I was interviewing women. I didn't always find them.

Signe Arnfred, a sociologist who worked with OMM for a number of years, did find replica Madonselas and Mohlangas. Signe visited Regadio de Nguri State Farm in Cabo Delgado, for instance, during the same period that I was interviewing women on state farms in southern and central Mozambique. Regadio, in an area that had been principal base for Frelimo during the war, has an unusual history as it was established out of political mobilization, from scratch, in a community that was ready for it. From the beginning there was a conscious effort to integrate women. There were 30 women among a permanent workforce of 200. The men tended to do the heavier work of digging and cleaning canals and there were no women tractor drivers. The latter was lamented by the farm's director. "The problem is one of schooling. Those who take the driving course have to have completed third or fourth grade. At this time we have no women with these qualifications. But this has to come." Two hours of literacy or adult education per day is obligatory and time is provided from work hours. In contrast to the management of Emocha, the director respected the women workers. "There are men who arrive in tatters, without shirts or pants. They want to make money to buy these things, and then they leave. Or they come to work because they need to pay a fine for adultery and afterward don't want to continue to work. The women are more stable. During the peak season when there is much work—transplanting rice, weeding, harvesting rice—many women come as seasonal laborers. Each year more and more want to remain on as permanent workers."[8]

Many of these women workers had participated in the armed struggle in different ways. For many this influenced their desire to get ahead. One had taken a first-aid course while a member of the Women's Detachment in the liberated zones and wanted eventually to continue her health studies and become a nurse. Said another: "I don't want to be a peasant. I think only of working, that's all. Even if I marry again I want to continue to work." One eighteen-year-old woman explained that she came to work at Regadio de Nguri to help her mother. "Then I married a man who also works here. He has another wife. We live in the same house in different rooms, but the relationship is not good. I do not like polygamy, but what to do when there are no men?" A sixteen-year-old began working to help her family. "I still send money to them. Meanwhile I got married. My husband is a worker here." A woman married to a man in the army came to work because her husband never sent her money. "He has two other women. Even if my husband returns, I will not stop working here. I like the work." This theme was repeated. "I want to work because I am able to provide for myself and also I am able to send money home. If I get married some time, I will continue to work."⁹

Over a half-decade later, in 1987, the agricultural sector that underpins the economy was in serious trouble. The state farm policy was judged a failure and has been drastically reduced. I could appreciate why on a visit to Matama State Farm outside of Lichinga, the capital of Niassa, around the time that these decisions were being made. Matama was considered a model farm in the area. Established in 1976, it typically comprised a number of smaller abandoned farms and plantations, covering 3,000 hectares. Over half the cultivation area was allotted to maize, with a good variety of crops grown on the rest of the land. In seven years Matama had not yielded any profit. The young director of the farm reeled off a litany of hitches and misfortunes that contributed to their problems. In 1983 the maize harvest surpassed the national average. But maize was left to rot in the fields. The combine harvester ran out of sacks. Weakened fourth-generation seeds had gravely reduced the yield. Insufficient pesticide was a chronic problem and beetles were attacking some of the crops at the time of my visit. Disease had destroyed part of the potato harvest.

A section of the farm was irrigated by a nearby river in the dry season, allowing workers to cultivate potatoes and wheat. This had run into problems early in 1983, the year of President Machel's fiftieth birthday. Wanting to show concrete evidence of advances, the district leaders decided to hurry plans to build a dam for hydroelectric power on that river in the dry season. But the dam was built upstream from the farm. The farm lost its irrigating water for the season and the potato and wheat harvests failed. In the end Machel had to cancel his visit.

The late 1983 harvest in turn was threatened by a shortage of workers to do the job. The farm was allocated 600 workers from the Operation Production program for relocating nonproductive urban dwellers to the rural areas. The harvest was saved. But as the salary allocations had been reckoned on the size of the previous workforce there was no money to pay the new workers. They waited week by week—for over four months—living off the basic rations handed out. Then when the figure for the number of workers per hectare was established at a national level, Matama had too many, and had to lay off 500. The new workers, mostly from Maputo, proved to be more diligent. They were, however, the last hired. It was not hard to conclude that the state farm program nine years after its inception was a mess.

Months earlier, in April 1983, the Fourth Party Congress reached the same conclusion, which resulted in a major overhaul of the agrarian reform policy.

When Frelimo came to power, Mozambique's rural transformation program was consistently cited as the country's number-one priority. With 85 percent of the population living in the countryside, and the vast majority of those living off the land, agriculture had to be a priority. The program was divided into three sectors: state farms, agricultural cooperatives, and family farms. Dovetailing with these were the communal villages, planned to be the backbone of the latter two and to provide many of the workers for the former. Large-scale private farming, explicitly market-oriented, was not even considered as part of development policy. Hopes for the potential of communal living and collective farming were high. "If the exploited peasant masses organize themselves in communal villages," stated a report to the Third Party Congress in 1977, "they will be able to integrate and coordinate their efforts and create a solid base for their political, cultural, economic and social development, and a general improvement in their standard of living."

The state farms were forged from abandoned settler farms and plantations, particularly those that were the most developed, the most accessible, and the least isolated. This sector was expected to provide food and cash crops quickly and abundantly, and thus was seen as the best way to feed the nation, while at the same time supporting the industrial sector. Like their larger counterparts, agricultural cooperatives were also designed to produce crops for sale, but on smaller and more isolated abandoned farms or those newly set up alongside communal villages, providing them with a potential source of income—beyond the family farms. Co-ops were also set up, somewhat later, in the green zones around Maputo and other cities.

State farms and cooperatives were seen as key to the socialization of the countryside: state farms would produce a rural working class, who would form an alliance with urban workers to lead the revolution; cooperatives would provide a model for working collectively, an example that could later be adopted by the family-farm sector. While each part of the three-prong strategy was given equal weight in principle and in rhetoric, when it came down to it, policy emphasis swung like an erratic pendulum between the state sector and the family-farm sector, more often than not bypassing the cooperative sector. In practice the pendulum came to a halt at state farms. They got the lion's share of the resources allocated to agriculture, while co-ops got 2 percent between 1977 and 1981. Family farms got nothing.

Yet family farmers by the 1980s were still producing three-quarters of Mozambique's crops, most of which were eaten in their own homes. But given the lack of official support, and the collapse of the marketing system after independence, family farming was in 1983 in total crisis. Said Frelimo vice-president Marcelino dos Santos, at the Fourth Party Congress: "We are not bothering about manufacturing the hoe, because we are awaiting the arrival of the tractor we must import. We are distributing tinned beans, that cost foreign exchange, in a communal village that produces beans and from which no one has bothered to collect surplus production. We overload the peasant with items he does not use, but do not provide him with a lamp, cloth, a file, or a hammer. Nonetheless, we expect him to exchange his production for goods he does not need."[10]

The Fourth Party Congress accordingly resolved to shift emphasis from state farms to smaller units, including not only family farms but also, for the first time, private, market-oriented farms. State farms were dramatically reduced in size, or subdivided, and private farmers were encouraged to put the unused land back into production. Foreign investment was encouraged, and price controls were lifted from many agricultural products in order to encourage production. Although in principle agricultural cooperatives were also to get a new priority, in practice they have again been sidestepped. As the main recipients of technical assistance from the state—fuel, tractors, pumps, and so on—private farms, in the end, are the main beneficiaries of the new policy.

The post-Fourth Congress years were to be a time of reorganization and consolidation, with the benefits being felt after 1985. I returned in 1987, and despite some promising signs, what I mostly witnessed was devastation. No sooner had the congress met and made their far-reaching decisions than the armed bandits began to spread chaos. The whole agricultural sector was in turmoil. Millions were facing starvation, thousands already suffering from famine. Moamba has been attacked several times. Gurue has been under a constant attack in one of the hardest hit provinces. One young army member from Gurue I met in Maputo told me that he has had no news from his family in two years. He doesn't know if they are still in Gurue, whether they are still alive, whether they have been forced to flee. When he talks about it, his youthful face looks old with worry. He just doesn't know.

❖5❖
Transforming
the Countryside

Mama Leia must be in her sixties, although she doesn't know the year she was born. Her hair, when not hidden under a headscarf, is more salt than pepper, and she has grandchildren in their twenties. She does know just how dramatically different her life has been since independence, bearing little resemblance to what she had expected for her later years.

Leia Manhique is her full name, but everyone calls her Mama Leia. It's a term of respect and endearment. She deserves both. Mama Leia was one of the strongest driving forces behind the establishment and construction of the Três de Fevereiro Communal village in the southern province of Gaza. As one of the leaders—she is the secretary-general of OMM for the village—she is constantly on the go, listening to complaints, trying to help solve problems, keeping an ear open for trouble.

Mama Leia was born in Xibonyanine, in the Xai-Xai district of Gaza. Her family were peasants. Her mother married young, a much older man who spent most of their married years working on contract in the South African mines. He used his relative wealth to pay *lobolo* two more times and to also marry the widow of his oldest brother. Leia was still a child when her mother died and as she did not get on well with her father's wives, it was her oldest sister, married to a miner herself, who raised her. Then her sister died. Leia had just "become a woman," old enough, in the custom of her society, to marry. Her brother-in-law proclaimed his love and said he wanted to marry her. She waited two months to see if he was still serious. He was persistent. In the end, she had little choice. It was a family matter and it was decided. Barely in her teens, young Leia switched from sister-in-law to wife.

Thinking back, Mama Leia can't say whether she was happy or not. When she got married, she said, she knew no other kind of life. He was her first man and she had no other. He treated her well. They had six children, four boys and two girls. Her children were still young when he died, possibly from tuberculosis, possibly from lung disease caused by the years of inhaling mine dust. It was a long illness and all she remembers from that period is the suffering as she worked in the fields so they could eat, looked after her husband who could no longer work, and cared for her children. Her nephew—her stepson—was good to her. After his father died, he helped Leia in the fields. He bought clothes for his little half-brothers and sisters and promised that she would never suffer so much again. She vowed never to remarry, and she never did. But her life got no easier.

It was not long before her stepson married. His wife was hostile to Mama Leia, so he built her a separate house and she began to work her own fields. Then one day a few Portuguese men arrived at her house, asking to see her *machamba*. They looked at the field and pointed. From here to here, they instructed, she would have to grow cotton, only cotton, and sell it to the Portuguese. "Here to here" was half her field. What was left was not enough to grow food for her family. Not enough to grow a surplus to sell for her basic needs. And the cotton production was so intensive she didn't have much time for growing food crops anyway. She had to carry the sacks of cotton to the store to sell it. There was a fixed price for the weight, but Leia found that, because she couldn't read, the buyers lied shamelessly about the weight of the sacks. Sometimes they were challenged by the occasional peasant who could read; then they confiscated the sacks and paid nothing. "Heh!" she exclaims when she talks about those times. "We certainly knew hunger."

Gradually news of Frelimo began to filter down from the north and out of the underground in the cities, to the people living in Mama Leia's locality. The rumors meant little to her: her horizons barely stretched beyond her immediate community. It was a waste of time to dream of change. And then it was 1974. April 25, the day of the Portuguese coup. The beginning of the end for the colonial power. On independence day, Mama Leia recalls, "we danced and danced. Hai! We never stopped dancing. We could begin to put our suffering behind us."

But she didn't stop when the dancing ended. She immediately threw herself into political work, to help build a new life for herself and her family. When the *grupos dinamizadores*—literally dynamizing groups, referred to countrywide as GDs—were organized in neighborhoods and workplaces during the transitional government, Mama Leia joined her GD and was made responsible

for social affairs in her locality. She was one of the many Mozambicans who took part in this process of "dynamizing" people, as
part of the ad hoc groups of ten to twelve members who took on a
variety of tasks—mobilizing people to work for the new government, organizing literacy classes, defending their communities,
running abandoned factories. It was one of the main ways through
which people began to respond to and work for Frelimo. Mama
Leia's experience with the GDs developed her leadership skills,
and she was chosen deputy secretary of OMM for her district,
before joining in the effort to construct her communal village in
1977. Since then, she has been the secretary-general of the village
OMM.

The village was established on February 3, 1977, the eighth
anniversary of the assassination of Eduardo Mondlane, Frelimo's
first president, and named Três de Fevereiro in his memory. The
area of which the village is part—known as the Baixo Limpopo,
the southern part of the Limpopo river in Gaza—has one of the
highest population concentrations in the country. By 1982, the
population of Três de Fevereiro numbered some 12,000 residents,
divided into five *bairros*. It was one of 130 communal villages,
totaling 150,000 residents, some 80 percent of the rural population of the area.

When Mama Leia moved into the communal village she, like the
other newcomers, had little else to go on than the dream promised
by a very new and hence inexperienced government. Two regions
of the country had unusually high concentrations of communal
villages—the old liberated territories of the north and Gaza
province. In the north experimental villages had already been
established during the war, providing a base to build on. Not so in
the south.

"We weren't mobilized by Frelimo," chuckled a Três de Fevereiro woman. "We were mobilized by water. The water never
stopped to ask us if we wanted to leave. We just had to run!" And
in a sense the water did mobilize them. In 1977 the rains, always
awaited with trepidation—would they come at all?—never
stopped. The banks of the Limpopo River were smoothed away as
if they had never existed. One hundred people died. The water
destroyed homes and drowned cattle. Crops were lost and the
agricultural infrastructure destroyed. These floods were the worst
in the memory of all but the oldest grandmothers and grand-
fathers, who told of the flood when the Portuguese just left them to

die and would not allow them to rebuild their houses on drier ground. Even in normal times, flooding was a way of life for the region. It 1977, however, government officials responded quickly to the disaster, plucking people from rooftops by helicopter, saving livestock, providing food. The relief efforts, aided by the Red Cross, sorely taxed the fragile resources of new Mozambique. But for those caught in the floods it was evidence enough that Frelimo was very different from the colonial administration.

To hear Mama Leia and the women she works with tell it, they jumped at an opportunity to be resettled in the communal villages on high ground, away from the flooded conditions that plagued the peasant farmers. "We were turning into fish, we had lived in water so long," said another Três de Fevereiro woman. But it was Frelimo's promises for new services that really made the mobilization work. Only when people lived in concentrated settlements, the government argued, could it begin to provide services such as water pumps, schools, clinics; to do so for a widely dispersed population was impossible. Once relocated, villagers elected their own local assemblies and their own justice tribunals. The women's organization also became active in the new village.

Within a few years, by 1981, the communal village program had spread throughout the country. Over 1.5 million people—15 percent of the entire rural population—had moved into more than 1,500 communal villages. The goal of the program was to have most of the rural population voluntarily resettled in communal villages by the end of the decade.

I remember the very earnest face of the young cadre responsible for communal villages in the district of Mossuril, Nampula province, when I visited the largest communal village in his district in 1981. His voice was certain: "All the people of our district will be living in communal villages by the end of the decade." He knew his statistics well: 5,200 people lived in eight communal villages, and a further eight were under construction. The village we were in at the time had a population of 2,300, out of the district's total population of 66,155. Close to half the district's communal village residents lived in one village, the balance settled in the remaining seven. Only 9 percent of the district's population had been mobilized into communal villages in the five years since independence and he seriously believed—there was no doubt about his seriousness—that 91 percent could be mobilized in the next ten.

This kind of optimism was widespread in the early 1980s, even as the government found itself unable to meet its goals for the villages already established. Três de Fevereiro was fortunate: access to the village was easy, as it was close to the main highway that runs north from Maputo to central Mozambique, but more than this, it was designated a model village. As such it became a testing ground for the communal village program. In 1981 it was one of the 460 villages to have democratically elected its own people's assembly; one of 300 served by a health worker; one of 375 to have an agricultural cooperative; one of a very few to have an electrically driven water pump, although a larger number had manual pumps of greater or lesser sophistication. But the water—one of the first priorities—turned out to be prohibitively expensive: clean water for the projected 10,000 communal villages for the country would cost $250 million (U.S. dollars). And presuming pumps could be installed, what would happen when they needed repair? There are virtually no trained Mozambican technicians to maintain and repair such a system, let alone foreign currency with which to purchase spare parts, gas for the vehicles that would take the technicians to the outer reaches of the countryside, mechanics to fix these vehicles when they break down, spare parts if a mechanic can ever be found. In Gaza, the Central State Farm Plan set a goal of sixty new shallow wells in 1982. By mid-April seven had been installed.

Even with the best of intentions, Mozambique was hard put to transform theory into practice. The chronic lack of resources was matched by a chronic lack of trained people, not only technicians, but leaders and administrators. The pool of human resources to draw on for putting into practice all the ideas and ideals, however urgent, was dismally shallow. While I met number of young responsavels—those in positions of leadership at local, district, and provincial levels—who were committed to change, there were some who were along for the ride. A case in point was a young district worker in charge of health who accompanied a team visiting a village in a drought area. As they toured the family plots looking at the onions struggling to grow, he stooped down and swept up a handful, close to half the crop. "I love young onions," he relished, while the farmer stood by saying not a word. At lunch the regional specialty, matapa, a stew of greens flavored with peanuts, was served. The same man pushed back his plate with irritation, and summoned the cook. "Where are the peanuts? How can you serve us *matapa* without peanuts?" he demanded. She explained that the harvest had failed because of drought and that they only had their seeds. "Then use the seeds. You can't serve guests so poorly." The seeds were not used. But the villagers must have wondered how much this man differed from the Portuguese administrators they had to deal with in earlier days.

Authority had gone to the heads of some, but *responsavels* were more likely to be overpowered by lack of resources and lack of training that rendered them impotent and incompetent. Mostly I was struck by their dedication and humanity. From my recent visit, the health agent in Eduardo Mondlane village in Boane district stands out. With his training he could have chosen to work elsewhere, somewhere safer, somewhere with easier access to food and goods. Instead he returned to his village to provide medical care. After our visit I heard that representatives from a private development organization came to visit. Impressed by what he was doing with so little, by the cleanliness and organization of his clinic, and by the fact that he rode his bicycle back and forth each day over miles of sandy dirt track, they promised to buy him a motorcycle. It was their idea. He would never have asked for it.

I spent many hours with Mama Leia and her co-workers when I visited the village at the beginning of 1981 and again in 1982. In the afternoons the women fetched a set of locally woven mats and laid them out under a large, magnificent tree that became the scene for the telling of many stories about their lives. "Ah," chortled Mama Leia. "We welcome Stephanie's visits so much! Only when she visits do we get to sit down and rest under the trees. And talk. Otherwise we never rest. Stephanie just calls us to come! That's her work!"

In Três de Fevereiro I felt welcomed as a friend. The women showed me their village with pride, each day a visit to a different place. In addition to the water pump, there was a grain mill, a consumer cooperative, an elementary school, literacy and adult education classes, electricity for lighting the main street (not the houses), and even a telephone. Mama Leia was particularly proud of the telephone, although she admitted that it was regularly out of order. "When there is lightening," she said, "I think: Which will go this time? The telephone? The electricity?" When either went, they could be out for months, even a year.

There was a determination in Mama Leia's face that could turn to stubbornness, with her jaw slightly jutted out as a warning to anyone who might cross her. It was this determination, I imagined, that had set her going in the first place, once independence was a reality. I could see her, jaw out, determination flushing her face, as she cajoled others into working as hard as she did to build their village.

Mama Leia was but one of the numbers of women who responded to the call to establish the villages. Often that initial decision to move into a village had to be taken without the approval of the husband. With so many men away in South Africa and a decision to be made quickly, it was impossible to consult. And once the women took that first step, they were hooked. They had a vested interest in making sure their village worked. Mama Leia was a widow and free to make her own choices, but other women had an uphill battle. Some men were antagonistic to such a move, worried that their control over their household would be threatened. Others were angered on their return from South Africa with money saved to procure a second wife, to find that the first had moved into a communal village where polygamy and *lobolo* were frowned upon and where a wife could get support in her demand that a man not marry again. And if a man insisted on his rights he might find himself with only one wife anyway, because the first would leave him.

In the northern provinces, where matrilineality and matrilocality were the norm, it was often the men who jumped at the opportunity to move into a village. A man hoped for the chance to weaken the strong ties between his wife and her family. But south or north, perhaps the greatest challenge confronting the communal village program is the realization of the nation's commitment to the emancipation of women.

Mama Leia's village, like the other large villages in the south, had many more women among its residents than men. Single and widowed mothers contributed to the imbalance, and the village was frequently depleted of its men by the draw of the South

African mines or work in Maputo. The economic impact of this work in South Africa was apparent the very first time I drove into the village: high electricity poles were set up at regular intervals down the center of the white sandy entrance road, symbolic beacons of progress. Neat cement houses, painted white or a medley of colors, were built side-by-side with mud-brick homesteads. Only money from South Africa and access to South African consumer goods could explain the corrugated iron roofs, glass windows, curtains, the children in shoes and new clothes who played in front of the houses. Even a relatively good wage from Maputo could not procure the better standard of living: goods such as paint or glass were almost impossible to find in Mozambique at any price.

Whenever I visited the family machambas, I saw women of all ages, some with babies on their backs or children playing nearby, working hard. In some fields groups of women worked together, in others women worked alone. Occasionally men could be seen hoeing and weeding. I asked one man working by himself where his wife was. "My wife is at home. She has other work to do. I can't say to her, 'Leave your work and come with me.' So I came ahead." He was unemployed, back from South Africa and unable to get another contract because of the severe cutbacks on migrant contracts by the apartheid government. He had looked in vain for work outside of the village. In a nearby field a man worked side-by-side with his two daughters and his wife's sister, who was on a visit. "When we wake up in the morning we don't feel well unless we come to the fields. It's a kind of sickness as well!" But mostly the workers were women. In a very overgrown field another woman worked alone. Her husband worked outside of the village and was away for stretches of time. She had nine children, but most were too young to help in the fields. Nearby in a very neat smaller field worked another solitary woman. Her husband worked in South Africa and she had no children.

Land distribution within the villages was based on the size of the family. Larger families had rights to more than one plot as long as they could work the land. But the land was on high ground, sandy, and dependent on erratic rain for irrigation. Mama Leia proudly picked some manioc when I visited her field, but there was little else that grew in abundance. Some peanuts. Some beans. As the drought progressed, even the relatively resistant manioc must have had a hard time coming up.

The longer I stayed in the village, the more I picked up an undercurrent of grumbling about land. There were some families who had very mixed feelings about joining the village. They wanted the services. They wanted the opportunity for their children to get an education. They appreciated the water and the sense of community. But in order to live in the communal village they were expected to give up fields that they had worked, perhaps for generations; a cut-off date was set for the end of 1982. Some had had mango and cashew trees, even cattle. The more alluvial soil was far better suited to producing food than the sandy fields on the high ground. They were caught in a bind. In an attempt to gain from both worlds, some built houses in the village that were never lived in; others were registered as residents in the village but when it came down to it, only one wife moved in; the other wife or wives stayed put and worked the family's land, living in the houses they had built years before. During the peak cultivation season, others traveled to their land—sometimes a day's journey—and spent the weekdays there, living in temporary shelters or in their old houses, now in need of substantial repair. How voluntary, I wondered, was the relocation of these families?

Yet other families had lost their family land to the Portuguese settlers when they were driven off the most fertile and least flooded land so that new Portuguese settlers could come to try to make their fortune. Any hopes that they might get back their land at independence were soon put aside. The settlers' well-developed land was incorporated into state farms. The fields in the village were poor compensation for these familes. On the other hand, for the majority of families who had lost their fields in the flood and whose land was so constantly under water that cultivation was nigh impossible, there was satisfaction. For them their new life in the village held unqualified promise.

In 1979 villagers in Três de Fevereiro took part in the first elections ever held in Mozambique. They voted for members of their local, regional, and national people's assemblies. For the first time in her life, Mama Leia was able to have a say in who would govern.

In village after village, days were set aside for the residents to question, criticize, and accept or reject a candidate. A man would be rejected for collaborating with the Portuguese administration; for beating his wife; for womanizing; for marrying a second wife after independence when polygamy was frowned upon. In one village close to Três a woman was accused of shirking her duties and after explaining that it was her mother-in-law who didn't allow her to do the work, she withdrew her name. In Três de Fevereiro, at the end of the day, thirty-two candidates were left after others had been turned down. Thirty-two members of the people's assembly it was.

After these elections, 894 assemblies were established at the local level, with a total of 22,230 members. Of these, 28.3 percent were women. Compared with figures from other African countries, Mozambique comes off pretty well. Data collected for the mid-decade conference of the United Nations Decade for Women held in Copenhagen in 1980 showed that—for the countries that had responded to the questionnaire—the median political participation of women at a local level was 12 percent. The percentage of women delegates in the National People's Assembly was 12.4, compared with 6 percent in national bodies for Africa as a whole. The results of Mozambique's 1986–1987 elections were even more impressive: 35 percent women at the local level, and 20 percent at the national. In the first election, no women were represented on the Permanent Commission of the People's Assembly, the body that must pass all laws before they go before the whole assembly. As a result of the latest elections, two women now number among the twenty-two members. Três de Fevereiro had an unusually high percentage of women in the people's assembly: 68.8 percent, or twenty-two women out of the thirty-two elected.

Once the members of the Três de Fevereiro assembly were in place, the meeting continued in order to elect five members of the executive council. Five men were elected. In the discussions of obstacles to greater political representation by women, mid-decade conference documents had pointed to precisely this problem: it is difficult for women to elect other women to positions of leadership. It was no less true in Três de Fevereiro, even though the majority of people living in the village were women, and the majority of people attending the meeting were women, and the majority of people chosen for the people's assembly were women. What was different was the way it was handled. "No," intervened the provincial representatives overseeing the Três election, "this isn't right. It is important that women be represented on the executive council as well." This was one of the many instances where Frelimo pushed for affirmative action, ideologically ahead of the population. Two of the names were withdrawn and replaced by those of women.

While Mama Leia is not a member of the executive, it is immediately obvious that she is a central figure. She exerted her leadership through a strong personality and a firmness that underlies her dealings with others. She was also, like so many of the women I met, ready with a laugh that in no measure denies suffering or belittles the seriousness of the subject at hand. It just makes it more bearable. It is her position as secretary of the village OMM that gave her authority and through this she has become an outspoken leader. Often I witnessed Mama Leia's tenacity as a leader, refusing to play a secondary role to men. Seeing her interact with a male *responsavel* for the agricultural cooperative, I appreciated how far she had come from the thirteen-year-old who married the husband of her dead sister because it was expected of her.

She was very eager to show me the work of the agricultural cooperative, as indeed I was eager to see it. It was a brisk sixty-minute walk to the fields from the village and we set off at 5:00 A.M.—only after I was able to match her firmness by insisting that yes, I really *did* prefer to walk rather than ride by tractor. Convinced that it was better for my work, she agreed.

We arrived at the same time as about a dozen women *cooperativistas* who immediately set to work with their hoes, preparing the ground for planting corn. However, there were no seeds to sow. They were safely locked up in the storeroom and the brigade leader—a man—responsible for the store had not yet arrived. He finally did, more than an hour later, to be greeted by an irate secretary. She launched in, accusing him of lying when he told the cooperative meetings that the reason the cooperative was functioning poorly was because the women did not show up. He did not come to work, she said, pointing out that the women had been there for some time. He responded, taking the offensive, that there was corn ready for harvesting. New corn should not be sown while old corn was allowed to die. All very well, replied the undaunted Mama Leia, but how could the *cooperativistas* know that if they hadn't been told and he wasn't there to inform them? He should have called a meeting the day before to designate the work. He left the field, with nothing more to say, but in something of a huff.

The interaction pointed to a crucial problem with the cooperative itself. When the co-op had been described to me before I saw it, I was told it had 970 members who were drawn from the village's five *bairros*. Working one day a week at the cooperative, women could continue to farm their own plots for the majority of the time. When the harvest was brought in and the debts paid—such as the rental of tractors from the state and payment for seeds—the balance would be divided among the workers according to how many days they had worked. The last time the workers had been compensated for their labor was 1979. By 1982 the harvest was barely sufficient to cover expenses, and the meager surplus was divided among the members. The co-op president blamed the tractors. "We had constant trouble with the tractors. They worked very badly and were always breaking down. They [the relevant state department] took a long time to do repairs. We were always quarreling with them."

Clearly the issue was more than tractors. Attendance was severely down. The day I visited, fourteen members were working, thirteen women and one man. The man, a member of the commission of the cooperative, was in charge of keeping the attendance records. He was quick to assure me that he often registered many more workers in a day. "Sometimes we have had as many as forty," he said with satisfaction.

The vice-president of the co-op, a woman, explained that many people preferred to work on their own land. On Mondays attendance was always lower because people had to get back from their own fields away from the village and the bus service was unreliable. She also pointed to a deeper problem: "People do not work together too well," she said. "We were used to working in our fields alone. We still have a problem of working together." And then at the end of the season there is only enough to pay for the expenses. "People complain a lot. We have to explain that we don't have a 'master' anymore. We try to tell them that it is *their* work and not the fault of someone who has vindictively held back the money." The failure of the cooperative in this village illuminates the failure of the cooperative movement as part of the rural development program. That the cooperative functioned at all showed that the promise of the cooperatives—a promise that met its demise with the lack of support from the state—still held to some extent in the village, as they waited for better days.

One morning at breakfast Mama Leia looked particularly tired and said she had hardly slept the night before. In the early hours of the morning two men got into a fight over an old grudge. They fought each other with knives and one was badly wounded. She was hastily called and arranged for the injured man to be taken to hospital. Mama Leia's work as a village leader was not confined to sorting out problems relating to women. When a difficulty arose between residents in the village she was invariably the first to be called in.

As with the urban *bairros*, the village *bairros* are divided into blocks of ten families. There are two people responsible for each block in Três de Fevereiro, one of whom is an OMM member. "We work with the five OMM secretaries for the *bairros*," Mama Leia told me, "and explain that they must encourage women to join OMM." Yet I found little evidence of active, ongoing mobilization of women to fight for their liberation. As far as I could ascertain, there were no longer any regular meetings of OMM and questions about the number of OMM members in the village were answered evasively. Listening to Mama Leia, I wondered how much of the long description of her work as OMM secretary related to changing social relations, and how much to getting women to be model wives.

"The OMM is an organization that has much work to do," she told me. "I must be ready to explain our work and why it is important for women to be involved to everyone—to women, to men, to the youth. The work of OMM here is to know what is happening regarding problems in the family, hygiene, health, drunken behavior." OMM visits families and tries to explain the importance of hygiene, teaching women to dig holes for garbage, to dig latrines, to keep their houses clean.

Indeed, most of the effort focused on women: "When I go to a house I look to see how the woman behaves, whether she has a clean house or whether she is insulting. At first I talk about the general need for cleanliness so that I open the way for her to ask questions. Sometimes when a woman is lazy I find out from her neighbors how she lives. Then we talk to her about her faults. In extreme cases, I go to her house when she is out and with neighbors weed the grass in front of her house. We'll take water to her house and wash the children's clothes and then her clothes. If necessary we take her to the bath huts and make her wash." Women are viewed as the ones responsible for good family relationships: "We explain the need for families to live in harmony, and for women to know how to live properly with their husbands and children. They must take care of their families. There must be respect between couples, as many problems are due to lack of respect."

Rather than helping women to work on this anger, through mobilizing for change, for example, OMM never seemed to get beyond self-help models. Nothing I saw in any of the dozen or so villages I visited in different parts of the country suggested the potential for a more dynamic organization. Nina Swaim, a *cooperante* who worked in Mozambique in the early 1980s, found a similar situation in a study she did of forty villages in Manica province: again women were being encouraged to keep the village clean and to be good housewives. When she questioned village OMM leaders about what village cleanliness meant, they said it was to mobilize women and men to cut the weeds around the houses; to supervise and encourage better cleaning habits among women and children (not men, it seems) and neatness around the house; and to mobilize women for clean-up efforts in the school, hospital, village meeting area, or guest houses. She was told that one way to do this was to walk through the village periodically and tell mothers when their homes needed cleaning or their family's clothing was dirty.[1]

The similarity between what Swaim found in the central province of Manica and what I found in Gaza gives the impression that OMM is indeed effective at getting its message down from the national to the provincial to the local level. If it decided to, it could be a far more dynamic, mobilizing body, sending down a directive for more serious change within the household; OMM could not only encourage women to keep their houses and the village clean or be chided if they do not, but it could pressure men to participate in this work as a first effort to changing family roles.

Despite a lack of leadership in pushing for the need for gender struggle, however, a strong message came through that women could take control of their lives. And women such as Mama Leia were given the chance to blossom as leaders and to dream and plan for their grandchildren's future. Certainly, from Mama Leia's viewpoint, the changes for women had been remarkable. "We feel we are liberated," she said. "We are free. And now we must work hard to develop ourselves." What was perhaps more important than words that encouraged struggle—words that could have been trapped by rhetoric—was the profound practical changes in women's workday, changes that in the end could free them from the never-ending intensity and drain of the labor to keep their families going. More time and more energy for pursuits other than basic survival could have more lasting impact on women's lives. This was abundantly clear as I watched women go about their daily work in Três de Fevereiro.

The women of Três de Fevereiro had been up early. Not long after the first roosters had announced the suggestion of dawn, the women had begun their day. There was water to be prepared for the family's ablutions, there was the fire to be lit for preparing breakfast, the children to be washed and dressed. The sound of wooden pestle hitting mortar as grain was pounded carried across the flat terrain of the village, a thudding-thumping that broke the stillness of dawn and provided a counterpoint to the afternoon sounds of the village. The even, rhythmic motions of a woman's body as she lifted the pestle and then brought it down into the mortar with a swinging, constant movement conveyed an effortlessness that belied the backbreaking nature of the work.

By 5:30 A.M. the sun had already risen when the women set off for their plots of land on the edge of the village, a twenty-minute or so walk depending where they live. Breast-fed infants were carried on their mothers' backs, while young children walked and skipped alongside if they could not be left at home with older siblings or members of the extended family. By midday, when the sun was uncomfortably hot, the women put down their hoes and set off back home. This might be time to gather firewood, which is bundled and transported on the top of the head. A family needs at least four large bundles of wood for their cooking fires for a week. Not enough wood could be found in the immediate vicinity of the village, and unless they had the money to buy a bundle (in 1987 about 200 meticais each), the women had to spend a good part of the day gathering wood and transporting it back to the village.[2]

The rest of the day was divided up between the many other demands of the household and the needs of the children. Pounding again. Cooking. Cleaning the house and the surrounding area. Laundry. And, of course, water carrying. A family of three uses about 125 liters of water a day for cooking and drinking (not laundry). Five trips would be needed for this water, and if the family is larger, the number of trips would be increased proportionately.

The women of Três de Fevereiro can get their water comparatively speedily from the center of the village. Their electrically generated pump with its storage capacity of 3,000 liters is one of the best in the country. A bank of faucets along the side of the cement-enclosed tank allows a number of containers to be filled simultaneously. The pump is open from 3:00 P.M. to 6:00 P.M. each day. Water can also be pumped at any time of the day from three manual pumps. In the later afternoon women would converge from all directions, swinging their twenty-liter buckets as they headed with long, swift strides toward the pumps. The return trip was slower, weighted down by the heavy cans of water, fresh leafy branches on top to prevent spilling. The can had to be full, otherwise the sloshing would unbalance it. It could take as little as fifteen minutes if the carrier lived close to the pump, longer from the outer reaches of the village. To one side of the pump are cement troughs for washing clothes, no longer used. The ease of having running water meant that the storage tank was overtaxed, and now water for laundry has to be carried home. Most women find it easier to carry their laundry to the river, where they can bathe as well.

I visited the pump square a number of times. I never saw a man lining up, although boys in their early teens or younger were occasionally there to help. Invariably, women were the collectors. The girls learn young. I watched as a six- or seven-year-old girl walked gingerly behind her mother balancing a small, one-pound vegetable can filled with water on her head. Her whole body was focused on the task at hand, as she concentrated on each step. Now and then, her hands would flash to the top of her head, hovering around the can in case she needed to save it. She would regain her balance, her hands would drop to her sides again, then when she took a few more steps up would go the hands again.

Women told me how they used to walk for as much as one hour in one direction for just one container of water, as many of their neighbors still must. Or how they would use gourds to scoop water from the river although they knew it wasn't clean. Few would boil the water, both from lack of appreciation of the health benefits and from lack of firewood. The promise of water had been a major incentive to move into Três de Fevereiro. "Many women laughed at us," recalled one of the village's women, "when we tried to encourage other women to join us in moving to our village. We told them we would have water pumps, and they said 'Your're *crazy* to believe that!' Now they cannot look us in the face when we pass them, because they know they were wrong and we live better than they."

The sight of women breezing down the dirt road on their way to the faucets, the long hot treks to water pushed into memory, is heartening. But a sobering shadow lurks behind them. The generator-powered pump was still new and had not yet broken down. But it surely would with the heavy use it was getting. Moreover, hundreds of water pumps have been destroyed by the bandits, and people have been forced to flee from their homes and their water sources in more secure areas.

Vying with water collection for the most labor-intensive task is pounding grain. In an attempt to ameliorate this on an experimental basis, UNICEF had provided Três de Fevereiro and a few other villages with electric grain mills. A neat, small mud-brick structure had been built with volunteer labor for the mill that arrived in the village in 1980. It was driven by oil provided by the province and was maintained by a local resident. He had no training but had acquired some skills working on machines in the South African mines. The mill hours were 7:30 to 11:30 A.M. and 3:00 to 5:00 P.M., when two teenagers were on hand in the small reed kiosk-type structure for collecting payment. A fee of 7.5 meticais (19 cents U.S. at the 1982 rate of exchange) was charged for grinding the equivalent of a fifteen-liter bucket filled with cleaned corn kernels. In two minutes enough corn could be ground to provide two meals for a family of six. Surely villagers would flock to the mill for the ultimate in labor-saving devices.

They didn't. When I visited the village a few weeks after its installation, fewer than ten people were using the mill each day. A few weeks after my visit, a nail buried in a container of corn destroyed a vital part of the mill, and it took a year to replace it. By my second visit it had been functioning only two weeks. During a five-day period fifteen people had brought their corn on three days, twenty-eight on another day, and thirty on the fifth. Some of these came from neighboring villages. Then the mill broke down again. This time a screw was discovered and immediately Mama Leia and her co-workers were certain that someone from a neighboring village had intentionally hidden a screw in their corn.

Their suspicion of outsiders clouded reason. It was unlikely that someone would risk losing a whole bucket of corn, but it spoke to the tensions between village residents and "outsiders," those from other villages. It turned out to be a screw from the mill itself and that much damage had been done, and the maintenance man thought he would have it working again within a few days. As soon, that is, as he could locate another screw.

Given the long periods of breakdown, a certain understandable wariness of this new-fangled system for grinding corn was to be expected. But there was a more pervasive cultural dimension to the problem that helped prevent the mill from being embraced as a time-saver, which hinged on the way in which the stiff corn porridge—*papa*—was prepared in the region. The corn is left to dry on the stalk before harvesting: only when the leaves are brown and brittle and look as if they may have been hit by drought is it "ripe" for picking. Women then knock the kernels off the cob by slow pounding, or rub them off by hand. Often the older women do this as they sit with the children in the evening telling stories. Women transfer kernels to the mortar with a cup or so of water and start the heavy pounding, adding more water every so often until the kernels are broken but still coarse. The course kernels are then placed in a flat woven basket for winnowing, returned to the mortar, pounded a while longer, and winnowed again, until they are properly clean. Finally, the corn is washed and left to soak for a day or overnight in special clay pots. There it begins to ferment, imparting the slightly sour flavor typical of the *papa* of the region—and absent when using dry-ground meal. Women take the fermented mash, rinse it once more, and transfer it to a large, flat, round dish, where they grind it with a wooden pestle to a thick paste. Then it is ready for cooking. That's the way it is done. That's the way it has always been done, and the women said the men complained that they had not eaten until they had eaten proper *papa*, with the sour flavor.

This saga reminded me of Nina Swaim's comment that the complaints by women about modern technology were really coming from the men, and that if the men did not insist on the old ways, women might use the easier methods. In several villages she visited, the hand pumps were not used as much as the original water source. It turned out that the men told the women not to use the hand pumps; they complained that the water drawn by hand pumps was *salgado* (salty).[3] There was a great sense of satisfaction and achievement in the manner of the women who took me to the mill, which was strong and well built. But I suspect the pride was more for its function as a status symbol—a demonstration of the new technology that no other village in the area possessed, and hence a sign of progress—rather than for its potential as a labor-saving device.

Watching the care with which women cooked and the pride they took in making *papa* or other local dishes "just right," I wondered how many women would welcome men around their fires, sharing their work. Until rural women have the actual experience and can appreciate the benefits from sharing work and responsibilities, they might well balk at the idea of losing control over their domain. If men were to suddenly walk in and say they would share the responsibility or even help, would women be delighted or annoyed? If men were to suddenly say they would carry water, would their wives be pleased, or would they feel they were losing out on an important opportunity for social interaction? More than any other task, water collection involves a strong connection between the women water gatherers. Whether women go to the central square of Três de Fevereiro, or line up for water at a *bairro* pump, or walk to a well a number of miles from their homes and meet the other women from the locality doing the same thing, the water source provides a place where information, gossip, and news is passed on and discussed, where women can laugh and complain and comfort. It's a place for fostering village or community cohesiveness that oversteps the boundary of family. Nina Swaim noticed when she was doing her Manica study that when a man did come to collect water, the women stepped aside to allow him to go to the front of the line.

Was this, I wondered, another example of the introduction of appropriate technology without first determining whether it was in fact appropriate? The mill was introduced without the collective capacity to maintain it, and without access to spare parts, which undermined its maintenance. It seemed as if Três de Fevereiro was chosen as one of the sites for the grain mill without consulting the women about what they really wanted or studying the social and cultural circumstances of the villages. The intent, nonetheless, was supportive of women: to try to break into the intensity of their days and free up some time.

As little progress has been made toward changing the sexual division of labor within the household, and there is little likelihood of such progress in the near future, an equally crucial change would be to relieve women of some of their duties and tasks by the judicious introduction of appropriate technology. But this needs to be accompanied by far-reaching change that can loosen the restrictive fabric of society and transform the daily lives of women so that the grind of production and reproduction ceases to be as taxing. For this to happen, attitudes that try to defuse gender struggle need to change at the same time.

By my second visit, in 1982, it was evident that the women of Três de Fevereiro were becoming demobilized. Attendance at literacy classes had dwindled. Mama Leia complained to me that she could no longer get women to do volunteer work, such as helping with the construction of a new village. "After all the help we got building our village," complained Mama Leia, visibly upset, "and I can't even find anyone to help with this one." Again and again it came back to the same problem of the failure of the rural development program to impact on women's productive and reproductive activities.

And throughout all, women's work is unending. Late one afternoon I sat with Anastaçia Guimerães, my translator, under a tree in what was the administrative center of the village, the weathered Mozambique flag waving slowly in the breeze. Women, carrying an assortment of containers, were scurrying by, heading for the water pump. One woman turned and waved to us. "There's never a moment's rest," called out Anastaçia. "We only rest in the grave!" "Ai," came the quick reply, "but how do we know? No one has ever come back from the grave to tell us!"

◈6◈

Contradiction
and Change

The pilot flew the five-seater plane in a wide circle around Xai-Xai, capital of Gaza province, alerting those expecting me to my arrival. I was taken by the beauty of the layout of this small town, spread around the mouth of the Limpopo, along which many large plantations had been established. I had not realized before—on my rumbling rides into the town over pitted tarmac—how attractive it was, and how many pleasant houses and mansions and open parks graced the town, where some of the richest settlers had lived, skimming the wealth off some of the richest land. The state of disrepair was masked by our height, and the early morning light played on the flat dark river water and lit up the whitewash of the buildings. As we circled I could pick out the party headquarters and the OMM office and the road to the beach that passed Mocita, a cashew-processing plant once owned by South Africa's transnational, Anglo-American.

The landscape contrasted with the one we had just flown over, on the way from Maputo to Xai-Xai—endless miles of hazy green clumps of trees and low scrubby bushes that gave way abruptly to golden dunes and a deserted ribbon of sandy beach that stretched from the south all the way north. No fields, no houses, no roads, no sign of life except for an occasional dirt track or distant cluster of homesteads. Somewhere below, in hiding, were the perpetrators of the attacks and atrocities in the south, the very reason for my having to hire this plane. It was the only way I could return to visit Três de Fevereiro, not far from the capital.

We landed in what seemed the middle of a field, bumping down on clumps of grass and taxiing on more grass to a standstill in front of a small, forlorn cement structure labeled in faded paint "Aeroclube de Gaza" and overgrown with grenadilla vines. There was one vehicle waiting, painted bright blue. Next to it stood a woman, her hand shielding her eyes as she looked toward the plane. It was Celeste, one of the members of the provincial OMM secretariat, whom I remembered with fondness from my previous visits. She was as charming and sweet-natured as ever and I felt a rush of relief. My program would actually take off. The Ministry of Information had sent messages to Xai-Xai, but as the phone link between it and Maputo was not functioning, they had received no confirmation. There were hugs and joyful smiles all around and I got in the front of the jeep with Celeste and the driver and we headed toward Xai-Xai.

"Do you want to stay overnight in Três de Fevereiro?" Celeste asked, hesitancy in her voice. No, I reassured her. The plane was scheduled to pick us up in Xai-Xai in the morning to fly us—Lina Magaia (with me as interpreter) and myself—back to Maputo. I couldn't risk missing it. Celeste gave a smile of relief. Their jeep, the same one they had acquired after it had been abandoned at independence, had no lights. It had served OMM well, despite threatening to break down regularly, but was very fragile—new blue paint job notwithstanding. It also had no side windows, I noticed, and the windscreen was made of plexiglass. The angle of the sun was such that it brought out an almost impenetrable film from the fine scratches across the windshield and I hoped the driver had better visibility than I. The jeep strained and hic-coughed into town at a slow, steady speed.

But when we finally set off for Três de Fevereiro it was not in the OMM jeep at all. At Xai-Xai I ran into the governor, who expressed his welcome by wanting to pull out all stops to make sure the journalist's visit was a success. "Make sure you see the canals," he said. And he instructed my new, all male, hosts to see to it. So we traveled in style down the highway at about seventy miles an hour in a new Toyota Landcruiser, accompanied not just by Celeste and Lina, as I had hoped, but by a virtual entourage, including party officials and Xai-Xai's mayor.

The superior suspension of the Landcruiser made the section of the highway appear as smooth as glass as we sped over the bridge and away from the town, enveloped in Cindi Lauper's "Girls Just Want to Have Fun" from the sophisticated sound system.

I rode in a somber mood, anxious about what I would find. Since arriving in Maputo I had focused on trying to get back to Três de Fevereiro, a task that sometimes seemed daunting. But here I was on the last leg of the journey and expecting the worst. It was five years since my previous visit and I expected to find the state of Mozambique in microcosm. The collapsed economy must have impoverished this once model village; the drought must have made it impossible to grow food on the dry, high ground; the war must have prevented those who still farmed their land in the valley—many a day's journey away—from making that trip now; and the reduction of the recruitment of migrant laborers must have harshly turned family economies into a downward spiral. What stories would I hear from the women who had hoped for so much? And what would they be prepared to say about their lives in front of the men who were now accompanying me?

The Landcruiser turned off the highway and drove past a new carefully carved sign announcing Três de Fevereiro and stopped in the village "square." A large group of joyful people were there to meet us, crowding around and pushing foward to shake our hands. We were ushered into the cement meeting place where many of my interviews had taken place and where a group of villagers were patiently awaiting us. The same local, elegantly styled sisal and wooden chairs were there for the visitors to sit on. The rest of the room was filled with chairs that had been carried from home. A small can of fresh flowers sat on a low table and a picture of President Chissano hung on the wall. I sat down next to Lina and eagerly scanned the group of about thirty-five villagers. There was an absence as loud as any shout: no Mama Leia. She was away visiting family.

This time it was two men, the village president and vice-president, who ran the proceedings. I had been so used to women in that role that it seemed quite odd. Did this augur a setback in women's political roles, I wondered uncomfortably.

I needn't have worried. The president was self-effacing, polite, and gentle. He smiled easily and a lot. His face semed constantly ashine with his pride in the village and he was respectful of all who spoke, men or women. The majority were women, who held their own. One would pick up where a man had left off to make sure all the information was given; another would interject, saying no, such and such wasn't so, and proceed to correct him; yet another would be the first to respond to a question. There was an easy atmosphere of give and take between all the villagers present. Better, in fact, than I had remembered.

This was confirmation of what I remembered from my last visit, and I hoped that it was a reflection of changes within the family as well. Even on previous visits, I had been aware of more equal social relationships emerging within the household. There was a sense, particularly among younger women, that men were showing more respect for women. Women told of husbands willing to cook meals for their families on primus stoves brought back from South Africa when their wives had to go to a meeting. At one of my first meetings with women in the village an older man, a member of the people's assembly, sat with us. He listened to the women speak and respectfully did not intervene. Toward the end he stood up and said in a soft and sincere tone, "Frelimo has taught us something we did not know, that women must be respected. We never used to value women. Now they must stand up and speak out."

I brought my thoughts back to the present and looked at the assembly in the crammed room. They were relatively well dressed. New *capulanas*. Fresh blouses and shirts and jackets. Some were wearing what could have been *calamidades*, the secondhand clothes that had come with the relief efforts. Rosalina, whom I remembered from previous visits, an OMM secretary of a *bairro*, sported an almost incongruous mix of clothing. She wore a smartly tailored red jacket, a crisp white shirt with fine black stripes, and a neat scarf tied around her neck. This executive outfit was topped by a headscarf wound around her head and worn with a brightly patterned orange and yellow *capulana*. Where were the signs of poverty I was sure I would find? The worn, threadbare clothes, the lack of shoes? Presumably, I concluded, everyone had one set of good clothes and this was an occasion for wearing them.

But as men and women stood up one after another to tell me about the changes that had occurred in the past few years, a picture of Três de Fevereiro began to emerge that was nothing like the devastated village I had been expecting. There were continued health-care services and improvements at the nearby rural hospital. A *chirindzene* had been built—a place of waiting—where pregnant women, nearing their due date, would go and wait for the birth. It was a response to the dropping off of the number of deliveries at the hospital due to lack of transport and the danger of traveling at night or long distances. Better to go early and wait.

The village had become the administrative center of three of the villages that made up the locality. There are bigger schools to accommodate the growing number of children needing education, and more teachers and new buildings. OMM members continue to take part in intensive literacy and adult education courses away from the village. As a sure sign of the times, an expanded militia was being trained to better defend their village and the locality.

Among them were women. The community provided the militia
with food as their work made it hard to grow their own.

Everyone talked about the hardships of the first years after I left
as if they were in the past. The drought had affected them badly.
"It was hard times," recalled an older woman. "We would travel as
far as Manhiça district, to look for food to eat. Sometimes we even
traded all but the clothes on our back so we could get food to feed
our children."

More than anything, they talked about land. For over a year they
have had new land, they told me, along the Limpopo River. Fertile,
irrigated, good land, in the valley as they have always wanted.
They can produce enough now to grow food for their families.
There was a drought all around, they said, but they had enough to
eat. Corn and couve (a leaf from the cabbage family) and cabbage
and sweet potatoes. They were no longer hungry. They could buy
some of the things they needed, even *capulanas*, which were
available in the stores for the first time in years, as well as hoes
and plows.

Lina queried the president at the end of the meeting, "Aren't you
going to ask Stephanie what she thinks about the changes you
have been describing?" He shook his head. "We must show her
first," he said, quietly, his face serious. "How will she know we are
not lying if she does not see for herself? We'll show her first and
then we'll ask her."

The meeting was brought to an end for a tour of the village. I saw
for myself the full classrooms where the children were sitting on
the ground taking an exam. The water pump was still working.
There were new fruit trees and papaya palms and special trees
planted as windbreaks to diminish the swirling sand on windy
days. Relatively good clothes were worn by the people we passed
on the street and most women had new *capulanas* as they went
about their business collecting water or pounding in their yards.
More children seemed to be wearing rubber sandals or shoes than
I remembered from before.

After our tour of the village, Lina and I were taken back to the
meeting room for a veritable feast: chicken stew, sweet potatoes,
matapa, rice, *papa* cooked the long way, and fruit. It was quite late
in the afternoon and we still had to visit the canals, of which the
villagers were very proud. When people gathered around for the
good-byes, and I saw some of the women's faces I knew so well, I

felt quite sad. When I left before I was always sure I would return. This time I couldn't be as sure. We climbed into the Landcruiser, picking our way around the gifts of papayas and manioc and bananas. As we drove off, the voices of the women singing a stirring "Kanimambo Macheli" were gradually drowned out by Cindi Lauper and "Time After Time."

As I drove away from the village, mulling over the changes I had seen there and the renewed spirit, I thought how much Anastaçia Guimerães would have loved to have been there too, to have the chance to visit "our" village once more. On the two previous visits to the village, she had been my interpreter from Shangaan, the local language, into English.

Anastaçia had spent her early childhood in South Africa, where her father had gone to work and had married a South African woman. When they returned to Mozambique her father applied for *assimilado* status, a bizarre arrangement through which the Portuguese administration created a hierarchy of status and privilege among the colonized. She remembers how Portuguese officials would knock on their door in the middle of the night as part of their investigation into whether the family was worthy of the status. If her mother came to the door in a *capulana* this would be a mark against them—still too Africanized; she should have on a nightgown. Similarly they would appear at dinner time to check on what food the family was eating, if they were sitting at the table, and if they were using a knife and fork. In the end her family qualified: her father was considered educated enough, with a high enough income, a member of the church, and severed sufficiently from his African heritage. She could then get the schooling her father wanted for her and her brothers and sisters. It was clear from the ease with which she adapted to village life, her unpretentiousness, her comfort in speaking and joking in Shangaan, and the total absence of "urban airs" in relating to the peasant women of Três de Fevereiro, that divorced from her African background she was not.

Soon after independence Anastaçia began to work with OMM and by the time I began my visits, she was in the national foreign affairs department. She traveled with me on many of my trips and had proved a supportive friend, sometimes ally, when my program developed inevitable and acutely frustrating hassles and she resorted to various tactics to sort them out. With Anastaçia I saw a Mozambique I had never imagined. Together we visited Ilha da Mozambique, an exquisite island off the coast of Nampula, where we stayed in a mansion previously owned by one of the richest Portuguese settlers in Mozambique and now a guest house for visitors. The house still contained the photos and furnishings he had left when he fled the country. We looked out onto the crystal sea and ate huge rock lobsters. We stayed in villages in the north and in the south where our hosts apologized for the simple meals, but fed us handsomely from their local produce, surprised that I was more than willing to eat *papa* and manioc. We slept one night in an abandoned house when we had run out of gas in Mueda. By the time gas was found it was dark and Anastaçia was adamant that we not risk driving at night—wise in that accident-prone country, where many a car did not have any lights, replacement parts being too hard to get. We stayed in hotels—only twice—with buggy beds and nonfunctioning plumbing and a stench that was a constant reminder of that fact. We sat squashed up against each other for hours on hours in old four-wheel drive vehicles, as we were taken long distances through the provinces of Cabo Delgado, Nampula, Zambezia, Maputo, Gaza. We found wispy shade along the deserted road in Zambezia when the jeep we were traveling in broke down, and ate the most succulent and delicious pineapples I have ever tasted, bought shortly before at the side of the road. Finally a car came by and took us to the district capital and onto Quelimane, where we just made our plane back to Maputo. The jeep remained there for days before it could be fixed. Transport was scarce, but nonetheless it had been provided to ensure the success of my program. It was hard not to feel guilty when it broke down.

In Gaza, when we were not in villages or outlying districts, we stayed at Chonguene, a long beach with magnificent golden sunsets. Outside the door of our room stood a large tree, trilling with the noise of hundreds of bright yellow weaver birds. They darted in and out of perfectly constructed nests that hung like large, unripe fruit off the branches. "Ah," said Anastaçia, "a communal village of birds!" In the rafters of what was once a recreation veranda, hopelessly untidy birds built the messiest of nests. The hotel had once been crowded with Rhodesian vacationers in its heyday during the colonial era, but now it was disintegrating and almost empty. Cleaners, on their knees, sloshed water around energetically as they washed the floor and toilets, but they had no detergent. There was water only a few hours a day. The ping-pong tables were covered in cobwebs, the curtains were stained with mildew, and the carpets were worn. Plans to renovate the area have been shelved since the MNR attacks. The shoreline is totally unprotected and the hotel stands out on the shore, connected to Xai-Xai by a dirt road that runs through bush and scrub. But the hospitality couldn't be better. And in between my visits and interviews I basked on the beach, swam in the sea, and took long walks alongside the endless dunes.

Anastaçia and I had lots of time for talk. She told me about her family, about how she met her husband, about her children and her still infant grandchildren, and her hopes for Mozambique. She was one of the few women I met whose husband had, without threat or question, immediately encouraged her in work that took her out of the country to conferences and on state visits. He assured her that he would be home to tend to the household. When I had lunch with her and her family one Sunday during my recent visit, Anastaçia was about to leave the country once again. I walked through the gate to their house and her husband waved to me warmly from the back yard, as he continued with the job at hand: folding the washing hanging on the line. That morning, while Anastaçia was visiting the grave of the young Mozambican guard killed in the recent South African raid, he had done all the laundry.

We sat in her living room while her husband and daughters finished preparing the lunch. Her face was sadder than I had ever seen it, her eyes pained. She told me how the young Mozambican couple so brutally shot in the raid had been close friends of her daughter. She sat in silence a while and said softly, as if talking about some distant, distant memory, "Ah, Camarada Stefan, remember how we traveled? All those distances by road, to all those parts of Mozambique? No more, no more. So many of those places have been attacked, so many people killed. It's hard to think about it."

Lina and I were driven to the fields in the valley, along the same road that I had walked to the village cooperative on my previous visit. With us was the village president, eager to show us the land, and most particularly the canals, which until recently had been part of the land owned by a large state farm.

Cutting through the fields and at right angles to each other was a network of canals that drained the land and stopped the Limpopo from flooding. Six to seven kilometers of renovated canals, at times rushing so that the water swirled and foamed, provided irrigation for the fields and stopped the flooding. Every now and then we would encounter groups of women, or men and women, taking advantage of the water to wash their clothes and to bathe, bright *capulanas* laid out to dry next to shirts and T-shirts and blouses and socks. The fields were high with corn, the tassels thick and swaying in the breeze. Where the irrigation stopped, the land reverted to fields in which the corn was stunted and open land was no more than dry, cracked mud, the result of the drought plaguing the area.

The canal system, almost wiped out in the floods and left pretty much untouched since, is still undergoing renovation. In fact, the work can never stop. To stop would give the overgrowth a chance to take hold once more and clog up the irrigation system, leaving the farmers to watch while the sand gradually filled in the canals. Much of the work is sheer manual labor—provided largely by the new farmers, assisted by excavators for the wider and deeper canals. I thought back to 1982 and Mama Leia's concerns about the resistance to helping construct a new neighboring village. Volunteers are easier to mobilize this time: the incentive is substantial.

While the cumbersome and distinctly unprofitable state farm of Unidade de Producão do Baixo Limpopo dominated the allocation of state resources, villagers were not eager to labor on infertile land. In a vain hope that more land would reverse the losing trend, the state farm continued to take more and more land away from the peasants or to reclaim land the peasants felt was theirs. This simply added to the alienation of people living in villages such as Três de Fevereiro and pushed the state farm further into debt.

Following the party's redirection of agricultural policy in 1983, it was not until 1986 that the policy began to be implemented in earnest, and changes were felt by the residents of Três de Fevereiro.

One of the first actions demonstrating that the government was serious about correcting past mistakes was the dismantling of the state farm, reducing its 26,000 hectares to 2,500, and restributing the rest of the land both to private market-oriented enterprises not previously envisioned, and to family farmers, as long as they would bring it back into production. With the land came technical support from the state. For the family farmers the new terms looked good. They finally had access to tools, such as hoes, plows, machetes, and pails, all of which could be bought from the consumer cooperatives in the villages. Also significant, a new policy permitted village residents to return to their own fields some distance away, and reestablish their homesteads if they chose to. In fact, despite the grumblings about this question back in 1982, surveys of a number of villages found that now that farmers have their own plots, the majority preferred to continue to live in the communal villages.

New land. Access to tools. Access to more—if still limited— consumer goods, most evidently *capulanas*. The result was a new mobilization of the community to work for the common good. A new infrastructure was set up to apply technology such as fertilizer and plows. I thought of the smiling village president and the new energy I sensed in Três de Fevereiro and wondered whether these changes meant that the agricultural economy was truly on the mend and that optimism was in order. There are problems, of course, some of them more immediately evident than others. There is a severe shortage of seeds and a faulty distribution system means that seeds often don't reach the family farmers. There are too few oxen to pull the plows, and tractors are unavailable, mainly due to the fuel shortage.

Otto Roesch, a Canadian anthropologist, writing on the effect of the new policy in the Baixo Limpopo, notes all these obstacles, and warns of possible long-range problems as well. The hydro-agricultural system, for example, needs constant, labor-intensive maintenance. Slackness on the part of just a few families on the canals that border their plots could compromise the whole newly renovated system. Failure to keep the canals clean upstream will lead to floods; downstream it will lead to the flow of the water becoming a trickle. There is another problem here relating to the goal of utilizing the areas for cash cropping—essential if the reforms are going to benefit the country as a whole. Besides, minimal maintenance will allow a family to produce enough for its own needs and a little surplus, enough to cover the goods that are available. But for cash cropping major maintenance is needed. If there is little apparent point in growing cash crops, few families will invest their labor in the more time-consuming maintenance. Added to this, South Africa has again increased its recruitment in Mozambique, meaning access once more to foreign exchange and unavailable goods and more reason not to rely on a surplus from the farms.[1]

Another long-term problem is the lack of a marketing system. The system that existed and functioned well before independence was set up by the Portuguese and consequently abandoned by them on their departure. Combined with the lack of consumer goods, this will continue to act as a disincentive to peasants to produce a surplus.

I walked around looking at the indeed impressive canals, and pondered what all these changes meant to the women of "my" village. Officials still talk about family farmers as if they are not women, eclipsing an urgent area of concern if the goal of women's liberation continues to be taken seriously. The fields are far from the homes, and for the woman farmer it means hours added to the day for the walk to and from the valley before beginning to tackle all the other household tasks awaiting her return. If these policy changes do result in a more viable family farming sector, able to market crops successfully, then who will get the needed training, acquire the new skills?

It is not likely to be the women. For one thing, their inability to speak Portuguese and to read and write could be perceived as a hindrance. When extension agents come to the area and cannot speak the local language, it will be the men they gravitate toward, undermining the equality that has evolved in villages such a Três de Fevereiro. In her report on Lionde, Merle Bowen notes an "overwhelming gender bias among extension staff." Most are men who prefer to deal with male farmers. Being men, they are more confident and have better organization skills because of their wage labor experience and their better education. They are naturals, then, to benefit from the extension services. The less assertive and less experienced women would find it hard to push for the same treatment from the already biased extension staff.[2]

Is the widening of the gap between men and women inevitable? I saw women of the village willing to speak out despite the presence of authority. They stood up with as much ease as the men to talk about their village, not only in front of Lina and me, but in front of members of the provincial government and party as well. While this is something of a monumental change, it is easier than overcoming the still-present inferiority complexes to demand equal access to training and technology. Maybe with concerted effort and support on the part of OMM and the party, that easy equality I watched between women and men, peasants and leaders on that June day will turn into something more. Meanwhile, the troubling issue of gender struggle is ever present. If it is played down—as it is—and if the sexual division of labor in the household continues to overburden women—as it does—how can the liberation of women progress?

While revolution is a slow process and "marches on its stomach," the emancipation of women is especially complex. It touches all facets of the revolutionary struggle, relying on advances in all fields for its own victories, and falling victim to the failures that occur in other sectors. Beyond that it has its own special obstacles, problems, and issues to confront and resolve.

We came to the end of our guided tour of the canals. The light was beginning to fade and those who had hosted us had to get back to the village. The village president pulled his shoulders back and stood straight as a rule, his arms hanging down to the sides of his body, at attention. His faced beamed, but his eyes held a question. He was proud of what he had shown me and was ready to ask me his question. "*Now,*" he said, taking a breath as a way of pausing for emphasis. "What did you think, Camarada Stefan, of what you saw?" His stance made me take the question seriously, touched by the memory of his earnestness back in the village when he said he must wait to ask me that question. I stood up straight myself, thinking before answering. Whatever my misgivings, the changes were impressive. "I am very, very impressed by what I have seen." I said, smiling back at him. "No, you were definitely not lying." His pleasure at my answer radiated from him, as if he was accepting a special gift.

This man had hoped for so much, worked for so much. To have gotten this far must sometimes have seemed akin to a miracle. Our handshakes, rough hand to smooth, was more of a clasp and neither of us quite wanted to let go. "You must always come to Três de Fevereiro. Then while we wait for you to return, we can say, 'Hau! We told her that last time were going to do all these new things. We must make sure we live up to our promise'."

The changes in policy toward agricultural development were starting to have an impact on the peasant farmers of Três de Fevereiro, indicating what might be achieved if the government could implement its new policy for the country as a whole, not just in secure regions. It was a thought I found myself gnawing over often, particularly when I visited the flourishing green zones, a large area of land that straddles the outskirts of Maputo. This success story—perhaps one of the biggest success stories for women—occurred even though the government is not concentrating on this sector. Because these are secure zones, the agricultural cooperatives here are doing rather well, some exceptionally well: development agencies, big and small, looking for projects to fund in secure areas, have directed funding to the areas where their success has in turn generated more support.

Just over five years separated my two visits to the green zones, which were set aside for farming as private farms or agricultural cooperatives by Maputo and surrounding area residents in 1980. It was hard to believe, this second visit, that I was returning to the same place. On both occasions I visited agricultural cooperatives run by women. The first, with Lina in 1982, was something of a disappointing experience, as I had gone there with quite high expectations. Instead I found women drained of all apparent incentive, barely fueled by hope for better times. The experience had left me puzzling over why the *cooperativistas* continue to put in their long hours of work for so little remuneration or reward. Surely it would not be long, I thought, before they would give up in despair and quit. But the women of the cooperatives held on. Their patience paid off. In 1987 the green zone cooperatives I visited were not only thriving but expanding. Their members were proud and hard-working. Something very special is happening here, and it is happening because of and for women. At the time of my first visit, there were 7 cooperatives. In 1987 the green-zone cooperatives covered eighteen districts, with a total of 194 cooperatives; together they had some 10,500 members, of whom 9,500 were women.

An organization of women has emerged that is strong, self-assertive, organized. Since my last visit, a members union— União Geral das Cooperativas Agro-Pecurias de Maputo (UGC)— was established to provide training programs, services (such as day care), and general coordination. Though not set up as a women's organization, it has in effect become one. A self-conscious union, whose president is a woman, as are all eighteen district presidents, its independence has at times brought it into conflict with the Ministry of Agriculture, the party, and even OMM.

At a seminar on women and the national reconstruction process held in March 1986, the contribution by the UGC showed a dynamic organization, ready to define its problems and the problems of women more assertively than is generally found in the national women's organization and in Mozambique. The leaders stressed the need to remember that the majority of the women members had had little prospects for the future, with no wage income, unable to farm their family plots, and no possibility of contributing to the family welfare. "These women were thus consigned to living in a state of complete dependence on their husbands, which in any part of the world, but especially Africa, is a bad thing for a woman," the document stated. By contrast, the cooperative offered an alternative:

> In the cooperatives and in their controlling body, the union, women are working, women are taking part in the decision-making process, women are running their cooperatives themselves, and themselves enjoying the fruits of their labor in total equality and democracy. This way the cooperatives are breaking definitively with the social basis of women's traditional subservient status.

All this creates new relationships in the family because the woman—contributing to the upkeep of the family in an equally or even more important way than the husband, and a way that is socially recognized—stops being just *"um ser familiar"* [a family being] and becomes *"um ser social"* [a social being].[3]

Through their new-found economic independence, women *cooperativistas* are moving away from their dependence on men. A *cooperativista's* productive life, being outside of the restrictions of the family structure, enhances this independence further, enabling the women to make their own decisions. It is perhaps here, more than anywhere in Mozambique, that a new set of gender relations is occurring within the family, occurring because women are demanding it.

I visited Che Guevara cooperative, which is contiguous with two others, Roberto Mugabe and 24 de Junho. Che Guevara is one of eighteen cooperatives in the district, with a total of 2,000 members, including 40 men. Members were growing carrots, cabbage, kove, and lettuce. When I arrived, local women were buying produce in bulk—as much as they could pile into a large, wide basket carried on the head—and transporting it to Maputo markets for resale. The irrigated soil looked rich and the crops were growing well, defying the region's drought. The irrigation pump, bought from their proceeds, hummed steadily in the background. During my visit there was much consternation when it was discovered that a nearby co-op had had its pump stolen overnight. It appeared that the lock to the shed had not been forced, causing a buzz of speculation about who could have done such an act: a possible insider, the second in the year. The theft was a sore blow to the cooperative, which depends on irrigation, has limited resources for replacement, and will find difficulty in locating another pump anyway.

Co-op members work six days a week. A few even work on Sundays. Che Guevara cooperative was doing well. The level of productivity varies from one co-op to another, depending on a lot of factors—good or bad luck in cultivation, leadership, ability to purchase equipment. Che Guevara was able to buy its own vehicle to transport produce to the parastatal department to sell it. It has bought its own pump and buys seeds. At the beginning of the cultivation year, the members meet to decide collectively what they think is realistic to plant that year and what they can afford to purchase. The salary that a worker gets is calculated on what is left over once the harvest has been sold and the overhead computed.

Che Guevara members receive a small but—relative to that of some other co-ops—adequate income. There are co-ops that still cannot pay their members. But I began to understand the tenacity of the members of the co-op I visited in 1982 when the perks were explained to me. Even back in 1982, co-op members were given preferential shopping times and access to a consumer co-op at the worksite. This significantly reduced the hours that a woman would have to stand in line. In 1987 the benefits were even more marked. For instance, members of Che Guevara have worked out a special arrangement with a textile factory. They supply the factory with produce for the meals in the workers' canteen and the factory provides them with *capulanas* at the official price of 400 meticais. It is not possible to buy a *capulana* for less than 8,000 meticais anywhere in Maputo. Co-op members are able to purchase produce from their co-op at well below market prices. Given the price of vegetables this is no small achievement. The director of a co-op day-care center could not hide her delight when she told me that all the children were going to get shoes the following day from the local shoe factory. Out of the two hundred children at the center I saw only one that was not going barefoot. Shoes were just beginning to be displayed in the store windows in Maputo, but there the retail prices were far beyond the reach of a cooperative mother; at the factory they would sell at wholesale.

It was 10:30 when we reached the day-care center. A sea of pale blue uniforms was taking shape as two hundred preschoolers between the ages of two and five, guided by two adults, were lining up for breakfast. One of the kitchen workers was pouring black tea into small metal mugs that had been placed in neat rows the length of the three shelters provided by UNICEF. Another was carrying chunks of fresh bread in large basins. When they were ready the children filed in at a steady and orderly pace, taking the piece of bread offered and sitting down in front of a hot cup. Their breakfast of black tea and bread was typical fare. Sometimes they have milk in their tea but supplies had run out. At lunch they would get rice and vegetables.

I watched, almost incredulous, as the two hundred children

knew exactly what to do and were sitting quietly eating their food. One youngster, one of the littlest ones, had been crying pitifully as he stood in line. He continued as he filed in with his schoolmates. No one came to find out what was the matter. There was no one available. For the 200 children, there were three teachers, and the center's director. In the kitchen, preparing the meals, were four more workers. That was it.

The children are divided into three groups—fifty two-year-olds, seventy-five three and four-year-olds, and seventy-five five-year-olds. Each group has its own shelter for taking naps, getting together to sing songs and to come in from the rain. The shelters were simple structures, with low cement walls, interspersed with posts that held up corrugated iron roofs.

Two hundred children and no toys. I thought of my sixteen-month-old back in New York in a day-care center crammed with equipment, where the adult-child ratio is one to three in the infant room. In the toddler room, the ratio would change to one to four. The enormity of what Mozambique is up against was in the face of that weeping, uncomforted child. My camera hung idle on my shoulder. I made a comment to my companion, a *cooperante* who worked for the green zones. She nodded, understanding. "And these are the lucky ones," said my friend. "Other centers have nothing but trees for shelter."

Walking toward our car I glanced into the small reed hut that served as an office for the director. Behind a glass-fronted cabinet were two shelves of toys. Some were still in their boxes. For a peasant society where manufactured toys are unknown or so expensive they cannot be conceived of for everyday use, they must have seemed better on display. In any event, twenty-five toys for 200 children would not last very long.

Despite the lack of manufactured toys, there is no dearth of so-called found materials. The playthings that the children had invented in the Maputo streets were often ingenious. I watched enchanted as a group of four- or five-year-olds played with small "windmills" they had made from the large stiff leaves of the gum tree and matchsticks. As they ran, the windmills turned on the matchstick fulcrum, faster as they ran faster, slower as they ran slower. Their laughter and enjoyment were contagious and I stood by grinning. Intricate cars and trucks are made from wire, and now that sodas are available in the foreign exchange store, the older children who build their treasured vehicles have a source of wheels—the lower third of the aluminium Coca Cola or Fanta soda cans, the bottoms facing outwards, are just the thing for broad-based wheels.

In the past five years, the cooperative movement in the green zones has produced women leaders who probably could not have imagined taking on such roles. Not only the leaders, but the workers too are reaping the benefits of their work, have derived a sense of independence that they could scarcely have guessed possible. Leadership development has been a conscious goal of the union. Ongoing training courses are held at a specially built center where leadership skills are taught, along with literacy and other training. There, too, day care is provided, but this time the ratio is three adults to forty children and there are some toys to play with, although just a few.

The transformation of gender relations that is happening for women cooperative members has not come without struggle. The president of the union, Celina Cossa, had begun her work in the cooperative with the task of organizing the selling of goods to the members. Her work kept her constantly on the go, traveling between cooperatives, often miles apart from each other. Her husband became increasingly upset. He said she was a "public" woman now, instead of a private family member, and he hated the fact that she was in contact with all those different men every day. He wanted her to stop. She ignored his criticisms and continued her work, but eventually he left her. She spoke to her family explaining the situation, but refused to change her work life in order to placate him. Her belief in the importance of her work gave her the strength to resist his demands. Finally he relented. He has had to learn to accept her work, which has now expanded to union president and delegate to the National People's Assembly. Her travels take her even further and she meets many men in her political work, where, unlike the union, women are not represented in great numbers.

The majority of the women are single or widowed or divorced or abandoned. But for those that are married or in common-law relationships, tensions between husbands and wives have sometimes led to women giving up their work at the union. Others, with support from their colleagues, stick to their guns.

Luisa works for the union and her work too takes her from one cooperative to another. She learned to drive and was given a car to use so that she could spend more time in the co-ops and less time walking between them. Her husband can't drive. He refuses to get into the car with her, he finds it so belittling. Even when she drives past him on the road he won't take a lift. He would rather walk.

◈ 7 ◈
Women in the Factories and at Home

Marta Tembe was fired early in 1974 after working at Investro Textile Factory for two years. Her problem was her section chief. She was eighteen and attractive, and he wanted to sleep with her. She refused. He persisted. She continued to refuse. He got angry. He looked for a pretext to punish her. It was during the time that miniskirts were popular among that segment of the city that kept up with fashions. She didn't like the new fashion and continued to wear longer skirts. "So you think you can be different, hey? You think you're a model or something, wearing those long skirts?" He told her to go home and change into a miniskirt. She refused. He reported her to the boss, alleging that she had refused to work. Her side of the story was never sought. She was promptly dismissed.

Then in 1976, a number of months after independence and two years after she had been fired, she returned to the factory to ask for her job back. Her co-workers corroborated her story, and she was back at her old work station a month later. The supervisor who had harassed her was still there and he was asked to account for himself. He denied being responsible for the firing. A month later he joined the exodus. Marta Tembe found the factory a different place. One of the more striking changes was her salary. Women's salaries, formerly lower than men's, were so no longer; further-more, they had increased from around 400–450 escudos to 4,000.

Marta Tembe found other changes. The pernicious overseers were gone, replaced by promoted workers from the shop floor. While the section heads were all men, the assistant supervisors were all women. This gave women the chance to earn a higher wage and to learn about leadership. A woman could, if she became pregnant, take two months paid maternity leave in addition to the one month of vacation per year, the result of the new maternity law. Marta could see real evidence of changing roles in the com-position of the production council—50 percent women. She could take time to attend the on-site adult education classes, where 30 women students are among the total of 263 taking the course. And

152

on the assembly line she found workers talking freely to each other while working.

How different from the earlier time, when the women sat at their work stations, sewing on buttons or sewing in sleeves or pressing finished garments in silence. The Portuguese section chiefs paced the floors, on the lookout for someone breaking the rules. Often, they didn't have to wait long. The rules were many, restrictive, and vindictive. Talking was forbidden. It was hard not to break this rule during the long hours of the work day, and workers tried to catch a few sentences behind their overseers' backs at opportune moments. When they were caught they were lashed out at and hit hard. Or they were fired. If, when the boss came in from his office to check their work, a worker stopped to look at him, he would walk up to her and slap her across her face. With force. From one day to the next the workers did not know if their jobs were secure. Firings were common and without warning, usually for trivial reasons, sometimes for no reason. In these new times, Marta joined in the normal level of interaction. Workers laughed, cajoled, but worked hard, for as one of Marta's co-workers said, "We are now working for our country. We are not working for the profit of the Portuguese." The goal charts that hung on the walls of each section were to remind the workers what should be achieved and what had been achieved. They were goals to help their country's development, not to line the pockets of the Portuguese bosses.

The colonial settlers left behind little in the way of industrialization in Mozambique. Some food-processing factories, textile and clothing factories (of which Investro was one of the largest), a tire factory, a steel mill, little else. Nothing very big or developed, most using rudimentary machinery and relying heavily on cheap African labor, among whose numbers only a few women could be found. Except in the cashew factories. Here the work was so unpleasant and so low paid that men shunned applying.

Investro Textile Factory was one of the three factories I visited at the beginning of 1982 to try to find out what the response had been to the party and government call for women to "enter production," what benefits were provided, and most particularly what impact a salary had on the sexual division of labor within the family. Party statements infer that as long as women "entered" production—be it factories or agricultural cooperatives—they would be on the road to emancipation, a move essential to building the new Mozambique. But women were not heeding the call and swelling the ranks of factory workers. In fact, most women workers had been at their workplaces since before independence. The state of underdevelopment in Mozambique meant that there were few job openings. Besides, the percentage of married women among the workers was small. For the most part, the reason women sought wage work in the first place was because they *had* no husbands and needed money to support themselves and their children. They were propelled into the wage labor force by sheer economic need. In most of the factories I visited, it was unusual to find a woman in a stable relationship with a man.

Investro, which I visited first, was something of an exception. A number of the women working here were married or were in common-law marriages. Investro was unusual too in that the women had some education, quite a feat in pre-independence Mozambique. Given the difficulties and expense of sending children to school during the colonial era, education generally indicated a better economic and social status. This might explain the readiness of these women to demand changes.

The Investro women workers got together before independence day to decide what they could do, as women, to mark their pending victory. The debate was enthusiastic before they decided on forming the country's first woman soccer team.

The passion that was vented in the city over this popular sport, this quintessentially male sport, was striking. The apartment I stayed in was high on the edge of a cliff that overlooked the sports stadium. The roars of response by the mostly male fans whenever a game was being played rose up in loud waves on a sunny afternoon, or a starlit evening. For women to play soccer really was a symbol that showed, as one of team's members told me, "that the situation of women would be changed for real in our country. Before there was a general attitude that women could not play such sports. We accepted the challenge and formed a team." Some had never played. Some had had quite rigorous if informal practice as youngsters, playing with their brothers in the dusty street or on rubbled and littered open ground that served as a soccer field. As the girls reached puberty, things changed. Adelia's mother stopped her from joining the boys' game as soon as she first menstruated. "She told me, 'Soccer is for men only.'" Another woman described how her interest had waned of its own accord as she realized she could never join a team. Now she could, and those years of battling it out with the boys of the neighborhood stood her in good stead.

Investro's team is in a league of ten women's soccer teams that have been formed since independence in Mozambique. They are seeded third. "Sometimes we win. Sometimes we don't. But we always enjoy playing," said one of the team's members. One of the women in the group I was interviewing listened to the sports talk with a look of disappointment on her face. She had recently married. "My husband doesn't mind me working," she said, "but he has refused to let me play on the soccer team." She was annoyed. But she didn't defy him.

This effort in the area of sports to show that "women can do what men can do" fell down somewhat in part of the factory. To really earn a lot more than the average 4,000 escudos, a worker had to be a cutter. In a room separate from the factory floor, the cutters expertly maneuver oversized pairs of scissors through deep layers of cloth, cutting out the suits and the skirts and the jackets and trousers that would later be stitched and turned and finished in the main area. Their salary is 7,000 meticais per month. All sixteen cutters are men. In response to my "Why?" I got blank looks, which made me wonder if this question had been seriously pondered at all. "You see, its very hard work," one cutter ad libbed. "It takes a lot of strength to cut through the thick layers of cloth."

The supervisor of the section disagreed. "Oh no, that's not so," he said. "Women can do this work. Its just that the Portuguese never allowed them to learn. Now they need training." Except that no women were being trained. Two women had been apprenticed briefly, but they, together with some men, had been transferred because there were too many cutters and too few workers in other sections. So the opportunity to virtually double their salaries and "show that women can do what men can do" was lost.

And out on the factory floor various sections were responsible for the various stages of completing a garment. Some of the tasks were drearily repetitive—sewing on buttons, for instance, or turning collars, or stitching zips. Other workers sewed more of the garment, using the sewing machines. The factory's ratio of men to women broke down here too, where considerably more men sat behind the whirring machines, earning slightly higher than average wages.

The conversation with the twelve women workers, who spent a good part of the day with me, took place around what was once the board room table and was now used by the production council. Their initial shyness dissolved as we got into a discussion about subjects close to their hearts: first work, then their families and the expectations of their spouses.

Viana Tomas had been a worker at Investro for two years before her marriage in 1973 at age twenty-two. Her husband told her she could no longer work. Forget it, he persisted, as she asked him again and again during the next five years. In 1978, he finally relented and she returned to Investro. "It was because of the revolution," Viana said. "It changed him. He now understands that I can work and should be allowed to work to contribute to building the country." They all accepted that they had to have their husband's permission to work—whether they were already working when they got married or not.

Many had stories of economic hardship to relate. I heard tales of fathers abandoning mothers with numbers of children to care for, so that the oldest child, sometimes as young as fifteen, went to seek full-time work. Tales of parents dying and leaving the children with no means of support. Rosa Sevene, at forty-one one of the oldest workers, had come to Investro after her husband's death. She hated having to do this and would have far preferred to continue growing food on her family plot outside of Maputo. If she had the choice, she'd still be home with her children. "But my children have to eat," she said. Maria Puala, on the other hand, who was forty-seven and the oldest woman worker at the factory, had been encouraged by her husband to work. In twenty years she had given birth to twelve children, nine of whom had survived. Her husband's salary at the Natural History Museum was 5,000 meticais and not enough to support all the children and make sure they were educated as far as possible.

But for most of the women I talked with—like Viana—economic need was not the only reason they continued to work even if it had forced them to look for employment in the first place. According to Alda Fernando, age twenty-three: "I also work to involve myself in development. And I like to work. I feel happy, fulfilled, when I work." Twenty-four-year-old Ricardina Massinga echoed these sentiments. "I began to work to help my family. But I believe that women *must* work. This is why I work." Their husbands supported them, these young women said. For political reasons, they said, they too believed it was good for the country.

This clarity of political viewpoint got shaky when applied to domestic relations. Here there was little intimation that household work was good for the country. Only three husbands helped with household work. One had his regular task—ironing. And that is all he did. Two others helped on an ad hoc basis. Amelia Seco's husband helped clean the house and do the laundry, on occasion, "because he wants to do it." Angelica Mabasso's husband "sometimes" helps her "because he wants to." Both agreed: "I don't expect it."

For the women living in Maputo's shanty *bairros*, domestic labor is time consuming and very draining. No labor-saving devices here, and no electricity. No water on tap. And the all-pervasive *bichas*, the endless lines: for water from the communal faucets; for shopping, sometimes hours long as women waited for bread one day, fish another, carrots yet another. *Bicha* tending was a task often given to the children. But the state criticized this, maintaining that children need to be in school, not in lines. But what is a mother who works all day, and has to travel a good distance to and from work, to do?

For many of those women workers who could not rely on help from extended family members, the only answer was to pay some of their hard-earned cash to domestic workers. The going rate at the time was about 1,000 meticais per month, a significant portion of their salaries. Some brought in young relatives from the countryside to live with them, who worked in exchange for food and lodging and sometimes education. The thirteen-year-old sister of one woman looked after her three children (aged one through five) for the whole day.

A new day-care center, with a capacity for fifteen children aged a few weeks to two years, was set up at the factory after independence. Except for the food the mothers brought each day, it was free. Mothers could continue to breast feed through the day. They were entitled by a recent law to a half-hour breast-feeding break in the morning and one in the afternoon, in addition to their lunch break. Despite the fact that this looked like an ideal solution, there was no waiting list. One reason was that once someone was looking after the older children, it cost no more to have them look after the younger children. But the main obstacle was transport. No woman relished carrying her child on the long journey to and from work, waiting for buses, squeezed between fellow passengers on overcrowded vehicles. It could be stressful enough without making the journey with an infant under two.

The day-care center itself was clean, with cribs, stove, fridge, and toys, all bought out of the proceeds from fund-raising activities organized by the factory's OMM and the local OMM. There were three workers, all trained in a special program in Maputo run by the Ministry of Health. They had been chosen from the factory floor and their salaries matched those in the factory. The large, airy room, with its tiled walls, had been built shortly after independence by the factory owners in response to worker demands and demands from the local OMM. (The factory owner left the country in 1979 and the factory was nationalized.)

With arrangements made for child care one way or another, the Investro woman worker can set off for the factory each day. But child care is but one aspect of domestic labor. There is still food to buy and to cook, water to fetch, laundry to wash by hand, housecleaning to do. "I get up at five every morning and cook the evening meal," explained one worker. "I leave for work at 6:30 and shop on my way home. Luckily the stores are open to 8 o'clock [special hours for workers] so there is time."

Time? How much time is left in a workday that begins at five and ends in the late evening? A day filled with housework, cooking, child care, and factory labor. Even with help from outside or help from women members of the extended family, there is little let-up. Even when this help is substantial, what isn't shared is *responsibility*—that unquantifiable reality that pervades family life, that drains energy, that promotes worry, not to mention guilt. With the hours so overfilled each day, how much time is left over to just be with the children? What happens when children are ill? Or when they injure themselves and need attention? Or when they need their mothers' attention and comfort? And when it's hard to find food for the evening meal?

On my 1983 visit I consistently heard of urban worker families (not only factory workers, but others such as government employees) who relied on rations from the consumer co-ops for their basic food. For the last days of the month, when these had run out, they lived on bread and tea. Often the bread was spirited away from the rations handed out at the workplace, even though this was not permitted. The food was provided at the factory as one of the benefits for workers. The benefit also meant that the workers would have energy to work and keep up production. But what mother, or father for that matter, could think of the abstract good of the country when children were hungry at home? This dilemma was addressed from the heart by two workers of the Companhia Industrial da Matola (CIM) who spoke about some of the difficulties they had in continuing at the factory school:

> When you think a lot about your life, you can't bring yourself to study. What do we have to eat in the house when I get home from work. Here I can go to the mess and eat well. There at home we have nothing. Here in the factory I have a uniform, I have something to put on, but there at home, there is no clothing for the children.

> You go to literacy classes just to be marked present. Your wits aren't there. They're at home with the problems of living. Your wits and your heart aren't there. At the end of each month, when the rations have run out, it's worse. You go out the door with your wife saying to you, "There's nothing here in the house to eat."[1]

For a brief period, until it was stopped by higher authorities, hospital workers caught taking food home were forced by over-zealous administrators to wear a sign proclaiming "I am a thief."

Of course, this is not only the worry of women. But when women work and do not have a wife back home to try to find food somehow or other, it is all the more anxiety provoking. The need to find time for all this work must surely cast a dark shadow over the life of working mothers. Men who fail to contribute their share of household work are even more likely to fail to take a share of responsibility. A subject that can jet-propel U.S. feminists into fury and resentful feelings of being exploited victims—namely, shared housework and shared responsibility—seemed to raise the level of heat around our table not one iota.

Marta Tembe's three children, all below the age of five, are cared for by an empregada—domestic worker—when she is at work. Marta cooks the family's meals and does most of the housework. "When I prepare the meals my husband is usually at home, but he doesn't help me. Sometimes he'll come and talk to me while I am working in the kitchen and help by picking bugs out of the un-cooked rice. But anyhow, I wouldn't like to see my husband doing the housework."

The three women who told me that their husbands helped them

with housework made sure that I understood that they did not pressure their husbands. What I was hearing here was in keeping with official party and OMM policy: don't bring conflict into the home.

The OMM secretary at Investro, Isabel Manhique, had been working at the factory since long before independence. At thirty-nine she had eight children, ranging in age from eighteen years to three months and including two sets of twins. She made herself clear on the subject: women should not demand that their menfolk help in the household. Neither should OMM factory meetings address the issue as a way of mobilizing women and men to break down the gender-based roles in the family. Sure, it would be better if men did help with these chores. That certainly is the goal. But it was something that should happen slowly. Meanwhile women should get up earlier and stay up later, in order to show the men that they could handle their various responsibilities. Then the men would change. She finds that since independence there is a difference. "Before independence my husband never helped in the house," she said. "Now I feel I can ask him and sometimes he helps. We need the money so I must work. But I am responsible for the house. I wouldn't demand that he helps. It is my work."

While Isabel Manhique was talking I reflected on my visit to Chibuto district in Gaza province at the beginning of 1981. Arminda Hombé was the district's OMM secretary and Frelimo district secretary for ideological work, the only woman I met to hold such a position. She was a popular figure in the district and when she took me to visit a number of villages, she was always greeted with particular warmth by both women and men. Her work kept her very busy, while she looked after her own three young children. Arminda explained to me: "Perhaps a young wife has three children and is breast-feeding the youngest one in the evening. The two older ones are playing at her feet. Her husband, just home from work, sits in a chair and reads the paper. The wife tries to attend to all three children at once. Then the toddler messes on the floor. The husband does not notice or ignores the exasperation of his wife. She then turns to him and says, "Dear, our second child has dirtied the floor. As you see, I am feeding our youngest.

Nutrition is extremely important for his growth, so it would be wrong to stop feeding to attend to the other's needs. Would you mind cleaning it up?" If she asks him politely, the husband will respond, and next time he will notice on his own accord and attend to it without being asked. This is how we explain to women at meetings the way to change men's behavior within the family." It's the same tune. "Speak with kind words." Continue to rock the cradle so as not to rock the boat. This approach was something I heard echoed in both rural and urban settings. I heard it so often that I ceased to be surprised. OMM cadres stressed that women must encourage change with "kind words," patient encouragement, and education of men; it is incorrect to speak out in anger.

Arminda Hombé impressed me as being anything but a meek woman, willing to pander to a man's chauvinism. Chibuto district had one of the highest concentrations of communal villages in the province, a province that itself had the greatest proportion of its population in communal villages. Her party work brought with it considerable responsibility, and placed her in the position of authority over men, as well as working side-by-side with male colleagues. I found it hard to imagine the scenario she described in her own home. Did she really believe in this soft approach? She certainly related it as if she did, comfortably repeating the line of the party and the women's organization, eager that I should understand their perspective.

While political mobilization remained vital—in all parts of the country—in encouraging women to take on men's roles, the mobilization of men to do "women's work" is absent. Where is the call for men to show they can do what women can do? There is an absence of the concept of gender *struggle* in the overall struggle for a transformed society. Demand for equality within the domestic sector is posed as a source of conflict, one that should be guarded against, not encouraged. While the need for more equality within family relations is not denied, women are urged to "speak with kind words" and bring about an integrated family work life through example. Work hard. Get up even earlier. Men will then see the need to contribute. The intensity with which women are at times exhorted to speak with kind words, to diminish conflict, while the demand that men take on household chores on an equal basis is labeled "mechanistic" suggests that women have in fact taken up this issue with energy, so that a need was felt to squelch it before such conflict become "destructive" in a society trying to forge unity. While class struggle is emphasized as critical to the transformation of the society, gender struggle is not. The former dissolves contradictions. The latter is threatening.

In the midst of war, political mobilization was energetically undertaken to make the long-term goal of a nonexploitative society—and not simply the replacement of Portuguese administrators with African administrators—a reality. Similarly, after independence, when the major thrust became development, development itself was not a sufficient goal. After all, development had taken place in neocolonial Africa, benefiting a favored few but not resulting in a new society for the masses. Hence raising political consciousness was considered essential to the process of economic transformation. But although Frelimo has stressed the importance of mobilization through the phases of its revolutionary struggle, its seems to be curiously absent from the strategy proposed for the emancipation of women. Women must be mobilized to join the current phase of the revolution, and not to fight for their rights as women, to *struggle* against their subordination.

It seemed to me as I spoke with different people and read Machel's writing on the subject that this view was very much a reflection of Machel's own attitudes, which he transposed into broader political concepts. It could be found in Machel's first speech to the founding conference of OMM, where he described the "mechanistic" division of tasks within the household as prevalent in the West, where "the aim is to transform the contradiction with men into an antagonistic one." He added:

> There is a profusion of erroneous ideas about the emancipation of women. There are those who see emancipation as mechanical equality between men and women. This vulgar concept is often seen among us. Here emancipation means that women and men do exactly the same task, mechanically dividing their household duties. If I wash the dishes today, you must wash them tomorrow, whether or not you are busy or have the time. If there are still no women truck drivers or tractor drivers in Frelimo, we must have some right away regardless of the objective and subjective conditions. As we can see from the example of capitalist countries, this mechanically conceived emancipation leads to complaints and attitudes which utterly distort the meaning of women's emancipation."[2]

"Some women use women's liberation as a weapon," I was told again and again, with accompanying stories about how this or that rural woman or urban woman had refused to cook for her husband because she interpreted the goals of the liberation of women as meaning that she did not have to do the housework any longer.

Mama Leia provided only one example: "After independence many women began to abuse their relationships with their husbands. They said they were emancipated, and talked to their husbands without respect. They would just shout at the man and even at their children. Even if the husband is in the wrong, it is necessary to talk it over. Women must not be free to abuse. We must be free to respect each other. Before women were angry and they could say nothing. Then after independence they began to express this anger. Husbands objected and said things like: 'You shout at us now because Frelimo says you are free.' The men would get very angry. We saw that women were losing respect for their husbands, and too many separations took place over small issues that could have been discussed and resolved within the family."

Nevertheless, many women do not have time to speak with kind words. They are too busy trying to put food on their families' tables. And to do this often requires working for money outside the home to supplement the man's income. From what I and others who have looked at similar issues have found, there is greater assertion on women's part than the OMM might have liked to believe in light of the organization's lack of encouragement to challenge men. They are challenging men nonetheless. While this often begins with women's insistence on working outside the home, it is transmitted back into the home with women's demands that their husbands take on responsibilities within the home. They begin to rock the boat. Some husbands adjust, some marriages don't survive. No doubt some women give in.

As our time together lengthened at Investro and the women and I got more comfortable with each other, some spoke out more openly. Two in particular began to express their unhappiness at the inequality they experienced. Juliana Barata was a few years younger than Isabel Manhique, with whom she worked as member of the factory's OMM secretariat. She felt differently. "Both my husband and I work. I am really happy when I get home and find my husband has helped with the chores. Sometimes I arrive home later than he and he has bathed the children and prepared supper. Ah, I feel good. But if I *ask* him to help and he refuses, I feel awful. "Am I nothing more than a slave in my own house?" I say to myself. "I work all day in the factory. So does he. But then I work hard at home as well. Does this not equal slavery?" When he helps, I find I enjoy doing the housework because I don't feel that only I am responsible. Many men are changing their attitudes because of the revolution. They are more ready to help than ever before. This is very important, because it is a real advance. Some men are changing because they are becoming politicized and realize that they are living in different times. Others change because it is the women who insist that they work in the house. But both are the result of a new society we are building."

Lucia Lalu is also a member of the OMM secretariat. She has two children, aged eight and four. Her husband is willing to help when he gets home earlier than she and sees that there are tasks that need doing. "In my opinion men should do much more than they do in the home. There are women who don't work and still they don't do the housework adequately. When their husbands come home at night, the food is not ready, the house is a mess. This shouldn't be. Men shouldn't have to help their wives if their wives are at home all day. But for working women, it would be really good if their husbands help. She comes home from work tired. The children haven't seen her all day. They want to play. They hang around her while she's trying to cook. Meanwhile her husband comes home and just sits down and surveys the scene. He does nothing. The father should look after the children, for example, while his wife cooks."

Despite their criticism of men's lack of help, neither woman suggested an alternative to OMM's direction. "Even though OMM is not working directly with men in discussing these problems," added Lucia Lalu, "it is the strength of OMM that is bringing about change. Men hear that women are needed in production and that women must be equal. This begins to make an impression on them, to change their attitudes." "We need a *men's* organization," quipped Juliana Barata, to a chorus of laughter. "Then men can discuss the social problems that exist and how they must help change them."

Among those who have little time for kind words are market women, who seem to have taken a stronger stand than some of their sisters working in the factories. Signe Arnfred, a Danish sociologist who worked for OMM for a number of years in Maputo, describes a particularly heated discussion between women and men in a market in a Maputo *bairro*. The women told her how they had to fight with their husbands in order to become market traders.

One woman had to find work outside the home to supplement her husband's income as it was not enough to buy food for the children. "He was always shouting because I wanted to start working in order to earn some money. He told me in that case I should return to my parent's house. I started working nevertheless. In the beginning he wouldn't accept it, but now he does." Another woman measured the change in her home life by the fact that her husband stopped beating her. "He was drinking, and he never gave me money. When I asked, 'Where is your wage?' he would hit me and say, 'That's none of your business.' So I had to start working. He used to beat me. These days he is only talking."

There seems to be room for optimism. "It is better now," explained another market woman. "When a family problem has to be solved, the man now will sit down and talk to their wife about it: 'What do you think. . . ?' Our husbands are not just ordering us around as before." A fourth woman had a different explanation. "The men complain that the women don't want to work because we are emancipated. But that is not the case. It is because we have so much work, taking the child to hospital, cooking, going to work, attending meetings and so on. The women really have very little time. And the men never think of helping their wives."

But it was the comments of the men, rather than those of the women, that showed that these women are not willing to sit back, shoulder an unfair burden of household work, and "speak with kind words." One complained, "These days, when a man is talking to his wife, and asks, 'Please do this and that,' the wife says, 'Why don't you do it yourself.' So the husband sees that they don't get along well together and he divorces the wife." "The problem is cleanliness," interjected another man. "My wife doesn't want to wash my shirt and my trousers. She says that she hasn't got time. It isn't that I myself am not able to wash my clothes. But my wife always did it, so why not now? It is a disgrace in front of my neighbors if my wife doesn't wash my clothes."

And so the contradiction persists, the contradiction between women's role in reproduction and their increasng role in non-household production. It became increasingly evident as I talked to women in factories. But it is a contradiction that could in the end give rise to its own solutions though the demands of women unable to cope with the pressures placed on them by their work and by the expectations of their commitment to the development of their country. It was the younger women I spoke to, the more educated women in their late teens and early twenties, who insisted that when they got married they would categorically refuse to accept that their husbands did less than an equal share of the household tasks. Their awareness was sharper. They point to the contradiction between the older and the younger generations of women. Like that in the poem written by fifteen-year-old Ilda Maria, which I read on my last visit to Mozambique, published in a collection of student poems put together by a teacher at Josina Machel High School in Maputo:

Mother: Carlaaaaaa! Carlaaaaaa!
          Where are you going, my daughter?
          Don't you see
          That it's too hot?
Carla: Mum, I'm going to school
          I'm going to learn
          How to read and write.
Mother: Carla, Carla, my daughter
          You have learnt enough
          Now even biology you know by heart
          But you . . .
Carla: Yes, mum
          I'm sorry to cut you short
          I know what you mean.
Mother: Carla, my daughter
          You shame me your mother
          Now you're big enough
          To be a mother.
Carla: Mum, I know what you mean
          What I must learn now
          Or what I should have learnt
          Long before I learnt biology
          Is "cookology," "sweepology,"
          And "washology."[3]

The sexual division of labor was not the only source of tension and contradiction for women workers. Even six years after independence, some factories were still paying women lower wages for equal work. One of these was CIM, a food-processing plant. When

I visited the factory at the end of 1981, it was hard to picture it as the thriving and expanding concern it was in the 1960s and early 1970s. During this heyday it had received a boost from the decision of the colonial government to encourage foreign investment and there was a steady flow of spaghetti, cookies and crackers, candy and chocolates, out of the plant.

In the chaos that followed the coup, settler owners abandoned the factories that they had brought to a standstill, leaving them to be taken over by the state. The Portuguese management of CIM was not part of this immediate exodus, but it slowly allowed the factory to run down. It balked at the democratic reforms the new government was demanding and refused to allow the production councils to participate in the planning and production decisions, or to allow party cells to operate and support the needs of the workers. The poor working conditions were left pretty much as they were. Tensions between the workers and administration mounted steadily, punctuated by a four-day strike for higher salaries, and the successive turnover of administrators just added to the confusion. While the strike did win a salary increase, it was one that continued to reflect the pattern of Portuguese wage discrimination, with women earning less than their male co-workers.

As the situation deteriorated, a crucial source of processed food for the whole south of the country was placed in jeopardy. The state stepped in as soon as it could and took over the factory in mid-1980. The new administration that took over was made up of dynamic and innovative managers and the following years saw CIM transformed from an apathetic, underproductive factory into one of the country's models of social progress for workers. However, it was to be a few years—well after my visit—before these reforms would be felt by the workers.

At the time of my visit, there were 1,200 workers, of whom 212 were women. The majority (137) were employed in the biscuit factory. The rest were dotted over the different sections, with 20 working in the spaghetti plant and nine in the day-care center.

The factory still seemed depressed. The central complaint was the low wages and most particularly the salary discrimination. The women earned 2,500 meticais; the men 3,000. For the women this was up from the average of 520 they earned before independence, but it was not enough.

Low wages resulted in a sense of malaise. Veronica Sumbane, party secretary for the factory, told me that after independence the energy level was high. Workers went eagerly to political education meetings; they read revolutionary magazines; they went to regular party meetings. "When I try to call a meeting now, the first question the workers ask is: 'Are you going to discuss what to do about the low salaries?' When I say no, they don't want to come." The commitment to political education petered out, and the brigades of the district's political structures seldom came to the factory. "They come only to know the problems. They don't come to solve them," she said. They would just listen, assure the workers they'd be back to iron them out and then not return. Although it was unusual to find a woman head of a party cell, particularly when there are fewer women than men members (CIM had 122 members, of whom 43 were women—a higher proportion than the ratio of women to men workers) Veronica Sumbane did not feel this was a blow for women's liberation. The acceptance of a woman leader was not necessarily a sign of progress, she said. "The men had no reaction. People are not deeply involved in party work just now. They are apathetic."

And OMM? I wondered aloud whether there wasn't support for OMM or for Veronica Sumbane's work among the women. This was negative, too. There had been an effective secretary for OMM at the factory initially, but she was too effective: as is the case whenever a woman shows strength and leadership, she was transferred to help remedy the dire shortage of qualified women. She was appointed OMM secretary for the province of Maputo. No one replaced her. The biggest concern among the women is the wages. It really distresses them. So they keep asking OMM to look into it, and OMM keeps promising that something will be done. "We are still asking and they are still studying," said Veronica. "This is why the women don't support their organization."

She had her own troubles relating to the workers. Some couldn't believe that she would take on the thankless job of party secretary unless she was being paid extra. Sometimes they'd ask to see her pay slip on pay day. "I show them. They can see that I earn the same as them but there is still tension." The secretary of the production council had the same problem. Before he left for his training course in Cuba he had been earning 4,500 meticais per month for the slightly more skilled work on the machines. The workers were convinced that he must be earning at least 8,000.

The bitterness about the wage differences became quickly apparent when I visited the biscuit factory assembly line. "Look at that boy," one worker said to me pointing toward a young man no older than eighteen or nineteen who, like the women I was talking to, was packing biscuits. "I have children to feed and a home to run. What does he have? Nothing! He has no family, only himself to look after and he earns 500 more a month. It's just not fair." "They say that the reason why men receive more money than women," said Helena Chirime, "is that men marry, and have family responsibilities. I have three children. I am the one, always the one, to feed them, buy their clothes, take them to the hospital when they are ill, pay for their school books. Their father never gave me anything. I have the same responsibilities as men. I should have the same salary."

The concern about wages tended to eclipse some of the real benefits for workers introduced at the factory that particularly affected women: the large day-care center, for example, with its forty children and its nine caregivers and service staff. Despite the problems of transport, it was a genuine alternative for women who could not arrange any other day care. For many it was the difference between working and not working, between surviving marginally and destitution. The center was well run. I remember the bright rooms at the side of the factory and the loving care the children got. The ratio was six or seven children to one adult. And immediately I think of the center I visited in the green zones with its meager resources and a ratio of fifty to one.

Other changes benefited women along with men, such as the provision of a substantial hot meal in the factory's cafetaria at lunch and daily tea breaks, a first-aid post, a social fund for workers to provide loans for family emergencies, one of the few retirement and pension plans, and a bakery that supplied bread for the workers. More recently, a housing cooperative and the right to buy factory produce at controlled prices has been added. These and access to other goods through the factory—capulanas, for instance, batteries, clothing—were de facto significant wage supplements.[4]

Even the fact that the chocolate and candy section was standing idle was an index of change. The problem was, the workers explained, that South Africa, the supplier of some of the raw ingredients, had not delivered them as part of the campaign of economic sabotage. Day after day the workers came to the factory, spent their shifts waiting, and collected their pay packet each week. They were astonished when I told them that in the United States workers would have been laid off without warning and entitled to only twenty-six weeks of unemployment benefits. In Mozambique there were no unemployment benefits, but the state did not sever its responsibility. Under the Portuguese they would have been summarily dismissed.

In the years following my visit, the new administrations' reforms began to take hold and the women workers won their right to equal pay. Women's salaries were boosted from 2,500 meticais to the new base line of 3,300. But the low salary level as a whole continued to be a point of contention. While the workers benefited from a range of services and perks well beyond what many of their co-workers at neighboring factories were receiving, the general economic failing of the country meant that these did not nearly compensate for the rapid deterioration of living conditions all urban workers are experiencing.

◆8◆
Outside the New Family

The Palace of Marriages is an imposing building set slightly back from Avenida Julius Nyerere. It is not out of place on this broad tree-lined avenue with its apartment buildings and many mansions and semi-mansions, as well as the grandiose Polana Hotel, famous during the colonial era for its excessive style and cost. The Palace of Marriages, formerly a Greek Orthodox Church, with its wide steps, high doors, all white and pristine, suggests another time and place implanted by the settlers, in the hope of recreating a lost European elegance on this very African terrain.

On my recent visit, I stop to watch a familiar Saturday afternoon ritual being played out at the palace. I stand among equally curious bystanders, quietly staring—small children dressed in rags, women with babies tied to their backs, a casual stroller like myself. A bride and bridegroom are descending the steps, the bride holding her white veil, an attendant scooping up the hem of her white bridal gown. Her groom is dressed in a neat dark suit. They are surrounded by well-wishers dressed in their finest. It could be a scene out of a glossy American magazine, celebrating the "church wedding." Except this isn't a church wedding. It is a civil wedding encouraged by a revolutionary government that has renovated the building for the purpose. I look on with some detachment and find myself wondering whether this couple is following political principle and marrying out of Samora Machel's—and the party's—vision of "revolutionary love." Will the family this couple creates replace the old concept of the family that has been identified in party documents as a major obstacle to equality between men and women?

The family is described as the incubator of an array of ills that result in women's oppression—particularly such customs as polygamy, *lobolo*, and so forth. In the new family, members will comfortably coexist in an environment of equality and mutual respect. At the 1984 Extraordinary Conference, the OMM recommended that "the family should be a melting-pot for the creation of the new man [*sic*]" and that "each family make an effort to create a new equilibrium, based on equality of rights and duties."[1] The party statements relating to family suggest that the definition of family means husband, wife, and children. Or perhaps husband, wives, and children, accepting that polygamy, even if the goal is to end the practice, is still a reality in Mozambique. This concept excludes another family configuration which is much a party of reality, particularly in the *bairros* surrounding the cities: single mothers and their children, often children with different fathers.

None of the CIM women workers I spoke to were in stable relationships, although there were other women in the factory who were in common-law relationships. They could think of only one woman who worked on the factory floor who was about to be formally married. The majority had children and no child support. Most spoke of having *companheiros*, a word that defies English translation. In a common-law marriage it might mean what we call by various inadequate terms for want of a word such as *companheiro*. For a woman at CIM it meant she had a man she could refer to as her boyfriend, even if she saw him seldom and even if he was married to and living with another woman. "If we don't have a *companheiro*," explained Salda Jonas, "people say we are prostitutes. If a woman decided to live alone, and chooses a different way of life, she is called a prostitute because she's different. It is not easy to be alone without sexual relationships. Then if she has many men, she feels like a prostitute. Men have it easy. They make the choices. Women have to wait and to accept the situation that men make."

The discussion of *companheiros* and the irresponsibility of men toward their offspring and their lovers became as intense as the discussion of unequal wages. It was generally agreed that it was better to have someone that could be labeled *companheiro* than to be linked to no one, even if this man was a shadowy figure in their lives. When I asked Julieta Fumo whether she had a *companheiro*, she said, "well, it's not easy for me to say whether I do or don't. He belongs to another woman. He only visits me sometimes." There were stories of being abandoned by husbands for infertility or for other women. Women with steady *companheiros* or with husbands were portrayed as being very threatened by single women, who would snatch their men away. They felt that these women regarded women workers as loose women and were quick to label them prostitutes. How stable were these "stable" relationships, I wondered. It was almost classic how anger was redirected toward the "conniving" women rather than at the men who flitted between women taking no responsibility for them or for the children they fathered.

Domestic chores, whether tackled by a woman worker at Investro or by a single mother at CIM, were similar. The work was possibly harder for the Investro worker because of the added demands of her husband. But many could and did employ help. For the CIM worker an *empregada* was way beyond her means, and she had to support as many children as her Investro counterpart on her income alone.

Veronica Sumbane, the Frelimo secretary at the factory, was twenty when she first arrived in Maputo from Gaza province, equipped with a third-grade education and little else. Her schooling ended when her parents, peasant farmers, could no longer pay the fees. She was the youngest of five sisters and a brother, who had gone to work in South Africa and was never heard from again. Her meager education provided the opportunity to work in an office and she found a job in a type-setting business, taking home a salary of 550 escudos. It was a struggle to feed herself. In 1970 she began living with the man she loved and had a child. Her parents, putting aside custom, had not pressed for *lobolo*, although they had expected and received it for her older sisters. "As you love each other," her father told her, "just live together. I won't ask for *lobolo*." When her baby was born she had no one to help care for it, so she stopped working. "I would have had to pay my whole salary to an *empregada*, so I had to stop."

By 1976 she had three children. It was a hard year. Her husband died, and soon afterward one of her children. It was a good marriage, and talking about it these years later she still fought to control her tears. Left alone with two young children of five and two she was desperate. She looked for work and eventually was hired at CIM, then still under Portuguese control. The salaries had improved as a result of a strike by workers two years earlier during the transition government but they were still only 850 meticais for women and 1,200 for men.

She was relieved to have work and excited by the fact that her country was now free. Much more was possible for her as a woman than ever before. She worked hard, both at her job and as a political activist. Within two years she was a party member and was then selected secretary of the factory's party cell. She lives alone with her children, now seven and ten, in the house her husband had built her and has since had another child by another man. This is a responsible father. But she is essentially in a polygamous marriage. She sees her *companheiro* regularly, but he lives with his wife, who also looks after Veronica's baby during the week. She fetches him on Fridays and looks after him during the weekends. When she was still breast feeding she had to get up very early to take him to his father's house and then pick him up at the end of the day. Her *companheiro* would not allow her to take the young child to the factory day-care center because he was concerned about the ride in a truck, with the possibility of breakdowns. As this was her only means of transport to work, she accepted his arrangement. It also lifted the worry from her shoulders. The two women get on well.

She still has her other two children to care for alone during the week. They cook for themselves and go to the market to shop for food. She does all the housework. Although her *companheiro* helps support their child, she would prefer to be married again. When she says this, she looks down, and the lips of this otherwise tough and independent woman again tremble.

My appreciation of what it means to be a single mother in Mozambique deepened after talking with women at Caju de Matola, the cashew-processing factory, where nearly all the workers are women. Women who, I found, had had such disappointing, sometimes abusive, relationships with men that they preferred being single, a status they often actively chose. They rejected the idea of marriage, registered or common-law, and unlike women I spoke to at CIM were unperturbed by the lack of someone to label *companheiro*. Take Marcelina Tsaquisse, for example, who has been employed in the cashew factory for many, many years.

Marcelina Tsaquisse was one of the first women workers to catch my attention soon after I entered the large hangarlike structure of the vast factory that stood near the highway that runs through Matola. Inside were rows of long wooden tables that stretched from one side of the factory floor to the other; women stood or sat on high stools sorting cashews by size and quality,

discarding the substandard. In the front corner, two women holding crude blow torches, with even movements, welded lids to the
large square tins filled with the processed nuts. They gave the
swivel mounts a push to set them in motion, and then with solder
in one hand they directed their flames with the other to the edge of
the lid to meld the solder and seal the cans. It was a simple system
that required some skill. They lowered the torch, rotated the tins
one more time to look for missed spots, and then lifted their arms
out of the way for a co-worker to remove the finished can and
replace it with the next. As they wore no protective gear, it was
easy to see that these welders were women.

One was young, in her twenties. The other was a lot older, her
speckled grey hair showing under a headscarf. This was Marcelina
Tsaquisse. She had begun work at the factory years before independence, joining the rows of women shelling cashews. There
were only a few men among the 1,000 workers, and they all held
administrative or skilled positions. After independence this
changed—and in the spirit of showing that women could do what
men could do, two women workers were trained to be welders.
The two male welders still held their positions, but now they
alternated shifts with the two women.

Marcelina was born in Inhambane, how many years before she
did not know. She has no birth certificate and has never learned to
read or write. She has grandchildren in primary school. She
worked in the *machamba*, got married in Inhambane, switched to
working the *machamba* attached to her husband's homestead, and
gave birth to four children. But they all died. Her husband blamed
her for the deaths. "As all my children were dying, maybe one day
it will be me," he told her, and sent her back to her parents,
demanding to be repaid the *lobolo*. Her parents were poor, and
had long since absorbed the brideprice. She left for Maputo to
seek work and managed to save the 4,000 escudos from her salary
of only a few hundred escudos a month, and sent it to her brother
to give to her husband. She continued to work at the factory. "Its
my responsibility to work," she told me. "I am not afraid to work
hard. This way I can support myself." She has never had a *companheiro* since, although she has had children. "I never wanted to
remarry. I never wanted a *companheiro*. Once was enough."

Marcelina was not alone in her attitude. Many women disdained the idea of marriage or *companheiros*, seeing in such
relationships an end to their freedom and the inevitability of

abuse and abandonment. The very fact that they had looked for a way out of their oppressive marriage and unhappiness, and resisted social pressure by going to the city to work, meant they were fairly tough to start with. Their sense of independence was strong and they were not going to relinquish it. Even if it meant they could stop working.

It certainly wasn't work that many women could have enjoyed doing. The conditions were so bad and the pay so low that most men did not apply. But the women had little choice, as there were few ways of earning cash in Maputo—domestic work and prostitution were about the only other alternatives. Many were desperate, like Marcelina, to find a way out of their marriages, and so filled the cashew factories' workforce in large numbers. In the factories where there were no machines for shelling, the conditions were particularly putrid. And it was hazardous. After the tough shells were charred, they would have to be removed manually. In the process a corrosive substance was released that ate into the hands of the sheller causing infection and considerable discomfort. They tied bits of rags around their hands to try to protect them, but this made it harder to work. Slowing down meant less pay, as their wages were calculated by quantity shelled and sorted, not by the hour. To make matters worse, men would complain that the smell of the acid never left the women's hands.

Conditions at Caju de Matola were a little better, because the shelling was done by machine, as was the rudimentary sorting. The roar of the machines was something else, and those working long hours must have surely lost some of their hearing.

One of Marcelina's co-workers, Felizmina Mafumo, described her experience. She began working before independence, earning an average of 150 escudos per months—about $5.00. She was told her salary would reach 300 escudos, but it never did. "Each day we would be given a large wooden box which we had to fill. I could hardly ever fill it in one day. So the next day I began where I left off. By the third day I would fill it and get paid. But only for one day's work. So I never earned 300 escudos."

After independence the salaries were reassessed on a national level and the cashew workers, such as Felizmina and Marcelina, began to take home 2,704 escudos. Unlike at CIM, the workers here seemed to have little to complain about. The improvements were real, and their salaries were the same as those of the men. They appreciated the change in working conditions and the benefits such as maternity leave and vacation time, the literacy classes and the political participation. And it was the exception who missed having a *companheiro*. Most had come to terms with and preferred their totally single and independent status.

Felizmina, for instance, remembers with pain her marriage to a man who worked in the South African mines. In the six years they were together she bore him no children. Her infertility angered him and he began to beat her. "Go to your own home," he shouted, "I don't want you here. You have no children. You are useless." In 1977 she came to Maputo to try to find work to pay back the *lobolo*. She has paid back everything owed, but she continues to work. "I want to work because I have to live."

She attends literacy classes at the factory and is learning to read and write for the first time. Felizmina lives alone in a *bairro* of Matola in a room she rents in a house. She sends money to her brothers and mother every month. Her father can't work because he is very old. She is satisfied with her life now. Although she is still young, she insists she will never remarry. "I don't need a man in my life," she said firmly. "I have a *companheiro* but I don't want any commitments. The first experience was enough. I don't want to repeat it."

Carlotta de Jesus Mahashane was born in Inhambane province thirty years earlier. When she was ten she went to live with her brother, a teacher. She had as much trouble with her brother as many women have with their husbands. As she got older and became interested in boys, he would not let her marry because he did not have a wife and needed someone to cook for him. When he finally married in 1963, she went to Maputo to live with her sister-in-law's mother. She was seventeen. She met a man who wanted to marry her, but as he wasn't Catholic her brother refused to give permission. Since then she has had the opportunity to marry. This time, it is she who refuses. She has seen the way her married sisters are treated, she explains. "They have such a hard life. They are not living well. I decided I didn't want to marry. I am better off alone."

Amelia Franice Chirore also had a hard life as a wife. She said her age was forty-three years, although she looked a lot older. She had been married twice. The first man she married mistreated her because she had no children. She left him. She soon got married again, *lobolo* paid a second time. She had five children. Only her first-born survived. She lived with her husband for many years before the trouble began. Her husband began to beat her. He took the money that was meant for their home and paid *lobolo* for another wife. Their relationship deteriorated even more. One day he beat her so badly he wounded her eye. She left him. Her son remained with his father.

In 1977, when she went to Maputo from Moamba, her first husband reappeared on the scene and demanded five cows in repayment of the *lobolo*. He began to nastily pester her mother, who was old and fragile and could not cope. To stop the harassment she began sending money to her mother so that she could buy the cows, using up her small savings to buy five cows for a man she hadn't seen in fifteen years. She lives with a third man, who has another wife. He treats her well, though, she says. Well, he doesn't beat her. She says too that he doesn't give her any child support for the child they had together. It is his seventh by four different women.

Lina, who is translating for me, is incredulous. "The first man beat you. The second man beat you. Why did you get another man?"

It's society, she answers. A woman is expected to have a man, reflecting the patriarchal attitudes that persist, coming from a combination of Portuguese-imposed mores and African traditions, attitudes left unchallenged in the new Mozambique. "If he was a good man, he would give me money. But he's not. Even if he doesn't give me any money, I still need a man."

Alda Abel Langa, district secretary of the OMM, who visited the factory with us, reinforced what Amelia Chirore was saying. Women like Amelia would rather be with a man even if he doesn't help support her because she finds it too difficult to go against social attitudes. She is afraid that if she is alone, she will be labeled a prostitute by the community. The men are very irresponsible, Alda Langa complained. He finds a woman, she's young. He convinces her to make love and as she's a woman she gets pregnant. Then he leaves her. She waits but he never comes back. The only men she meets are married. It all begins again. The men are just interested in sex and they don't tell the women about their wives. It is common for a man to have three, four, five women he has made pregnant. The women are abandoned and get no financial support for his children, like the majority of women working here in Caju.

"Society does not blame men if they abandon women," Lina

added. "Women are seen as responsible. So women have to work to support their children. People condemn women if they don't look after their kids. Men are never condemned."

Amelia Chirore was the only woman I interviewed who felt a *companheiro* was necessary. Most felt they could do without, thank you very much, after the bad experiences they had had with their men. None seemed to hanker after a life without work, either. Lina asked a group of women we were interviewing, "If a man comes to you and says he will give you the same amount of money the factory pays and he will look after you but you must give up work, would you agree?" The answer was unanimous and unequivocal. "Never!"

There was a chorus of responses. "By working we have discovered our lives as women." "I feel independent. I can buy my own clothes and educate my children." "I would never stop working. Perhaps he will give me money for a short while, but then it'll stop. And *then* where will I be? Men can't be trusted. This way I earn my own money. It's not good to have to ask someone for money. If they want to give it, that's all right. But I wouldn't ask." "Because I work I feel more free than other women. I am able to solve my own economic problems. I can educate my children. I don't depend on anybody for anything." "I believe I *must* work. It's important to contribute to increasing production. My work produces foreign exchange for the country to buy things we need."

While Lina and I were talking to a group of women who had moved away from their work stations to surround us, a young woman working close by was listening intently. As we were breaking up she rushed over to us, her face flushed with the desire to throw in her own opinion. Adelia Cossa was thirty years old and had two children, one ten years and one seven months. She was not married and did not live with either of the fathers of her two children. Both of the men were no good, she complained to us. When she was pregnant the first time, the father ran away. Her uncle called him to tell him he had to take responsibility for the child. He refused to register the child as his. The same happened the second time. "These kinds of relationships are bad," she said, the words rushing out as she spoke in more and more angry tones. "Men are not human. They are animals. The problem is that women like these animals and they get pregnant. Then the men run away and the women are left alone. Men don't have any kind of value. They don't accept their responsibilities. Look at me," she said, pointing in rapid motions towards her chest. "I am thin because I work so hard to support my children. I am considered the lowest of the low because I have children alone and I have to work. I am nothing in society. But I know I have more value than the men. I have accepted the responsibility of my children, the result of these relationships. *I did not abandon my children when they were born.*"

Adelia Cossa was as adamant as her co-workers about not giving up her job for any man. "If I give up everything for a man to go and live with him, I would be dependent on him. I never want to lose my independence." Then she thought a minute and added, "I wish I knew how to change this. I would work very hard to do it. But I don't know where to go."

There is a way, insisted OMM secretary Alda, to force men to take responsibility for the children they bring into the world and then abandon. Use the children's court. "OMM has given women a tool for their victory. Women can organize themselves and punish men who act like this by forcing men to take responsibility for their children. He's not so free as he was before. Nowadays we can catch up with him."

Since independence women have been able to sue. Not enough women know that they can get this support. If a woman is not involved in OMM it may be hard for her to hear about the courts and her right to sue for child support. But even when they do know women are fatalistic. They feel that they don't have the power to make any change, bemoaned Alda. "What can I do?" they say. "It's society that lets him do this. I can't change it."

But women can change it, insists Alda. She should know. She has done it herself. Alda Langa was born in Gaza, thirty-nine years earlier. In 1963 she came to Maputo with the man she loved and he began to pay her parents *lobolo*. In 1966, before he had finished paying, he was called up for military service. Two years later he returned—but to another woman, not to her. Eventually in 1979 he returned and stayed with her long enough to father three children, before abandoning her again. She went to court. As as result, 1,500 meticais is deducted directly from his salary for her each month. "If any son of mine makes a woman pregnant and refuses to take care of his child, I'd *insist* that he does. I'd tell him: 'Your father ran away and I had to take care of you. Do you mean I must take care of your child too?' The main thing is to educate your children right." The problem is that not enough women use the courts, laments Alda. There must be more publicity and education about this option. She would like to see OMM call meetings and talk about how the courts can force men to take responsibility for their children. "I've seen men crying in court because their salaries will be used for their children. If every women goes, then men will change."

None of the women at Caju had taken up this option. One woman, Alice Fumo, after complaining that the father of her three youngest children refused to help, shrugged off the option to go to court. "I've told her often that she can go to the court," said the party's assistant secretary of the factory. "But she won't do it. She really knows that it is possible this way to force the man to help support the children. But she has no education and as she never trusted the colonial laws she finds it difficult to trust Frelimo's law. She's afraid to go to the court and doesn't believe it will be of any help."

One Sunday morning I saw one of these tribunals in action. It did not hear cases for child support—those were assigned to a different local court—but it did hear a number of cases that day, which showed that the mistreatment of women by men is taken seriously by the state. The court I visited was one of the many set up in the *bairros*, and to facilitate the community, meets on Saturdays and Sundays. We drove through the dirt roads of the typical Maputo *bairro* with its cramped reed and tin shanties and stopped in front of one of the few cement buildings in the area, with a low front veranda and dark inner rooms, one of which served as the court and had been decorated with a flag and fresh-cut flowers. The judge-president was a woman, supported by five judges, including two women. All been elected and worked voluntarily. At the back of the room sat a policeman, who also contributed his services voluntarily, "just in case."

One of the cases heard that day had been brought by an older woman. This was her second time before the court. She had been living with a man for nine years, not legally married, but in the eyes of the community they were man and wife. Then her husband was transferred to Manhiça, where he was a clerk in the district department of education, returning weekends to the *bairro*. There he found another wife and ordered his first wife to leave the house so his new wife could move in. The complainant had nowhere to go. Her own shanty home, which she had left when she went to live with this man, had long since collapsed from lack of upkeep.

She had little independent income, only what she could make from buying tobacco in the market and processing it into snuff.

At the first hearing the court had ordered her husband to build her another house and that he give her 500 meticais per month. As yet he had done neither. He dismissed the court as "a piece of rubbish" and refused to attend. Now she was asking that the 500 meticais be deducted from his salary and given straight to her. And she did need that house. It didn't have to be a big house, she said. Just a bedroom and a living room. The judge-president was firm. She said that the abandonment of women is a grave problem in Mozambique. She would send a court order to Manhiça to have him brought to a hearing as he had willfully disobeyed the decision of the court. If he continues to defy the court and impairs its responsibility and dignity, the case will go to the provincial court and he will be jailed. "He is very obstinate," said the wife, looking down, her hands resting on her *capulana*. "He'll refuse to obey the order." "Don't worry," the judge-president responded. "In this court we use popular methods. But when its necessary to exercise our power, we exercise our power."

It was this same sympathy for the abandonment of women that could help women with children find support. And however many men declared the court "a piece of rubbish," they would still be deducted directly from their salaries. But still the women at Caju de Matola were reluctant to use the system. Partly this was a result of traditional attitudes, which came from women's responsibility for production. It was they who provided food for their children through their own daily labor in their *machambas*. The men were not expected to help. This work gave women self-respect. Now in the city, although the circumstances and social problems were very different from those of the rural areas, women still felt this sense of responsibility to provide for their children's upkeep.

What I witnessed at the local tribunal in the Maputo *bairro* was the carrying out of the spirit of the as yet unratified Family Law. The first draft of the new law, which was completed at the end of 1980, was greeted with a very mixed response by party and government leaders. By 1982 it was clear that the debate was too heated to put the law out for general discussion without more revisions. Nonetheless it was sent out to the local and district judiciary with the directive that its basic principles should act as a guideline in judicial practice until a revised family law could be passed. Then for a few years little further was done with it. By 1987 a commission was established to begin these revisions for presentation to the Council of Ministers. Ultimately it will be circulated for popular discussion and feedback throughout the country, before the final draft is completed and presented to the National People's Assembly for adoption.

The law met with opposition for not sufficiently reflecting the realities of Mozambique, on the one hand, and on the other for being too radical on some points. A major area of contention was the recognition of common-law marriage. If the ideal is for all marriages to be legally registered, it was argued, then how can common-law marriages be accepted? No one will bother to get married, argued the critics. If common-law marriages are not recognized, went the counterargument, a Mozambican reality is being denied—despite campaigns advocating marriage at the Civil Registry only 10 percent are registered. The first version recognized only two kinds of marriage—registered and common-law—with the inference that they were monogamous. The second includes marriage under customary and religious law. One of the issues being discussed for the final draft is whether divorce from a polygamous marriage should be made particularly easy for women who wish to initiate the move.

The recognition of common-law marriage is a means of supporting women, giving them a right to have the informal relationship recognized so when abandoned with children, they can sue for child support. It also takes into account the unpaid domestic work of the wife (legal or common-law) by dictating that the contents of the home, regardless of whether they were procured through the man's wages, should be shared by both. It reflects the general tenet of the law that promotes equal rights for women and men, within as well as outside the family.

And yet contradictions persist. In a better world, with men who would respect them and in whom they could trust, maybe the women workers at Caju da Matola would have chosen to be attached. Certainly their independence did not come easily. They extricated themselves from restrictive, painful relationships, found jobs, paid back the *lobolo* to ensure a divorce, and worked hard trying to earn enough to feed their children and provide the care they needed. It was a reality that led them to, in the end, opt for and actively prefer their single status, in which they took comfort and pride. Although they do not articulate it this way, this independence is an important aspect of their liberation as women. But it is not something for which they are praised for their courage and conviction, the way women who are proving that they can do what men can do are praised for the contribution they have made toward equality for women. They are more likely to be criticized and looked down upon.

When we left the cashew factory to return to Maputo I was driving a friend's small car, giving a ride to Lina, to the OMM secretary Alda, and the assistant secretary of the district Frelimo, also a woman. A short distance from the factory I had to swerve to avoid a man who was wandering inattentively at the side of the road. I honked furiously. He still did not seem to notice. "Ai," chuckled Alda Langa. "That man has many, many worries. He doesn't care to live. He has made four women pregnant and *all* have taken him to the children's court. And now his salary is gone to support his children. Ai, he has worries." We drove on, laughing together at the idea.

◈ 9 ◈

Operation Production

In Maputo in 1983 I often heard about families such as the Ndabas, who lived in a reed house somewhere in the *bairro* of Mavalane. After the Portuguese left and restrictions on enlarging one's home had been lifted, Mr. Ndaba had spent many a weekend looking for materials and extending his little home, adding a bedroom and extending the kitchen area outside. He worked at the General Tyre factory, Mabor, and his wife had at first spent her time looking after the four children and working on the plot of land she had outside of Maputo. Between his salary and what she could grow for their table and sell on the side they made ends meet.

Then in 1982 and early 1983 the drought ruined her crops. She was very lucky and managed to get work as a cleaner in the hospital, and they brought in a young cousin from the countryside to live with them and look after the children while they worked. Together their salaries just managed to cover the cost of the extra person. But soon more relatives came to live with them, Mr. Ndaba's brothers' children. Unable to farm because of the drought, they chose to seek work in Maputo. Each day they went out looking for work, and sometimes found an odd job here and there and would buy food on the black market to supplement the family diet, but times were lean. Mrs. Ndaba became particularly worried about her children, who were getting thinner, and she set off to work each day with a heavy heart, beginning to resent the hospitality they were expected to show her husband's brothers' sons. But what could they do? You didn't turn your *family* out of the house. She had to forgo the clothes she had planned to make for her children, and hope that at least there would be bread and black tea for the last week of each month. She felt crowded by the young men, who couldn't find jobs and hung about all day, worried that they would get into mischief. She longed for a time when they would have their home in order again.

I never met that family; I am not even sure they were a family as such. But for people in Maputo they represented what was happening in one household after another, not only in the *bairros* but in the center of Maputo as well. The food situation in Maputo was tenuous at the best of times, although the government rationing program managed to provide almost enough food for city residents. Most months they could rely on a supply of rice, beans, and sugar and sometimes oil and a few other basics. With the drought in the countryside, the situation was getting out of control. People headed for Maputo and other urban centers such as Beira in unprecedented numbers. The government got very worried. Hunger began to threaten an ever-increasing number of urban residents.

And so *Operação Produção*—Operation Production—was introduced in a desperate response to a fast-growing crisis. The program was jointly administered by the ministries of Interior, Defense, and Security. In principle it sounded OK. There was no work in Maputo. Unemployment was growing. There were fertile areas in the rural north of the country begging to be cultivated, but not enough workers. If those who could not find work in Maputo were sent to these areas to work on state farms and agricultural cooperatives they could earn enough to survive and at the same time help to produce more for the needs of the country.

So in mid-1983 the program was put into effect, to remove the "nonproductive" people from Maputo and other major urban centers such as Beira. Three documents were required to stay in the city—an identity card, a work card, and a Maputo resident's card. Government workers went on house-to-house checks and those who could not produce all three were presumed nonproductive and taken to detention centers before being sent north. In principle a system was established for appeals. In practice, there were so many people brought into the centers that it was impossible to go over every case. Within days people were rounded up and put on planes heading north.

City residents at first welcomed the program. They thought it good that the people who couldn't find work would be given the chance to work and to produce food, and when things got better no doubt they would be able to return. Above all, they were glad to be relieved of the extra burden. But then things start going wrong. People who never should have been rounded up were taken, and the program was instituted so hastily and on such a scale that appeal was very difficult. This became more and more prevalent, touching almost every family, and their relief turned to outrage. But there was little they could do—except complain.

I arrived back in Mozambique on my third visit just a few months after the evacuation of thousands of people from the urban areas, when it was still a subject of debate and discussion. One of the most virile expressions of deep-seated patriarchal attitudes could be found in the implementation of *Operação Produção*.

This program was not aimed specifically at women, and in fact far fewer women than men were caught up in its net. According to official pronouncements it was only prostitutes or idle women who were evacuated. Yet the term "prostitute" is used far too loosely. There is an exaggerated concern about prostitutes among many leaders that seems to have little bearing on reality. Perhaps it is a leftover worry from colonial times when Lourenço Marques was a haven for prostitutes and their customers—Portuguese soldiers and white South Africans. But prostitutes are no longer seen on the streets of Maputo, and haven't been for years. There is no doubt that some system of selling favors to foreigners in exchange for goods from the foreign-exchange store still exists, but on a small scale. The label seems to apply to single women with children. A general sense of morality—misguided morality—colors the way in which these single mothers are viewed. Such women are considered "loose" and their behavior tantamount to prostitution, synonymous, it would appear, with "promiscuity." The single mothers I spoke to did not fit such a definition, not in the factories, not in Niassa. I got more and more uncomfortable each time I heard the term.

And how does one define "idle"? It is one thing to define a man as nonproductive or idle. A man without a Maputo residence card, without a work permit, with no rent receipts, can be presumed to have moved into the city recently and to be out of work, living with relatives. But a woman who has none of these documents or a marriage certificate could as easily be living in a common-law relationship, with children, running the household, and hence heavily engaged in productive labor. What about the young women who came as teenagers to live with relatives to help care for the children while both parents were out at work, enabling the adults to be productive? They too should have been defined as productive even if they did not have the necessary papers. The opportunities for vendettas and corruption in a program instituted so hurriedly with impossibly limited resources was enormous.

It was a number of weeks into the program when Minister of Interior Armando Guebuza visited the evacuation center in Machava on the outskirts of Maputo to talk with women. What he heard concerned him. He ordered the immediate release of pregnant women. He promised that all the women who wanted to present their problems would be given the chance to do so, and their situation reassessed. His visit coincided with statements from the Central Operational Command that the family and the moral stability it represents must be defended: even if the family in question is based on retrograde values, it is still an important social unit and must not be broken; special care should be taken to examine every case of women who don't work or study but are living with a family; women who are effectively housewives or doing the work of housewives so that the man and woman with whom they live can go to work should not be taken to the evacuation centers. A spokesperson for the Central Operational Command emphasized that it is absolute contrary to the principles which guided Mozambican society to violate the family. Operation Production must reinforce the family.

These words came too late for those women already caught up in the relocation process. Once evacuated from Maputo, few could return home. And the centers were so overpopulated and lacking in resources—both human and economic—that a sensitive investigation of each woman's case was well nigh impossible. In effect, then, the term "nonproductive" was applied equally to both men and women, and many actively productive women found themselves sent far from home, trapped in a program that failed to recognize their worth as the most fundamental producers and reproducers in the society.

It was on my trip to Niassa to interview women sent from Maputo that I discovered some of the injustice and tragedy that had befallen many women, a result of the abuse of power and the patriarchal attitudes that still lie just beneath the surface of Mozambique's new society.

I set off to Niassa with my friend Teresa Smart, a British *cooperante** who was also doing research and writing on women, and

---

*Teresa Smart was a British *cooperante* in the Ministry of Education, 1979–84, teaching in the Industrial Institute and developing new curriculum materials. In 1983–84 she was registered as a journalist for the purpose of covering the preparations for the Extraordinary Conference on Social Issues.

was willing join me and act as my interpreter. Permission to interview women in the centers in Lichinga, the capital of the northern province of Niassa, was refused by the Central Operational Command. However, nothing was said about our interviewing women already allocated to farms and communal villages. This is where we asked to go.

Lussanhande is a communal village seventeen kilometers from Lichinga and is reached by driving for ten of these kilometers over a bumpy dirt road. It is a pleasant village. The houses are close together with neat thatched roofs, some surrounded by thatch fences. There is the occasional large tree, and well-kept gardens are dotted about. We arrived when a truckload of fertilizer was being unloaded. There were other signs that this village was doing well: a school has recently been built, along with a health post for the 276 families living there. And there is water. The Lusso River is wide and never dries up, and the village also has wells and two water holes with manual pumps, all dug by the state. Lussanhande had a successful agricultural co-op, which had been incrementally expanded from 75 to 250 members, the pace of expansion planned to ensure that the co-op didn't grow too fast and jeopardize production and profits. The first residents of Lussanhande had come from an *aldeamento*—one of the "protected villages" surrounded by barbed wire and patrols into which people had been forcibly relocated to "protect" them from Frelimo. It was a cohesive, stable, and productive village, born out of the desire for a community built on the friendships that had arisen out of the hardship of *aldeamento* life.

This was a village picked to receive seventy-five women from Operation Production—women who had been given a day's notice of their transferral from the spartan transitional center, women who could not speak the local language. The village youngsters, having learned Portuguese in their school, acted as interpreters for those who could speak Portuguese. Houses were to be built for the newcomers, and they would be given land to cultivate their own *machambas*. Eventually, if they wished, they could join the cooperative.

Teresa and I spent a few hours under a large tree in a clearing at the center of the village, talking to three of the newcomers. Here as elsewhere we were left alone. Wary of official ears that would inhibit the women from speaking openly, we had explained that as Teresa spoke Portuguese we needed no translators; it would be hard for the women to talk in front of men, unused as they were to speaking out. I wondered if male journalists would have been given quite the same freedom. In any event, although it was sometimes a battle, we always managed to do our interviews unimpeded by officials.

The women spoke with soft voices, but their quiet did not hide the pain. Eliza Ernesto was twenty-one. She was born in Namaacha, near the Swaziland border, and aided by the postindependence changes, had studied to sixth grade. When she was seventeen, her mother and brother arranged for her to marry a man who worked in a factory in Matola. She described their life together, living in an extended-family arrangement with his parents and a brother, as having no conflicts. He always gave her money and even now in Niassa he sends letters and money. Trouble came from his first wife, who would come to see her children (the divorce decree had given custody to her husband) and pick fights with Eliza—once Eliza hit her. His wife had influence with the local officials, who decided that Eliza had to go to be reeducated in Niassa for two years. One day after she was taken to the evacuation center she was on a plane to Niassa. She hopes she will be able to return home after two years. Her husband said he would come to Niassa on his holidays and try to get transferred there if he is unsuccessful in getting her case reviewed in Maputo.

Gloria Alexandria was forty-four years old. Her husband had long since died and she lived with her son, who was a policeman. Her problem was her relationship with her nephew, whom she had raised from infancy after her sister died. He never had a proper job though he worked occasionally. He was married with one son. His wife did not work either—outside the home, that is. When the brigade arrived to take her nephew, he wasn't home, so they took his wife. When Gloria went to take the woman food and clothes, the chief of the block that included her house told her she had to stay too, until they found her nephew. They did find him, but Gloria was still put on a plane to Niassa. Her son tried to get her out of the evacuation center but she had left by the time he got there. It took Gloria Alexandria a while to tell us what she thought the real cause of her evacuation was: the block chief wanted her.

He would come and knock on her door, pestering her, at all hours. She refused. She did not like him. But now, with Operation Production, he had power, and like other corrupt petty officials, he jumped at the chance to abuse it.

Rosa Zeffenias told her story as quietly as the others did. She was a lot older. She had eight children, the youngest already in his early teens. She sold produce in the market and her husband gave her money. Later the husband took another wife, but they got on well and the husband spent every other week with each. Rosa Zeffenias gave a detailed if complicated story of her evacuation, telling how her husband had begged for her release after the chief of the block had ordered her transferred to the evacuation center. Her youngest son had pleaded with the judge to allow his mother to stay. "Who will look after me, if she goes?" he had cried. She gave us her husband's name and told us where he worked in Maputo, asking us to go and tell him we had seen her and send her greetings. We said we would try.

Operation Production was a fertile ground for abuse of power, power that was more likely to be used against women who had scorned the advances of petty officials and who, by the very fact that they are women, have little possibility for redress. Those in charge of the program were cognizant of these abuses, and some of the abusers found themselves sent off north. But the work of verifying the stories case by case, given the vast numbers, was beyond the capacities of the officials running the program.

We spent hours with these women, listening closely to their stories, feeling pain for their plight. They were soft spoken, so lacking in open anger. There were no harsh words about their hosts. And their hosts? Whatever the discomfort with this intrusion from the south, it was never hinted at. Whatever disruption must be felt by what seemed a cohesive and stable village by the influx of so many women, some of them young and attractive, was impossible for us to judge.

Next we were taken to Unango, originally a reeducation camp, now transformed into a small town populated by camp residents who worked on the state farms or in the agricultural cooperatives. They were mostly men, the majority unmarried. The population had almost doubled with the arrival of 500 *inproductivos* in July and August.

At first members of the administration were loathe to let us interview alone. The women here were ex-prostitutes they said, and they might not tell us the truth. But after all the persuasion she could muster, Teresa managed to convince them it would be better for our work. Four young women were ushered into a room for us to interview, for as long as we needed. Eliza was twenty-two years old, had completed sixth grade, and had tried to look for work but had never been successful. She had a boyfriend before leaving, but she wasn't ready to marry, she said. Ana was the same age, had completed third grade and lived with a man she said was her husband. They had two children. He was in the army in Chokwe and seldom got leave to come to Maputo. Presilhina was nineteen, had completed fourth grade. She had had a boyfriend for two years earlier and they had a child of close to two. The three women talked animatedly, with a certain breeziness, although at times Ana would fight back tears. The fourth, a young mulatto woman, would answer no questions. We never learned her name and she sat deep in her private misery throughout the time we were together.

Presilhina and Eliza had already gotten married in the short time since their arrival. They did not tell us the circumstances, but laughed when they told us. Nothing seemed to affect them too much. When we asked if they wanted to return to Maputo, Eliza said she'd prefer to stay. She liked her husband. She was the only one of the three who did not have children in Maputo. Except for the young woman who cried, and the occasional tears of Ana, their stories were not punctuated by the pain that we had found in Lussanhande.

At Matama the pain was the most raw. It was Matama that finally broke any residue of detachment Teresa and I might have hoped for. At Matama it was hard not to cry with the women, hard not to feel their anger, hard not to feel their impotence to change their situation. Among the 1,900 workers was a new influx of 600 evacuees. Of these there were 30 women from Maputo, bringing the total number of female farm workers to 100. The fact that we ourselves were from Maputo gave them hope that perhaps, just perhaps, we had the power to help them. And so they poured their stories out.

One of the women who spoke to us was twenty-four-year-old Regina Jaime. It was Regina, the strongest, the most articulate among the group of eight women we talked to, who best described the conditions they were experiencing. Her outspokenness, her refusal to be broken, made her a natural leader. Her defiance was keen, no tears here, and her young face was firmly set as she talked to us about her experiences. But she laughed too. Despite her hardships, she was able to chortle at what she found hilarious in the grim stories she was telling.

Regina Jaime was born in Maputo and had always lived there. She had finished fourth grade and found work at the Maputo Central Hospital as a custodian. Two years later, in 1974, she got married. Her husband would not allow her to work any longer. Still wanting her own income and some independence, she began to crochet garments and sell them. Her husband was from the north and they lived with her father, after her husband's family paid *lobolo* of 4,000 meticais to her father. They had one child.

There was no love lost between father and daughter. He was an alcoholic and domineering. Her husband drank as much as her father and they were constant drinking companions. He started beating her and she decided she had had enough. She took her child and went to live with her mother. They got along well and it was then that she met her second husband. He didn't drink. He treated her well. They fell in love.

Her first husband would not let go. He would come to her house and abuse her, shouting at her, telling her that he would not allow her to be with another man. She began to pay back the *lobolo* through her local authorities. Her father, as block chief, had some influence and reported her to the tribunal. The judge who heard the case sided with her first husband. On July 10 she was taken and on July 22 she was sent to Niassa. She left her three children by her second husband with her mother. The fourth, her youngest, had died a few months earlier. "I don't want them to suffer. It's better they stay with my mother."

Soon after arriving in Niassa she was sent to Matama. She had nothing but the clothes on her back—the dress, *capulana*, and headscarf that she was wearing when she was taken four months before. They had yet to receive any pay: they arrived after the wage allocations had been made to the farm and there was no money to pay them. The administration was trying to correct this, but meanwhile they had no money. She could buy no clothes. "We wash the clothes and then wait for them to dry or put them back on wet so that they dry on our bodies. We don't have any soap for ourselves or our laundry. We were told to put our names down if we needed soap. When we got to the store, all the soap had already been sold."

"We have to work. If we don't we are told we'll be beaten. Already two men were *sjambokked* [a long, flexible, leather whip] because they went to town on a Saturday night. We have to go far for our water and we don't have buckets. We have to carry our water in cooking pots and they are not very big." They slept in an empty shed that had been used to store sacks of wheat. The roof leaked, the walls had gaping holes. It was very cold at night, and most women didn't have mats or blankets. They covered themselves with sacks. Every day they ate beans and maize. Just beans and maize—no tomatoes, no oil, no onions.

This she could try to live with. What she couldn't live with was the insistence that the new women arrivals get married. Soon. There was an attempt to make such marriages obligatory. Women in other blocks had already married. Women in Block 2, led by Regina, had refused. The men were told they could take these women and get married. So the men pestered the women mercilessly. One woman was even chosen without her knowledge and her marriage was registered. She made such a fuss that it was rescinded. Sometimes the men tried to use force. Regina's cheeks flushed as she sat in her faded clothes, talking about the plight of the women. Her face showed a mix of emotions, upset but still laughing as she told us how she carefully kept every letter from her husband as proof that she was attached. "It's a long way," she said simply. "It's not a life."

Later Teresa and I had the opportunity to interview a prominent member of the party and government who had recently visited the evacuation centers and places of resettlement such as Matama. He was a man well versed in Frelimo ideology with a long history of involvement that began early in the armed struggle. Hence, he was someone who did not speak only for himself.

He was positive about the program. He spoke of how people from the south had brought their cultures with them, and already within a short time cultural experiences were being exchanged to everyone's benefit. The people of Niassa were eager to receive these people, and put themselves out to help them establish new lives. "Well, with such a big relocation, of course, friction comes with it, but I will say that its negative impact is very small. It doesn't really have any impact." Any mistakes—in bringing people who did not qualify as nonproductive—had been or were being corrected. Perhaps 2 percent of the people that arrived should not have been there, he estimated, shaking his head, saying it was a complex situation. Some came up with stories that sounded as if they needed special consideration, but delving deeper, he found discrepancies in these stories. However, he acknowledged that not all the stories were false, and already some wrongly categorized *inproductivos* had been returned.

After listening to a description of Niassa as very fertile, a potential breadbasket for the nation, how it is hampered by a small population and so how opportune such a program is for Niassa, we ventured to mention some of what we saw and heard, asking for his reactions. We said we were troubled by the application of the definition "nonproductive" to both men and women, given women's productive role in family life, which could be overlooked. He insisted that while women's work is important, "our society can't afford to have people who eat, who consume and don't produce. . . . I say to you and I insist on this point that it is more important to have the meat to put in the pan than just standing, waiting for the meat to *come* to the pan. You take from the pot what you put into the pot."

I think of the work that women do to put that "meat" in the pot. I think of the single mothers who have no financial support to get meat into the pot for their children. But as I am there to get his opinions, not to debate mine, I say nothing. We tell him how appalled we were at the conditions at Matama. "I don't think it takes much imagination to appreciate what can happen in a situation where there are 1,600 men, most of them single, most of them young, who are clearly eager to have wives and into that setting you place one hundred women." He quickly agreed that this was a problem. He shared our concern, he assured us. "It is easy for this small group of women to *slip into prostitution in the present conditions.*" I start. He was envisioning a setup where one hundred prostitutes or potential prostitutes are being given the opportunity to once more "slip into prostitution." I was envisioning a setup where women are suffering sexual harassment, perhaps even rape. When we protested and said that many of the women we spoke to had husbands, albeit common-law, that they had children they had to leave behind in Maputo, his voice did not hide a condescending tone: "Actually they didn't leave boyfriends or husbands. They left, most of them, *several* boyfriends and *several* husbands."

I knew that not all high-ranking Frelimo officials would be quite as insensitive to women's position as productive workers, and would be less hasty in labeling unmarried women prostitutes, but in my last days before leaving Mozambique I was unable to set up the interviews I wanted to get an antidote to this one opinion. By then I knew that there was considerable debate in government circles about the wisdom of this program, despite the urgency of the situation. There was growing awareness that the scale of the operation was a task far too great for the capacities of Maputo's small civil service and local authorities. The minister of interior's visit to the evacuation centers and his special concern for the women who had been rounded up came four days after Regina's detention, and eight days before she was sent from Maputo. And she had been born in Maputo. It may have been one of the easier cases to resolve. And yet I too had to admit the limitations in taking such stories. I was there only briefly. Two white, expatriate women sitting for a few hours on chairs under a tree in Lussanhande, in a small room at the center of Unango, under a makeshift shelter at Matama, who could not corroborate what they heard.

These limitations became sharply pronounced when we paid a visit to Rosa Zeffenias' husband at his place of work in the Maputo *baixa* to tell him we had seen her at Lussanhande. He lacked concern for his wife's plight, although he was not hostile. She was an alcoholic, he said. They had not lived together for a long time. Perhaps it was better for her and for her well-being that she was in Niassa, he said. For a moment, Teresa and I were taken aback. We went over our material carefully, remembering how we had heard the stories in enough different ways to feel they were true. And we did not only go by the stories were heard firsthand. We heard many like them second- and third-hand from people working in Niassa, and from people in Maputo who had known some of those rounded up. I have been doing interviews with women for many years, trying to piece together the stories of women's lives, in Guinea-Bissau, in Mozambique, in South Africa. Teresa had also had some of this experience. A journalist tries to look for clues, almost instinctively. The looks that dart across faces, the eyes that are lowered, the flush of cheeks, the tone of the voice. We did not doubt that most of those women really believed what they were telling us. Most really felt they were accused wrongly, were suffering pain from being wrenched away from children, from parents, and from lovers. If most of the women were prostitutes, then why wasn't this major activity visible on the streets of Maputo?

And now over three years later, I can still see Regina's face and hear the urgency in her voice. I think of how the women would ask, "When are we going to return home?" We could not answer. We were in no position to answer. We had come to gather information. We were incapable of acting on it.

In 1987 I asked about the program. It is no longer discussed. It has been pushed into the past. Top-ranking government officials in the interim openly admitted that the program was a mistake, never to be repeated. And when I talked with OMM leaders they still expressed their unhappiness over the program and how the issue of common-law marriage was not taken into account, leaving women unprotected against earnest bureaucrats overefficiently carrying out a decree. However bad the problems are in the urban areas—and they have gotten much worse in many respects because of the war's escalation—Operation Production will never be revived. But while this may be an important commitment, it does not help the majority of the evacuees, who never made it back home again.

Since our visit, Niassa, that fertile province, so underpopulated and its potential so undeveloped, with its western border shared with Malawi, has become a territory for bandit operations. It is said that many of those sent from the city, so disillusioned by the way their government treated them, joined the bandits. Others escaped. But even without the war, the only way to get back the long distance to the south is by air. A *cooperante* picks up a hitchhiker on a road outside of Lichinga. "Where would you like to go?" he asks. "Maputo," comes the reply.

⬧◀10▶⬧
Fighting Polygamy
and Lobolo

"*Lobolo* has really made women suffer," said Mariana Cossa, speaking from the pain of personal experience. She had dutifully accepted the marriage arranged by her father. Immediately, the custom began to insert strains into her marriage, distorting her relationship with her husband's family. The years that she lived with her in-laws she remembers with rancor. She moved in soon after the wedding ceremony, and not long after that, her husband went to work in South Africa. He was away for a year at a time, sometimes more.

The first time he returned, his family rushed out to welcome him, and whisked him away to ask him about his work and his life in South Africa. They wouldn't let her near him. When Mariana tried to enter the room to welcome her husband, they chased her away. They wanted to be the first to have his news. When she asked them what they were discussing, they were hostile: "You came to our house only because we bought you," they said disparagingly. "We paid for you." Just as if she were a coat! Her husband wasn't quite as bad as some who gang up with their parents against their wives. He did repeat to her what they had talked about, but it was a scene reenacted each time he came home.

Mariana's mother-in-law treated her no better than a servant. She had to ask permission, often through her husband, for the littlest thing, even for sugar or soap. She was not allowed to kill a chicken unless her mother-in-law gave her permission. "Then I would run after it, catch it, kill it, clean it, cook it. But I would be sure to pick leaves to prepare for myself because I knew I wouldn't eat it."

After her husband died, Mariana Cossa left the family and came to live in Três de Fevereiro. Here she could become her own person. She entered the political life of the village in earnest, and was elected to the executive council—one of two women members. Now she speaks out strongly against the practice of *lobolo*:

201

"We agree we want to stop it. Our children will get divorced because they will not put up with it. They must start a new life."

During the war of national liberation, Frelimo began an offensive against customs that were viewed as restricting women's free choice and placing them in positions of subordination. After independence and most particularly during the second OMM conference, the party took up the problems of polygamy,* *lobolo,* initiation rites, and premature and hereditary marriages, among others, with some fervor, and began a campaign to end them.

Not many governments have been willing to take such a stand. In newly independent African states, at least, the tendency was to give legal backing to these practices, trying to counter the way in which the nation's culture and history had been disdained and denigrated by their colonial masters. Frelimo views the problem differently: while part of the process of freeing Mozambicans from the colonial mentality is to revalue their culture, it is also true that this must not proceed blindly. Just because a custom is African does not mean that it unquestionably enhances African life, and therefore fails to oppress. It is important to identify what is positive, what is benign, and what is detrimental and should be disowned. Hence practices such as polygamy and *lobolo,* because they serve to ensure the subordination of women and foster inequality, must be fought.

It was, and remains, a tough nut to crack. Polygamy and *lobolo* were not simply adopted into the society because men liked the idea of having more than one sexual partner, or because women were so denigrated that they could be bought like a coat or a cow. As Frelimo recognized, they arose directly out of the nature of the peasant economy. Because women's labor is so relentless, it was in a household's interest to have more than one wife to share the work, ensure the household's survival, and give it the chance to

---

*Technically polygamy means marriage to more than one spouse by either the wife or the husband, while polygyny refers to the marriage by a man to more than one wife. Because polygamy is commonly used to mean the latter, and Frelimo uses the word *polygamia,* I have chosen here to stay with the word "polygamy."

accumulate wealth. Because women's work was therefore valuable, her parents were compensated for its loss at the time of marriage. With such customs comes a set of social relations, which people, after a long history of acceptance, cling to tenaciously.

Lobolo, which often amounts to a practice of buying women—after all, they can't quit their jobs—gives stability to the marriage, which many women value. The husband is less likely to abandon and physically abuse a woman whom he has had to pay for. But it places the man firmly in a position of power over his wife. It entrenches subordination. Both customs came implicity with another: arranged marriage, which Frelimo and the OMM refer to in their documents as forced marriage. It was common for a father to arrange a marriage for a daughter when she is as young as thirteen or fourteen, often with a man considerably older than she. In many areas of the south, this is still common: the older man, particularly one who has worked in South Africa, is considered particularly desirable because of his relative wealth and economic stability.

Polygamy and lobolo, as well as arranged marriages, originated in the south, where patrilineality and patrilocality provided the basis for social interaction. North of the Zambezi River, where matrilineality was traditionally the way of reckoning descent, it was the mother's brother in whom power was vested. While this was still a man, the relationship of the woman to the family with whom she was economically integrated was as sister, not as wife. She was surrounded by her own kin. Indeed, the experience of Mariana Cossa would have been inconceivable here. Because divorce was relatively easy for both husband and wife, the wife had more freedom to choose her husband and more freedom to get out of a marriage that had broken down. I was told of men who arrived home to find their belongings sitting outside of the wife's house. The message was clear: "leave."

Despite the campaign against them, lobolo and polygamy are being absorbed into life in the north. While the matrilineal system is no longer so strong in the north, it has not yet been replaced by patrilineality or patrilocality. Thus polygamy, in the north, is an apparent anomaly, lacking its original economic significance. The husband will divide his time between his wives, spending some days in the house of one, then moving to the other. His roots are with his mother's brother's group. The machambas of his wives are part of her family's household. The custom has clearly caught on strictly because it is advantageous to men, not the household as a whole, yet since divorce is still relatively easy, a wife can opt out of a polygamous marriage when she chooses. In the south divorce was rarely initiated by a woman.

Ironically, this spread of southern norms, especially polygamy, may be influenced by the fact that the majority of the party and women's organization's leadership view patrilineality as the norm. They come from the south, where stronger colonial and missionary presence meant a better chance for education. Today they view patrilineality not only as normal, but as "modern," or at least more in tune with the modern nuclear family. And although they are opposed to *lobolo* and polygamy, they grew up with them, so they view them too as normal. Divorce, which might have acted to check polygamy, is frowned upon, especially when initiated by women. Some women complain that divorce has become more difficult since independence, "because Frelimo doesn't want unjustified divorces. They say that the children won't know their fathers. The *bairro* secretary doesn't like divorces. He punished people that want to divorce. They have to do public work in the *bairro*. In the old days the women divorced more easily."[1]

Divorce is one of the few ways women can retaliate for men taking a second wife. Yet there are many instances of women who asked for a divorce because their husbands wanted a second wife and were refused. They were told that they should not disrupt the family. A provincial judge, newly appointed in the north, declared: "The attitude of the provincial court to polygamy depends on the economic conditions of the man. If we find that he has the possibility of supporting two women, we don't see it as an evil."[2] Here is an instance where women's rights, already in place, are being tampered with, and the women's organization seems unable to protect them.

The spread of *lobolo* into former matrilineal areas is more difficult to explain. It operates to give the husband, rather than the wife's relatives, control over his family. And certainly it acts as a check on divorce by women. In fact, the strict opposition to divorce is apparently in conflict with party policy on polygamy—which remains unchanged. The second OMM conference recommended that new polygamists as well as their wives be excluded from positions of responsibility in the mass organizations and the state sector, as well as in the leadership of communal villages, cooperatives, state farms, and factories. The party accepted these recommendations, and new polygamists could not be considered for party membership. During the elections for the people's assemblies men who were new polygamists were rejected as candidates.[3]

The ideological campaign has also been supported by some legal changes and concrete help from local OMM and Frelimo bodies that provide a place where women can bring their unhappinesses. I collected many descriptions of how this support worked. The OMM secretary of one of the *bairros* at Três de Fevereiro went into detail about one domestic dispute they had helped resolve.

A woman came to her to complain about her husband. He was not treating her well, and had announced that he was going to marry another wife. She was very upset. She and her husband had five children, but now he wanted to marry this woman from outside the village. She was young and impressionable and thought the man was rich. He was not, and he would not be able to support two families, his wife insisted. The OMM secretary took some other women from the neighborhood to go visit the husband. They began politely: "Before we talk to you, forgive us for what we are going to say. It is your private affair, but as we live together we must help each other." The women went on to explain that his wife had come to them concerned about their marriage. They explained that he should not marry another wife, and that he should rather use the money he had saved for *lobolo* to improve his life with his wife of long standing. He understood, the OMM secretary said, and had not gone ahead with his second marriage, building a cement house instead. The man was caught in a bind, due to his respect for community opinion: he was being pressured hard by the community and the possibility of losing his first wife was very real.

This kind of story was repeated to me often, but it wasn't only the OMM that intervened. In the district of Bilene, Gaza, a male schoolteacher became concerned about the protracted absenteeism of one of his students, a fourteen-year-old girl. So he went to visit her home to try to uncover the cause of the problem. It turned out that her parents had arranged for her to marry a thirty-five-year-old man who already had one wife and that *lobolo* had already been paid for her. The teacher took the case to the district OMM in the hope that they could intervene, and the district party also got involved. They sent representatives to talk to the family.

"We are fighting against *lobolo* and young marriages," they told the parents, explaining that they were trying to build a new society without these oppressive customs. "We are suffering very much in our country. We have no technicians, no doctors, no nurses, but here you are preventing a young girl from becoming any of these because you want the *lobolo*."

The daughter was then asked her feelings on the matter and whether she wanted to get married to this man. She replied an emphatic no. "I had listened when he started to tell me that he loved me. But I didn't know he would pay *lobolo* for me and arrange to marry me," she replied. Both parties to the arrangement gave up in the face of the pressure. Her parents returned the *lobolo*, the marriage was canceled, and the daughter returned to her studies.

In fact, in the early years following independence, party and OMM support was a trifle *too* much. As Sarifa Amati, a young district OMM leader, described in 1977, when parents resist, in some instances, a daughter is sent to another province to work in a Frelimo project. Liberated from her parents, she is able to develop a new political consciousness. In extreme cases pressure is also put on the father so that he is isolated at work, passed up for promotion, and refused membership in the party. When a woman has agreed to be a second or third wife she is called before OMM and criticized heavily, and must attend reeducation classes held by OMM. Sometimes the girls will be sent for reeducation outside of the locality.

There was an initial tendency to call for change rather stridently, accompanied by many an "*Abaixo* Polygamia!" or "*Abaixa Lobolo!*"—Down With!—but with not too much in the way of examining and understanding *why* people, particularly women, held so tenaciously to customs that seemed so obviously detrimental. It was out of this spirit Sarifa Amati could talk of reeducation programs, and Mama Leia and Arminda Hombé could tell me that polygamy has vanished from their communities.

Mama Leia was emphatic. "The only polygamists we have," she said referring to her village in the south, "are old polygamists, men who married more than one wife before independence. We have no new polygamy in our village." And from Arminda Hombé, the OMM and party leader in Chibuto: "When we organized the mass organizations, we explained that polygamy must end. OMM explains that we women must be careful not to love a man who already has a wife. Since 1977 we haven't had this problem of polygamy."

I was not sure whether to be impressed or skeptical. How would it be possible to transform, on such a wide scale and in so few years, practices that have been woven for centuries into the very fabric of society? It wasn't. From other OMM local leaders I got a different picture. "*Lobolo* is still one of our biggest problems," said the district secretary for the neighboring Bilene district of Gaza. "This is one of the main problems we discuss at meetings."

Skepticism won out as I began to talk to other women in Três de Fevereiro, to secretaries of the *bairro*, for example, and asked them when the last polygamous marriage had taken place. "Oh, so and so married another wife last month," I would be told. I also began to hear how *lobolo* would be exchanged at night or in secret so village officials did not hear about it. Or of a practice gaining some popularity, particularly in Gaza province, that replaced *lobolo* with a new custom of "gratification gift," implying a voluntary, spontaneous transaction offered out of gratitude to the family of the bride, such an exemplary daughter-in-law-to-be.

That Mama Leia's declaration of victory over *lobolo* and polygamy was still a goal rather than a reality became even more evident during my second visit to the village. One morning, she came to us preoccupied about what had happened the night before. A young woman had been arrested. She had attacked her mother-in-law, shouting in uncontrolled anger that she wanted to kill her and she didn't care if she went to jail. Her neighbors, hearing the fracas, rushed off to call in members of the militia to intervene. The young woman punched one of the militia members in the eye and he was taken to hospital. She was removed from her home and put under guard for the night. The following morning serious-faced village *responsavels* began to gather in a long reed- and mud-walled shelter that had been built for such meetings. Among them were members of the justice tribunal, the people's assembly, and the OMM. In all about fifteen people—including the young woman, her mother-in-law, and witnesses—were present for the proceedings, which went on all day.

The young woman, Maria, who had two preschool children, lived with her mother-in-law, while her husband, a miner, was away for long periods of time in South Africa. Throughout the proceedings she said very little in her own defense. Her mother-in-law was the one who did most of the talking. She said that since her son had left on this latest contract, her daughter-in-law had been very hostile toward her. She didn't understand it. When she finished her work in the field, she said, she would go and offer to help her son's wife. Her daughter-in-law shouted at her and ordered her off her field. If she collected water for her daughter-in-law, the younger woman threw it out. Worse, said the mother-in-law, was that when she asked for water or food for herself, she was refused. Then to cap it all, this ungrateful wife of her son beat her. She spoke as if she were completely innocent and mystified by this sudden change in behavior. She had only been trying to help, as any mother-in-law would do.

Maria said little more than admitting she had acted badly. She promised she would mend her ways. The impromptu court decided not to press charges to a higher court, but asked the neighbors to keep an eye on the situation. For punching the militia member she was sentenced to three months of labor in the field just beside the meeting place. Mama Leia assured me that she would not work longer than two weeks. "We want to make sure she understands what she did and that she is really sorry. So we tell her three months."

The next morning there Maria was, bright and early, weeding the field. Her children were left with the mother-in-law. Anastaçia, tightening her *capulana* around her waist, walked over to the field, and bent down with the accused to help her work and to talk to her. She sensed there was more of a story there and wanted to find out. Maria opened up about her woes. Her mother-in-law only pretends to be friendly and helpful, she complained, when in fact it is she who is the hostile, mean one. Her husband had saved up money in South Africa and sent it to his mother asking her to find him a second wife and make the necessary *lobolo* arrangements. A marriage was subsequently arranged with a young woman in a neighboring communal village. The husband now sends his wives identical dresses, and she has to deliver them to the second wife. She feels humiliated. When a letter arrives from her husband, his mother, who is illiterate, takes it to someone to read it to her. After she replies to it, she gives it to the daughter-in-law to read. Now her husband says he intends to build a new house next to hers for his second wife when he returns from South Africa next time.

As unhappy as she is with the arrangement she kept her side of the story to herself. In all probability her defense would have reached sympathetic ears. She would have exposed polygamy, *lobolo*, traditional oppressive relationships between mother-in-law and "bought" daughter-in-law, all issues that OMM is trying to eradicate. But then Maria might have had little option but to leave her husband, who was already married to the second wife, which she apparently could not bring herself to do. Too late for intervention. But it is possible that some compromise could have been made that would have supported Maria. The OMM representatives who sat through the hearing and joined in with the questions to try and solve the problem did not push for the whole story. If it was clear to Anastaçia, an outsider, then it must surely have been clear to everyone there that there was more to the problem than met the eye.

The unhappy, sulky expression etched into Maria's face said much about her hurt and her hatred for polygamy. I remembered a similar expression on the face Juliana Caetano, an older woman I met in a village in northern Zambezia province. After twenty-two years of marriage her husband had decided to take another wife. A very, very young wife. Juliana Caetano was the OMM secretary-elect of Mutanga village in Manacurra district. But Juliana Caetano, in contrast to Maria, did not suffer in silence.

We sat on chairs under a newly built pole-and-thatch shelter, with five women, and an empathetic young male district *respon-savel*, interpreting from the local language. He lived in the village and was Juliana's son-in-law. My questions about polygamy were getting nowhere. The women were not anxious to share their views, despite the young man's assurances that he knew they did not like the practice. He felt they were worried that their husbands would find out what they had been saying and be angry. I turned the questions away from the personal to the general. After a while the reticence seemed to vanish and was completely broken when Juliana began an impassioned speech propelled by her antagonism toward her husband and her feelings of abandonment.

For twenty-two years Juliana had been the only wife. During that time they had one child, a daughter who was married to our interpreter. The family was among the first forty families to move into the village in 1977 and three years later, at the time of my visit, the population had increased to 236 families and was still slowly growing.

"Polygamy is bad," said Juliana, her thin, tired face tightened by her anger. "*Bad*. Why do men want more wives? Sometimes when the first wife won't accept this she quarrels with her husband. And then he leaves and starts a new life with a second wife. It is hard on the first wife. A woman has to organize the house. Life is difficult and there is not enough—not enough food, clothes, other necessities. He can't even support the one wife, how will he support two? But when a man has decided, the woman can do nothing. When a man takes two wives, each has her own house. But the first wife is left alone, alone. Her husband no longer takes good care of her, or even thinks of her.

"I am a woman, just like the new wife is a woman. Why does he want more than me? He thinks he is young, although he is old. Otherwise he wouldn't marry someone so young. I love him because he is my husband. He can go out whenever he wants. When he comes home, I am always there. I love him, but he is ceasing to love me. Why am I not allowed to love my own husband?"

The political education campaign to try to change the customs that caused the sufferings of the Marias and the Julianas struck an sympathetic chord among many, particularly the younger generation. It was among their ranks, more than the older women, that determination not to follow in the footsteps of their parents could be found. It was here that the customs, while certainly not eradicated, could be found on the decline.

I spent an afternoon talking with two workers for the Três de Fevereiro consumer cooperative. Both Virginia Mtevuye and José Sitoye were in their early twenties and had a high level of political consciousness. Both insisted that women suffered gravely because of polygamy and *lobolo*. "When a man has two wives it is impossible for him to love both equally," said Virginia, reflecting one of OMM's most common criticisms of the practice. "Perhaps he buys something for one, but not the other. Or perhaps the gifts are the same but one wife gets jealous because the other gets hers first. These are the kinds that develop tensions between wives. We can't forcibly prevent a man from marrying another wife, but we try to explain that it is wrong and that he is damaging his marriage. We have had problems like this, but we find that most of the men accepted the change after we spoke with them. Those that didn't still got married, but often the marriage did not last for very long."

José Sitoye felt that one of the most significant changes in the village is the decline of *lobolo*. "Now we don't have to buy our wives and this is very important. I fell in love with my girlfriend and I asked her to marry me. I didn't ask her father for permission.

We registered our marriage in Xai-Xai. We hear so many troubles that our parents have. If a man beats his wife he feels he has a right: 'I gave such a lot of money for you. You must obey what I say.' When we try to discuss the problems with them and ask 'Can't you solve your difficulties without beating her?' The husband protests: 'No, I paid for her.' We must end this custom. There may still be beating but the men won't be able to use this as an excuse. The woman is particularly concerned, so it's easier for her to see the need to refuse to be *lobolado*. She saw the problems that *lobolo* created between her parents or among her neighbors. She understands that if she accepts *lobolo*, the same problems will be hers." Virginia added: "The men always say, 'I bought you.' But we know you can't *buy* a person."

The new generation. The generation not willing to blindly accept the customs of the past, or so I thought, as not only a young woman but a young man began to articulate their opinion about the need for change. It turned out, however, that "gratification gifts" had been given in both their marriages. They felt there was no contradiction between this and their abhorrence for *lobolo*.

Two young women, not politically active, expressed their feelings about *lobolo* in no less strong terms. When I interviewed the two they sat on wooden chairs in front of me, still and straight-backed, looking down at their hands on their laps often, talking in soft voices. José and Virginia had been so relaxed, leaning comfortably in their chairs, their body language speaking of self-assurance, that I expected the second interview to produce much more traditional views. I was wrong. Lisa Matusi was twenty-one and had been married for over three years. Her husband, who worked in South Africa, had been away for the past two. She was his only wife. They had met when they attended literacy classes and she moved from a neighboring communal village when they got married. When he went to her parents to ask for Lisa's "hand," they asked him about the *lobolo*. Lisa did not like this at all, and she wouldn't get married if a *lobolo* was arranged. Her husband-to-be passed this on to his parents, who later came to the family bearing gratification gifts on a day a special feast had been arranged. While the gift remained, Lisa saw it differently. The gift did not transfer authority and power into the hands of her husband and his family, as Mariana Cossa had found when she married. "We as the youth of today," she said, "cannot be married with *lobolo*. This is a custom for the older people. It was practiced during my mother's time, the time of oppression. Now we don't want to be oppressed any longer. Lobolo is a form of oppression."

Her friend Marta Nkuna, also in her early twenties, had married for five years. Her father refused to accept the *lobolo*, she said, although when she described the gifts brought in gratification, they were of similar value to the *lobolo* in that region. "If a woman is married with *lobolo* then you feel that you are only in the house of your husband because he has paid for you. You are not free. It is like being in prison."

Is gratification simply *lobolo* in disguise, a maneuver to try and hide the real thing from the "*Abaixo Lobolo!*" criers? Actually, not quite. There is a real change in perception—as reflected in the comments of the young marrieds of Três de Fevereiro here—which points to an emergence of new relations within the families of the younger generation. As far as the couple is concerned, the wife is no longer regarded as bought or as property. The husband no longer therefore has the right to patriarchal behavior toward the wife. She feels freer to defend herself against acts of oppression. It allows—at least and importantly in the woman's head—for her to enter the marriage as an equal partner. The four were adamant about this. José, while condoning the gratitication gifts, had asked his wife whether she wanted to marry him. He had not gone to her father to ask the permission, obligatory under traditional custom. They had registered their marriage in Xai-Xai, in keeping with the new marriage practices provided for by the state and encouraged by the party. And he had accepted the transference of gratification in keeping with the economic needs of the patrilineal peasant economy.

Gratification gifts allow perpetuation of a practice that is based in the economy of peasant life—at least in the south: the need to reimburse the loss of a worker and the expectation on the part of the father that comes with the birth of a daughter. So in a sense, everyone's happy. Father's continue to benefit from customary law through the acquisition of critical and long-anticipated goods; young women benefit from the spirit of Frelimo's ideology that removes some of the restrictions of the culture of *lobolo* that would otherwise perpetuate her subordination. Problems are bound to arise when a woman wants to divorce her husband and does not feel she should be liable for reimbursing the *lobolo*. It is then that the system of gratification is likely to revert to *lobolo* as the question of control ultimately becomes an issue. In any event, it still is the unmodified *lobolo* that is most common.

It was almost two years after my interviews in Três de Fevereiro when, in 1984, I accompanied some of the Gaza brigades preparing for the OMM Extraordinary Conference on Social Issues concerning women, to the localities, communal villages, and work places to hear what people had to say about these concerns. The party and the women's organization faced a tricky question: How could they more effectively change the circumstances of women, young like Maria and older like Juliana, who had suffered such personal pain because of these customs? By the time the 1984 conference concerning women was conceived, it was clear that the customs were still firmly in place for the majority of the country. The *abaixo* phase was criticized for being too didactic, replaced by the view that it is not possible to simply eradicate the customs without an understanding of the social and cultural context. Once understood, this analysis could help shape the new policy. The goal of the preconference meetings throughout the country was for the leadership at a local level to listen and then transmit their findings to the national office.

Two of the villages I visited were in the general vicinity of Três de Fevereiro. The third was beyond the northern boundaries of Xai-Xai. I also attended meetings in the town of Xai-Xai itself. Mama Leia was not the only one to have asserted that polygamy and *lobolo* had ended in the villages. It was in listening to the proceedings at these meetings, however, that I finally appreciated how widespread the customs of polygamy and *lobolo* still were. "If any one says that *lobolo* has decreased in this village, they are lying," challenged a village elder at the Julius Nyerere meeting.

Meetings were a regular feature in the lives of the villages' populations since independence. Over the years they had met together under a special tree, in a clearing, or some other favorite meeting place to greet and meet with visitors, to elect village officials, to discuss party documents, for a variety of other reasons. They were already used to speaking out. The call to discuss issues so close to the hearts of the men and women living in the villages, issues such as polygamy or *lobolo*, meant a good turnout. There were more women than men attending the meetings; although the men were generally—and expectedly—more outspoken, the women were by no means close-mouthed.

The themes for the Extraordinary Conference included some

dozen items—initiation rites, *lobolo*, premature marriage, polygamy, adultery, divorce, disruption of the family, prostitution, relations within the family—between spouses, between parents and
children; women in production. Over 2,000 meetings took place
throughout the country, including the furthest reaches, and information was collected from interviews with another 2,000 small
groups. The brigades emphasized that mistakes had been made. In
a spirit of self-criticism, leaders acknowledged that their previous
strong condemnation of the practices had either backfired—sub-
terfuge was resorted to—or just failed. To try to remedy this,
honest and frank discussions were called for at the meetings.

At gatherings I attended in Gaza, the topics of polygamy and
lobolo aroused the most interest, leaving little time for the discussion of other issues. While both men and women spoke out,
women were generally less forceful than men, and sometimes had
to be urged by the person in the chair to give their opinions. They
did find other ways of expressing themselves. At 24 de Julho there
was a persistent groundswell of muttering whenever the men
defended polygamy, the equivalent of hearty boos. Sometimes the
women's loud murmur crescendoed into jeering and some of the
local leaders would rush around, gesticulating, shouting at the
women to behave themselves. It obviously disturbed them that the
women should be so "unruly." It had little effect, and the women
continued to express their antagonism collectively.

Some of the men's support of polygamy rested on arguments
repeated in the different meetings, particularly men's need to have
at least two wives to cater to all their personal needs as well as the
need to produce. This is a familiar refrain used since the early
days of Frelimo's mobilization. At Marien Ngouabi, a man stood
up to say: "It is better to have more than one wife. When one goes
on a journey to visit her family, then I can stay with the other wife.
When one is ill, the other can cook for me. If I only had one wife,
who would stay with the children, who would cook, who would
pound when she is ill? Without a second wife I would suffer too
much." As at 24 de Julho, the women expressed their feelings by
jeering and shouting him down while he talked. An angry buzz of
comments continued after he sat down while the woman in the
chair tried in vain to bring the meeting to order. An elderly woman
got slowly to her feet and the audience became still. "I heard what
the speaker said. Women don't want polygamy, but when a man
says that he is going to take another wife or another lover, the first

wife is passive. She cannot protest. But if a man has five wives, how can he satisfy them all? How can he provide for them all?" The women responded with energetic applause.

"The reason why we marry more than one wife is because of our poverty," explained one man at 24 de Julho. "When our mother died [when we were still children], who pounded and cooked and fed us? If one wife is ill we need another to feed the children, cook, collect water, and so on. We need more than one woman to help with these tasks. We learned from the way our fathers and mothers lived that having more than one wife is necessary." Again it was an older woman who responded. "The question is not whether one woman cooks when the other is ill. I am the only wife of my husband. When I am ill, *he* cooks the food." When a woman stood up later and said: "Every woman must be with one man only and every man with one woman only," there was hearty, spontaneous applause from the women. A buzz of objection greeted a man at 24 de Julho when he said that "I believe men marry two women because there are more women then men. If a marriage consists of one man and one woman, then women are left over."

Not often did men stand up to denounce polygamy. But at times they did: "Now we don't want more than one wife. We must end this, or a woman is nothing more than a *capulana*. You buy one today, another tomorrow. It cannot be like this any longer." This man, in his fifties, was, however, a village leader, who had only one wife. I thought of the saying of Amilcar Cabral often quoted to me on my travels through Guinea-Bissau, when he was talking about men's casual attitude to women. "Women are not shirts. You wear one today, you wear another tomorrow."

In general, the debate around polygamy was clear: men for the "yeahs" and women for the "nos." The debate around *lobolo* was less clear. Because of political education, *lobolo* was regarded by many women as a "sale," one they did not want to be part of. The feelings expressed in my interviews showed an unhappiness with a practice that so forcefully transferred male domination from the father to the husband, clinched in an economic deal. This custom more than any other made women feel oppressed, leaving them impotent to express their rights. But at the same time, many women argued for the custom as a way of strengthening marriage bonds and protecting against abuse and desertion. Men, on the other hand, like the power it bestowed on them over their families, and fathers, from the time of the birth of their daughters, looked forward to the economic transaction that would come with the marriages.

However, what dominated the preconference discussions was not the custom but the rising price, which also made the new system—with its important consequence for women's perceptions—harder to maintain. The cost of *lobolo* rose sharply in the years following independence. When Frelimo came to power *lobolo* was in the vicinity of 5,000 to 15,000 escudos; by the end of 1982 it was as high as 40,000 meticais (the metical matched the escudo in value when the change of currency was made). The higher prices were more than an average factory worker earned in a year. It was fast becoming a crisis for younger men, who are unlikely to have access to this kind of money. The men who are the most likely to have more money are those who had worked in South Africa for a while. "It is not for nothing that fathers wish to marry their daughters to men who work in the South African mines," said one woman at the Marien Ngouabi village. "It is because of the hunger."

"*Lobolo* has always brought us many problems, but if it is 2,500, then it is manageable. Then it is not a question of selling the woman, but of gratification. We could live with 2,500." This was a common call. If *lobolo* was a low amount, then it could serve the purpose of bonding a marriage, rather than making the women feel as if she has been bought, tied into a relationship that she can never get out of. As one young woman said: "I don't want *lobolo* even if my parents want it. My parents are old and they will be gone when I want to leave this husband. They won't be able to return the money. I only want to get married." For sure, the women workers at the cashew factory in Matola would have had immense problems cutting loose from their unhappy marriages if they had to pay back at the current rate. Their salaries were far too small. And what about women that are infertile, a fairly widespread problem that has many painful social implications? When *lobolo* is presented, it is presumed that the chosen wife will be a bearer of many children. Childless marriages are the source of the gravest conflict between spouses. "When a woman does not get pregnant," observed an older man, "the husband gets angry. It is difficult for a wife to return large amounts of money."

When the brigades had completed their work in collecting data, the reports were sent to Maputo for analysis and summation. Finally, after a number of delays, the Extraordinary Conference on women was held in November 1984. It was a mix of the encouraging and the discouraging. Discouraging was the way in which the male leadership of Frelimo, particularly President Samora Machel, tended to dominate the meeting. His long speeches took up time that was to have been devoted to discussion from the floor. So women from the provinces, some illiterate, some never before out of their provinces let alone in the capital, missed an opportunity to be heard, to make a contribution. These women had become part of something of a national movement, which had involved thousands and thousands of people, both women and men, as they involved themselves in intense and ongoing discussion of the social issues relating to women. I thought of the meetings where I had witnessed this, and sadly contrasted it with the deflation of this enthusiasm at the plenary.

On the encouraging side were the meetings and workshops; these were vibrant as women thrashed out their feelings and criticisms of the social conditions and the way in which the leadership had responded to them. President Machel's role was not the whole picture. OMM leaders were not disappointed by the preponderance of male leaders, but rather regarded the attention given to the conference by Frelimo as an honor and a clear indication of Frelimo's ongoing support for women's issues. And indeed, I remember well the enthusiasm and support of the Frelimo *responsavels* I met when traveling to meetings with the brigades, which others found in many other districts. It was this enthusiasm that was rekindled in the workshops.

The heavy Frelimo presence at the highest level, with top leaders besides President Machel taking time from their work to devote all their energies to the women's conference for its duration, can certainly be interpreted as an important signal. For while this might be interpreted as party control over OMM, it made clear to the country that Frelimo and the government continue to take very seriously the issues of women's liberation and the problems that must still be surmounted. It was a statement of renewed commitment to both women and men all over the nation that the issue has not been put aside, despite war, famine, and economic difficulties. As such, it gave OMM renewed strength and respect. The problem ultimately was that the plans for follow-up have been slow in materializing.

But where to go from here? By November 1984 the war was already superseding the goals for transformation as the country's resources and the population's energies were going into fighting that war. Women's concerns have been taken off the immediate agenda, and replaced by the concerns of the nation as a whole. Even the conference resolutions were geared toward this, ignoring the potential for building on the experiences of the mobilization around these social issues that highlighted the preparations for the conference. While the need for focusing on rebuilding and defending the nation can be appreciated, it could be hoped that the resolution would have reflected both.

The general resolutions of the conference, however, called for women to commit themselves to solving the broader crises of the nation, and not to take up the fight for liberation as such. Even the resolution relating to the home does not indicate that the call is for an end to the sexual division of labor. It seems more confining for women than liberating.

The conference resolved to address the fight against hunger; the total liquidation of the armed bandits; the building of new relations within the family and the consolidation of the home; the conquering of new knowledge through education in order to conquer the concepts of science and technology; and the glorious task of being a comrade, wife, friend, and loving mother in the home.

In the end, what was absent from the conference's agenda and remains absent from the overall agenda is a program for a women's struggle. While class struggle is called for as a constructive force, women's struggle is seen as divisive. The absence of mechanisms for the transformation and reorganization of productive labor through rural development, and of sexual division of labor through gender struggle, continued to dog progress here as much as in the other areas of women's lives. The goals of freeing women through the lifting of oppressive customs such as *lobolo* and polygamy are important in the long-term transformation of women's lives.

The persistence of these customs provides a particularly cogent example of why the reorganization of women's productive and domestic lives need to be done in tandem. When an adequate level of development makes the peasant household less marginal, both customs will lose their original importance. As one man stood up at a preparatory meeting and averred: "Of course we need more than one wife. The Portuguese only had one wife because they could hire workers. We cannot afford to hire workers. Therefore we need to marry more than one wife."

If men were to pull their weight within the household, on the other hand, the accumulation of a surplus would not be dependent on the exploitation of numerous wives but on the work of all members of the family. And when women's labor is respected within the family as well as outside, women may no longer fear desertion, and the party might have to accept divorce. While political education plays an important part in ending these customs, without reorganization of women's role in production and without gender struggle, it can go so far and little further.

⋈11⋈
Beyond the Family

At independence, Adelina Penicela, a fifty-year-old Maputo market woman, could not read or write. She was one of many: 90 percent of the population—closer to 100 percent for women—was illiterate. Even before its literacy campaign launched in 1978 OMM established special courses for women, and Adelina Penicela was one of the first to sign up.

"I began to learn to speak Portuguese with Frelimo, with the OMM in its first literacy course," she said in an interview recorded by OMM. "The course at first astonished me. We women in our fifties who knew no Portuguese, when they called us to come eat, we couldn't understand. We had to speak with gestures because we spoke only our maternal tongues. But after a month, we began to understand our first words. We came with our eyes closed, but little by little our eyes and our ears began to open and we began to understand."

Horizons opened along with eyes and ears. "We learned many things—about our provinces, the largest river, the mountains. Before, we found each other strange, we didn't mingle. But there at the center we learned that we are all equal. We participated in cultural activities and sports, we saw many films, some about women in other countries. Many of us didn't even know that women also worked alongside men in factories."[1]

Adelina joined the increasing number of those learning to read and write; by 1980 the illiteracy rate had dropped to 72.2 percent of the population as a whole. For women though, the rate overall was still high: 84.6 percent. And in Adelina's age group (50–59) 95.9 percent of women were still illiterate. Among 15–19 year-old women, the rate looked better, dropping to 66.7 percent. On the other hand, as Adelina was from the urban area, she was part of a significant statistic: only 40.3 percent of the urban population (male and female) was illiterate. In the rural areas this figure was 77.1 percent, including 94.6 percent of women between 25 and 39 years of age, 97.7 percent of those between 40 and 59.

The reasons for the discrepancy between men and women are repeated throughout the African continent: patriarchal cultures that do not see any purpose in educating girls, effectively silencing women; mothers who can't afford to lose their daughters' labor by sending them to school during the day when they could be helping in the fields or tending the younger children; the belief that girls, as potential wives, have no need for education, for their work will be in cultivation; the fact that many girls drop out of school in order to get married at a young age to men chosen by their fathers. It is in peasant societies where these norms tend to be the most persistent, a major contribution to the low literacy rates. It is easier to set up literacy classes in the urban areas, where the population is denser, and new skills can be quickly turned to jobs than among the dispersed, largely agricultural population of the countryside.

Frelimo inherited a grave problem. Few schools were provided by the colonial administration, except for the tiny network of state schools catering to children of settlers and the minute percentage of Mozambicans who had acquired *assimilado* status (in other words, were considered sufficiently civilized and fluent in Portuguese to be classified as second-class citizens of Portugal).

Education of the "indigenous" was through mission schools, which were few in number and very exploitative of the young students. Boys and girls spent as much time working in the fields and kitchens of the mission as in the classroom. "The girls who were sent to school," recalled a worker at the Companhia Industrial de Matola, Alicina Macuana, relating her experiences at Santa Maria Mission, "were made to collect firewood and cultivate the fields. Only the boys were allowed to study." Said another CIM worker, Cristina Mavale, "I went to school as a child—just up to first grade, then I quit. Schools in those days were just work in the fields and cooking in the teacher's house. It was only work. Eh—in cashew harvest time—it meant staying in the bush, making local brew for the teacher."[2]

There were other problems. The teachers had little if any training; the schools were underfinanced. The language of instruction was Portuguese. Strict age criteria blocked the few who did pass from moving on to the next level. In 1975, on the eve of independence, there were still only 600,000 children enrolled in primary schools out of a population of 10.5 million.

During the armed struggle and in the early years of independence, the importance that Frelimo placed on education could be seen in the schools for adult literacy and for children that were set up under trying conditions in the liberated zones, and extended into Mozambique after independence. Education could achieve, Frelimo stressed, the freeing of the minds of the oppressed from the indoctrination of the oppressor.

A poem written during the war by Sergio Vieira, a young militant who rose quickly in the ranks of Frelimo and subsequently the government, captured how education had fueled the revolution.

at night in the bases
deciphering letters
in the shadow of mango trees,
spelling out words

under the cry of bombs
scribbling sentences . . .

word was made bullet
and the bullet was guided by the word . . .

from words
hurricanes were born
which annihilated the companies.

With the sentences they wanted to hide from us
we lit the great fire
of the Peoples' war.[3]

Throughout the colonial period Mozambicans had been labeled "idle," "uncivilized," "uneducated"—labels implying innate qualities. These labels then were internalized. By insisting that this was an imposed ignorance, consciously depriving a whole population of access to information, and hence—at least for a good number of decades—from fighting against their oppression, Frelimo used the literacy campaign as part of a process of enabling Mozambicans to see that they were victims of a colonial policy. In the process of freeing themselves from a mentality of inferiority, they would be able to establish people's power. In 1968, the Second Party Congress resolution on education included a call to promote intensive literacy campaigns among the masses—men, women, and young people—and to encourage young women to complete primary school. Bush schools and literacy centers were set up in the liberated zones, as people eager for education came in large numbers to learn to read and write. Then came the end of the war.

The very word "revolution" in relation to education conjures up visions of hundreds of school students and young literate adults fanning out over the countryside in a concentrated, one-shot effort to do their revolutionary duty by teaching their fellow countrymen and women to read. It is an inspiring idea that has met with success in countries such as Cuba and Nicaragua. And indeed, some of the euphoria that came with the transitional period and independence found an outlet in education. As Judith Marshall comments in her study of literacy in Mozambique, "literacy seems to have been the central activity into which those identifying with Frelimo placed their hopes and energies."[4]

One of the ways to channel this energy was to work with the *grupos dinamizadoes* (GDs), which sprang up under party guidance in workplaces and communities throughout the country and took on a variety of responsibilities, including education. From one province to the next, the GDs enthusiastically began to organize literacy classes.

Men and women, tired after their day's work, would flock to the rundown school buildings, now empty of the younger generation, and in crowded classrooms take their turn to try to master the skills of reading and writing. In the factories, classes were set up and workers given the right and encouraged to participate. Those that already had the basic skills were urged to study the higher grades. In the communal villages, literacy monitors arrived with the schoolteachers and began to teach the peasants after a hard morning's work in their fields.

OMM was particularly active in the period from 1976 to 1978, possibly an outcome—at least in part—of the special emphasis on the urgent need for women to overcome illiteracy and gain access to information. "These difficulties," reads the OMM 1976 resolution, "were evident even during the course of the Second Conference; because of illiteracy, a large proportion of the delegates could not follow the reading and discussion of the reports." The resolution went on to state that as "women play a fundamental role in educating the new generation," eradicating illiteracy among women "must be one of the priorities of OMM."[5]

It was in this early period that women such as Adelina Penicela learned to read and write. But they learned more than these skills. Judith Marshall describes the impact of OMM involvement:

In the period of 1976 and 1977, the Mozambican Women's Organization had put particular stress on literacy for women, and had organized special residential course for their own provincial and district level OMM activists. These courses, which drew women away from their normal responsibilities to concentrate only on literacy had had phenomenally high results. For the women who came, the course marked a dramatic expansion of their worlds, starting from airplane travel to reach the national capital to a three month period of new experiences. Freed to concentrate only on studying, recognizing how their newly acquired speaking, reading and writing work could feed into their regional organizing of other women, getting enormous support from the national OMM staff during the course including regular Friday night newspaper reading sessions and frequent visits, being exposed to films and study trips to local factories and child care centers, the women in the courses progressed remarkably.[6]

By this time, the enormous tasks of national reconstruction were more firmly in view, as was the appreciation of the length of time needed to create a literate population. Both these factors ruled out a one-off campaign as in Cuba and Nicaragua, where both the size of the populations and the numbers of those who were illiterate were so much smaller. In Cuba, for instance, at the time of the revolution, out of a population of 7 million, 23.6 percent were illiterate, while of the 2 million Nicaraguans, the figure was 53 percent.[7]

In Mozambique, with a population of 10.5 million and 90 percent illiteracy, this type of onslaught on illiteracy was not an option. The staggering illiteracy rate meant that the one of every ten Mozambicans who did have minimal reading and writing skills could not be spared. They were needed immediately by the government and the myriad of new projects being established. Instead, Mozambique adopted a series of literacy campaigns.

The success of this program from 1974 to the launching of the national campaign in 1978 can be seen from official estimates. The number of people who learned to read and write in these short years is estimated to be as high as 500,000. But it was something of an ad hoc system, depending on the resources available in a particular district, and the willingness and charisma of individuals to ensure that it was carried out. It took two more years of preparation to launch the first of a series of national campaigns, which concentrated on workers in organized workplaces but was also geared to a lesser extent toward members of the party, people's assemblies, and mass organizations—particularly the women's organization.

With the decision to focus on the workplace, rather than the community, potential women students were effectively excluded because of their small numbers in the workplace. The enthusiasm that marked the first few years of the campaign quickly dissipated. Certainly, the increasing MNR violence took its toll, ultimately crippling the literacy campaign outside the cities. There were also, however, real problems in the campaign itself. Weak planning at a national level, compounded by the difficulty encountered in trying to produce the necessary books and to train literacy monitors quickly enough, meant that much of the treaching was not up to standard. It was hard to hold the students' interest. The campaigns were more and more formalized, integrated into the academic year, which differed from the production timetable, be it on farms or in factories.

But as in so many other areas, the difficulties for women were even greater, resulting in a significantly higher dropout rate. It was the rare woman who could find time for her own productive labor, plus domestic labor, plus about two hours of classes a day. In the rural areas, for instance, few women could speak Portuguese, the language chosen for the literacy standard.

Even in the one year that separated my visits to communal villages in Gaza, I could see signs of decline of interest. I could also appreciate how difficult it was for women to commit the time to literacy in the context of the day's work. I have a vivid memory of students taking the end-of-year exam in a village in Chibuto district, Gaza. They sat on the ground in a clearing under a tree, pencils in hand, printed exam papers on their laps. The majority were women, who sat for hours in typical Mozambique style, their legs straight in front, their bodies held at a perfect right angle. But it is one woman I remember most. Her baby—perhaps twelve months old—was full of the zest of life, and brimming with the curiosity and mischief of her age. One moment she would be tugging at her mother's pencil, the next she had crawled over to another exam-taker to bother her, then she was back, playing peekaboo with her mother's body as her shield as she tried hard to distract yet another of her mother's classmates. Through it all, her mother's face showed only deep concentration as she tried to answer the questions. She managed, somehow managed, to ignore the antics of her child. Around her sat women tackling their exams while their infants nursed at their breasts.

In Três de Fevereiro, the village in which I spent the most time, the situation was quite typical. In 1980 over a hundred students attended the literacy classes, and seventy passed the exams. Another twenty-three attended adult education; fewer than ten passed. The following year started off well: 164 enrolled for the literacy classes, 37 for adult education, almost all women. But none sat for the exams. The literacy monitor, a concerned older man, was very discouraged. When he asked his students why they stopped coming, they told him that they had too much work to do. Two hours a day for literacy training is a large chunk out of a woman's workday. He didn't seem quite convinced that this was sufficient reason, and bemoaned the fact that there was no way to enforce attendance. But he was also sympathetic. "Sometimes the students leave their *machambas* and come directly to class. They have no time to do their homework, they're tired and their minds are still with their fields. Then they can't keep up and they lose interest."

The reason for the preponderance of women in the classes was that many of the men had learned to read and write while working in South Africa. But there were other reasons. "The men are ashamed that they can't read and write," the teacher said, "and don't want to show their ignorance in front of women. Men are very proud. They think that they are the heads of their families. When a man goes to class with his wife and he doesn't know the answer and she does, he feels shown up. So he stops attending."

Some of the older people drop out because of their eyesight. They had been unaware that it was failing until they found they could not see the letters on the blackboard or read their manuals.

To try to help those who would most benefit from literacy—members of the OMM and other leadership groups, for example—a special class was established in Três de Fevereiro, drawing students from neighboring villages as well. Twenty students attended the classes regularly. Fourteen had said they would take the exam. In fact only seven took it—four men and three women. OMM was encouraging its own women leaders to go away to study in special programs they had set up, so they could complete intensive courses unencumbered by the pressures of their day.

I visited one of the OMM centers in Macomia district, Cabo Delgado. Each three-month course was attended by OMM secretaries or assistant secretaries drawn from the four locals that comprised the district. The goal of the program went beyond literacy to include training on how to conduct meetings, how to work collectively, and how to better understand and promote the work of the women's organization. In addition, local representatives of the Ministry of Health gave sessions on nutrition, infant and child care, first aid, the importance of building latrines, and so forth. The director was a young woman who had passed fourth grade. She told me that at first some of the women were very shy and reticent about participating in the classroom, or even singing with the group. They gradually gained confidence and in time learned to interact freely with the others.

The classrooms were small reed structures, each with a faded blackboard propped up in front, with neat rows of small desks for the students. There were three teachers, two of whom were the director and assistant director. Sitting in one class I glimpsed how real is the problem of the lack of adequately trained literacy monitors. The monitor had chalked a sentence onto the board from the students' workbook: "A luta do Povo é Justa" (The people's struggle is just). The monitor pointed to each word with a long stick she held in her hand, and the class repeated them back to her in the singsong tones of rote. Despite the fact that the word "povo," the people, was the key word for the literacy lessons, from which the students were meant to identify other sound and words, no one noticed that it was mispelled: "pvo."

The second center I visited was in Nampula province, where a more developed program had been established with the help of United Nations and nongovernmental agency funding. Simple, airy brick and cement buildings had been constructed, housing classrooms and dormitories. It was an ambitious program, with courses on nutrition and latrine-building, hygiene, the importance of bathing children regularly and breast feeding, trying to keep the mosquitos down, and general household cleanliness. The course was designed for women who had passed third or fourth grade, so that they could take notes and use the booklets handed out during the course once they were back home to train others in their villages. It was a manifestly unrealizable goal: so few women had any education at all in the north, and those who had reached this level would have already been absorbed by the state sector or in other desperately understaffed areas that it was highly unlikely that any such qualified woman would be available. For the two sessions of the course held by the time of my visit in 1982, none of the women students had been able to read or write and only a very few of the twenty students spoke Portuguese at all. They spoke seven different languages, none of which was spoken by the instructors, who were from the south. To try to address this, the prospectus for the course had been put aside and replaced by a three-month literacy course, with the hope of cramming as much of the coursework as possible into the final month.

I interviewed a group of four young women who spoke Portuguese fairly well—all learned at the center. When I asked them what they hoped to do with their new knowledge when they got back to their villages, they said with emphasis that they would make sure that *both* women and men benefited from the information and skills they would be passing on. They did not regard this as women's work only, they said. I wondered how the men in their village would cope with the almost defiant assertiveness in these young women when they got back to the village and began to demand that men participate. Would OMM intervene and tell them to speak with "kind words?" Or would OMM encourage this newfound confidence and appreciation of the need for more equality? I hoped I was wrong in presuming it would be the former.

Soon after my visit the center was closed for urgently needed reassessment and redesign. It never reopened. By 1983 bandit activity was beginning to be felt throughout the north. And with each year it became more difficult for villagers to travel to the center, which was in an insecure area in the countryside a distance from Nampula, the provincial capital.

On my first visit to Mozambique, a special meeting of women from *bairros* of Xai-Xai was held and for hours I listened to women who stood up to tell me how their lives had changed since independence. Others acted out skits to show how their lives had been transformed. At the end of the meeting a small, thin old woman came up to me. There was one thing she had to tell me, which she felt explained it all. She looked me straight in the eye, her smile exposing the gaps between her teeth. "I can write my name now," she said.

Factories eventually all had literacy and/or adult education programs. At Investro, most workers, including women, joined the workforce with some basic literacy skills, but they needed a post-literacy program. Workers had the right to attend classes, getting some time off from work and using some of their own time at lunch. The education programs in the factories were instituted as part of the national policy of educating the workers, who could then play a more decisive and conscious role in the development of their country. For the first time in their lives, women workers were given the chance to learn to read and write, to widen their horizons, to advance. Yet few women at the factories continued to take advantage of this opportunity after the initial years. None of the women I interviewed at Companhia Industrial de Matola (CIM) in 1981, for example, were studying, although some had completed first or second grade before dropping out. (With the subsequent change in the factory's administration, a revitalized school for literacy and adult education was established, which became something of a model.) Those that stayed in did so at some cost. Few men had to face the range of obstacles confronting women in their quest for literacy.

My friend Judith Marshall spent six months assessing the literacy and adult education program at CIM, gathering material for her own research. I had the opportunity to look back into CIM through the window provided by her work and sharp insights. Judith had worked as a *cooperante* with the Ministry of Education for six years before beginning her own research. She was concerned to understand how women actually use literacy skills in their day-to-day lives, to see the extent to which the inability to read had shaped their choices and whether literacy-training would create the confidence that would help them enter the arena of public discourse formerly confined to men.

Some of the problems identified by Judith at CIM are similar to those I found in Três de Fevereiro, while others are not. Some are either specific to women or effect women more adversely than they do men. Judith found that few women spoke Portuguese, and those that did were hesitant to use it in class, fearing that they would be laughed at for their mistakes—a fear based on experience. One woman worker described how women who spoke Portuguese in public places were ridiculed for their efforts. Others talked of the self-consciousness women felt. "Some women really don't know how to speak Portuguese. Others are just embarrassed. As to why they have such complexes, how should I know? In my experience, women who don't work are especially afraid."[8]

Women workers bring their particular collection of insecurities to class, and are afraid to speak out and participate. They sit in silence, walled in by their fear of speaking out in the face of authority and out of the belief that they are incapable. This was often handled sensitively by the male teachers. But not always. Judith witnessed class situations where women's inability to speak out or to give the correct answers were chided by both male teachers and male co-students, reinforcing this lack of confidence and the sense that they were hopeless cases.

Women were far more likely than men to drop out or not start at all because of the socialization they had received as children, which assumed that girls would not go to school in the first place. All these combined to make women feel incapable of learning, whereas men were more inclined to tackle their lessons with confidence—and hence a self-fulfilling prophecy—that they could do it. "I like to study but nothing stays in my head," complained Adelaide Mulengo, who dropped out after repeating third year. "When I close the book, my head also closes. I don't think I'll go anymore. I'm just going to irritate the teacher. Not even a little bit stays with me—nothing enters."[9]

Many women dropped out after just a year of classes because of the pressure of their double day. What the women at both Investro and CIM told me about their domestic work load leaves little doubt that adding literacy classes to their day is more than most could handle, particularly women with children. This was poignantly described by thirty-seven-year-old Leonor Benjamin, a clerical assistant who had worked at CIM for twenty years: "I really want to study but social conditions don't make this possible. Senora Judith knows how it is with men. I'm alone there at the house. I don't have any household help. If I study here, I'll get home only at 9 or 10 at night. My husband is without food or water. He could decide to get another woman, saying 'This woman is prepared to cook for me. You don't want to.' These are the social problems we face. I want to study a lot. I'd like to do up to at least the sixth grade—but I can't because of the social situation. Employing somebody costs a lot. . . . My husband lets me work. Many husbands wouldn't do this. He accepts that we don't have children. Because of this, I can't stop being a good woman for him."[10]

Amelia Cossa, now forty-three, had worked at CIM from the age of fifteen, when she had passed grade three in a Maputo school. Her day begins at four in the morning when she sets off to work for two hours in her *machamba*. Between 6:00 and 7:00 she gets ready for work, before boarding the bus. She returns home at 5:30. "I'd like to do fifth class," she explained. "My problem is the time. I get home too late to do the cleaning and feed the children. A woman is always being squeezed. She's always in the middle. Always given orders. When she gets home, she has to do this but she can't do that or the other. She's the one who always gets ordered about."

But even the most elementary ability to read and write began to open women to a whole world from which they felt excluded, a world that ceased to be mysterious and foreboding. "With literacy," one woman told Judith, "people don't earn more but everything they know is in their heads. They can go anywhere, do anything, ask for things, enter in. When people don't know reading and writing they are afraid." And once this fear begins to retreat, there is elation in the power they derive from their newfound skills.

"Once my husband sent me a note saying, 'Meet me at the corner of July 24th Avenue and Lenin at four o'clock. No sooner said than done, off I went there to meet him," said a delighted Serafina Alexander. "Afterwards, I was really pleased. This studying has its uses!" She was totally illiterate before beginning to study in 1982 at CIM, while caring for three children under five, she reached third year after three years. The birth of her youngest prevented her from writing the third-year exam. Her situation is repeated many times over. Women give birth to children about every two years, further drawing on their time and energy. Out of thirty-seven women interviewed, twenty-two had had to interrupt their studies because of one or more factors relating to motherhood: pregnancy, maternity leave, or illness of toddlers.

Women bringing with them to class their low self-esteem, their insecurities and fears, women coming out of a situation where they are dependent and subordinate, arriving in class with less education than men, have so much more to overcome; a set of invisible bonds is wound around them by the social and economic conditions that are endemic to the situation of women in Mozambique. The slower progress in literacy for women has as much to do with these realities as it does with problems in the organization of the literacy and adult education programs, or the ongoing war. On a day-to-day basis, it is the women, not the men, who shoulder the worries of bringing up children in a war-torn society, of getting home on time to attend to their household responsibilities and getting up before dawn the following morning to begin the grind again.

Here again, the issue of literacy is a cogent example of how the failure to confront the sexual division of labor in the home limits a woman's potential, and keeps her locked into old patterns of overwork and subordination. These limits on women's ability to become literate are another sharp reminder of the need for gender struggle, a struggle waged in the context of literacy that will assist the quest for self-empowerment.

For those who manage to persevere and overcome these obstacles, horizons widen progressively; lifting the veil of ignorance is a series of small victories. These women gain a new sense of self, which, when combined with the encouragement of women to speak out—be it in the classroom or in other settings: at political meetings, as members of production councils at work, of peoples' assemblies in their community, as members of the party, while "showing that they can do what men can do"—go far toward realizing the goal of the new woman. The elderly woman who came up to me at the meeting in Xai-Xai to tell me she could write her name had listened, as I had, to woman after woman standing up to tell her story of how life had changed since Frelimo took over the country. She listened too as one woman, an OMM district leader, stood up toward the end of the meeting to press a point.

"We have talked a lot," she said in a clear voice that carried across a packed hall buzzing with the interaction of the women. "We have related many stories. But I must talk about something we have forgotten. We have forgotten to say that women had no voice. Where matters of importance were being discussed, there were no women. Men said women could not think. But after we got our independence, this changed. In the past days we never had a chance to have a hall full of women talking about our lives. But today we can be together from morning to night discussing our problems. Frelimo says that all of us, women and men, can develop our minds, all of us can work. Frelimo knows that women can think very well, that women are as capable of making decisions. A woman can be somebody."

⬖12⬖
A Decade in
Women's Lives

Lina Magaia is one of the very few Mozambican women who, as a girl, made it into the Portuguese schools. Her father, a meteorologist, married a woman from a peasant family and they had three children, two daughters and a son. Lina was born in Maputo in 1945. Her father made sure all his children went to school, even the girls, even though the only schools they could attend were the overcrowded and pedagogically stifling schools for Mozambicans. When Lina was twelve her father was reclassified as *assimilado*, and with this status came the privilege to transfer to the superior schools for the Portuguese. As the only African in the class, Lina had to contend with daily humiliations. Her teacher, racist to the core, could not accept her as equal to his other students; when she could not answer a question or understand a problem it was because she was intrinsically inferior. When one of her classmates could not answer a question it was a part of the learning process. Lina challenged him constantly, refusing to sit and take the abuse, and in the process she learned how to fight for herself and for the rights of her people. It was a lesson she never forgot.

In 1961 Eduardo Mondlane visited Mozambique while he was working at the United Nations. He traveled widely and spoke to many people. Like many of her compatriots, Lina was inspired by his words and ideas. It was as if he was talking a new language and his words fell on ready ears.

At the end of 1961 Lina began to publish short articles in the local newspaper, her first forays into journalism. At the same time she began to talk out about the oppressive regime. In 1965 she planned to leave and join Frelimo in Tanzania. Knowing she might be searched, she asked a friend to sew her documents into a hidden part of her handbag. She was saying an emotional farewell to this friend when the secret police came to arrest her. With a casual "Ciao!" her friend swung Lina's handbag over her shoulder and left the house. Because they couldn't find her documents, her prison sentence was short.

After three months she was released with a heavy threat over her head. If she made any trouble at all, if she took part in politics, whether inside the country or out, they told her, her father would be arrested. They meant it. She gave up the idea of joining the armed struggle.

In 1967 Lina won a scholarship to a Portuguese college and left for Portugal to study. So new and exciting was the world outside the confines of colonial Maputo that her work suffered. She almost lost her scholarship, but with the pleas of her father, she settled down. Still, all was not smooth. She was dating a Mozambican, a football player, and in 1971 she became pregnant. They fought over Lina's father's disapproval of the match, and they separated. With a small child to support, she had to stop her studies. But she stayed on in Lisbon.

Her little boy was just two on April 24, 1973, the day of the officers' coup in Portugal that changed her life and that of every Mozambican. Lina immediately reentered politics, joining a group in Lisbon that was disseminating information about Frelimo and supporting an end to the war and independence for the colonies. The right-wing forces were not about to give up the colonies without a fight, and the house that she and her comrades were working out of was shot at. Her friends became anxious for her and her young child. It was agreed that she should go directly to Tanzania.

Once there, she immediately joined Frelimo, fulfilling a dream of many years, and started her military training. Her son went to Tunduru on the Tanzanian border, where Frelimo had set up schools and a child-care center for children of their militants. But he wouldn't eat. He eventually became very ill with dysentery. By the time Lina entered Maputo with the army in triumph at independence day, her son had died. She planted a tree on his grave, so that his death could symbolically fertilize the growth of a new Mozambique. It's a loss she still bears with pain. She married after independence and gave birth to three children, two girls and a boy. Later she adopted two young orphans, expanding her family to five.

After independence, Lina's first task was to work on the establishment of a new education system, at the request of Samora Machel. In 1980 she helped set up the first cooperatives in the new green zones. Two years later she was transferred to Manhiça, in Gaza, to head the economic department of the state sugar farm and factory, Maragra. She moved there with her children, back to the area that her family had come from, while her husband remained to work in Maputo, over an hour's drive away. When Maragra became a target of attack after three years, she moved to the district capital, but this area also began to be attacked. Fearing for the lives of her children—all the more because they traveled back and forth between Manhiça and Maputo regularly—she sent them to live with their father in their house in Maputo. Now Lina travels back and forth between her two homes. Regularly, often every weekend, she drives, risking ambush, to see her husband and children.

Each new position Lina took on represented a challenge to try to set in motion a different aspect of development. But the hardest job came when she was appointed director of agricultural development for the district of Manhiça, with a dense population, a good potential for agriculture, and a major target of MNR attacks. It is here, in the home area of her grandmother, which she knew well and where she still has relatives, that she began to record the stories of the MNR atrocities, taken from the peasants.

In her book *Dumba Nengue*, literally "trust your feet" (implying that those who do survive), she describes the day she decided to begin this documentation, when in May 1985 she arrived home in Maputo in the afternoon, stunned by what had happened earlier that day. Her children rushed out to greet her, but all she could do was throw herself on her bed in tears. When her eight-year-old son, Ivan, came to ask her why she was crying, she said:

"Today I saw Sonyka killed by a bullet in the chest, my son," referring to her second youngest.

"But isn't Sonyka there outside?" he asked, astonished.

"Yes, our Sonyka is outside. The bandits killed a child even smaller than Sonyka."

The children went to get the tangerines that she had brought for them out of the car, and Ivan came running back. "The car is covered in blood," he said. "Whose blood is it, Mama?"

Only then did she realize how much of the little girl's blood had spilled in the car. "Blood of that pretty young girl in her red skirt. Blood of that child whom I had wrapped in my black blouse, a blouse that I could never bear to wear again. It was the blood of the children of Mozambique. . . . And I saw my children crushed, disembowelled, rent with bayonets or their heads blown open by a burst from a machine-gun."

She wanted to understand. How was it *possible* that people

could do the things she had heard about? And so she began to document the horror, to tell the stories of the victims who are illiterate and have no access to microphones or other technology to report what has become the reality of their daily experience.

Lina continues her work in Manhiça, trying to rebuild what has been lost and establishing new development projects to improve the lives of those living there. Her commitment is strong. Her friends and colleagues in Maputo keep urging her to return to work in Maputo. Manhiça is far too dangerous, they argue, not without reason. She could transfer in an instant, to one of many different jobs in Maputo. Few women are as educated and as experienced as Lina, few Mozambicans male or female, in fact.

Worrying that she was neglecting her family by her decision to continue to work in the countryside, Lina went to talk to her father, the one person she always turned to with her troubles and her confidences. It was 1984, just after the first attacks on Manhiça. "Lina," he said, "you have to stay in Manhiça. What you're doing there is good for the people, good for Mozambique. Don't come back before your work is completed, just because people are pressuring you."

He died a month later. In some ways, she still hears these words as his final message to her, she told me. She wants to honor them. But more: "I, Lina, am lucky because I have another place to live. But what about the people from Manhiça? What place do they have to go? I have work to do. I would be a coward if I left now. If I was forced to go to Manhiça, then maybe I would wonder if I was being sent there because they wanted me to die. But I *asked* to go. How can I suddenly say I am not staying because there are attacks? I have not finished my work there. I was given the unique opportunity to get an education. I must use it. And always, always I ask myself: 'What about the people?'"

From the low land of the green zones just on the outskirts of Tete City it is possible to watch the tanks roll by and the trucks and cars hurrying on the elevated road to join the military convoy that will escort them across Tete province to Malawi. For the women who sow and weed and with their hoes cultivate the ground of the green zone cooperatives, the convoy is a constant reminder that the war never stops. Many of the few hundred women who work in these co-ops have had much more direct experience of the war and came to Tete City after fleeing the bandits. They are proud of their cooperative union, with its fourteen member co-ops, 90 percent of whom are women. These co-ops are flourishing, as they are in the Maputo green zones, because voluntary agencies with money for development projects have had to find projects in secure areas. Despite the lack of peace, a new equality and the beginning of development can be seen in small pockets of Mozambique, seeds that wait to multiply once peace breaks out.

On June 25, the thirteenth anniversary of independence and a public holiday, Lina and I visited the cooperatives around Tete City. Even though it was a holiday, the president and treasurer of the "Filipe Magaia" cooperative were there. They were eager to talk about their work, speaking in halting Portuguese to Lina, not knowing that she was the first cousin of their co-op's namesake, one of the first martyrs of the liberation struggle, a top strategist for the guerrilla army.

Eulalia, the treasurer, was eager to talk. She had passed third grade in Beira, she told Lina, the city where she was born. There she met her husband, who was later transferred to Tete City by the bank where he worked. Then he was laid off and they remained. "And who supports the family now? *I* do!" she said very proudly. She had never anticipated that she would even be able to continue her education. But she did. "There is our school," she said pointing to a large tree among a clump of shady trees. "Under that tree we have studied, only women together," she explained. The school was set up for co-op members only. Now the upper grades go to study in Tete City, but those just starting, like the president of the co-op, study under the trees. "We women have organized ourselves," she added. "We don't need men," she said.

"We don't want this war," Eulalia told us. "If it wasn't for the war we could produce so much, so, so much, that we could send produce to Beira, even to Maputo. Then we could buy from the cities what they produce. We suffer because the war doesn't let us have *capulanas*, shoes. But the war will end. When we had our first war, we couldn't believe that it would ever end. In the same way we can't believe this war will end. But it will. It will."

Eulalia reflected on the *matsanga*: "It's very complicated today because the *matsanga* are Mozambicans. It's not easy to identify who they are, unlike the Portuguese who were white. But the matsanga don't produce their own guns, their own ammunition. Someone gives it to them. *That's* our real enemy. *That's* who we must fight. But those that actually appear in front of us are the matsanga. So it's the matsanga that we have to kill." She went on: "This war is delaying many of our possibilities. But nonetheless, we're very happy in our work here. We have achieved so much. Even our co-op president has gone to a meeting of the Union of Cooperatives in Maputo! I didn't know where Maputo is, or whether it even exists! But she went. And she went on a plane! One day, maybe I, myself, will go. All of this we got from Frelimo."

Carolina, the president of Filipe Magaia, also wanted to talk. She told us how things had changed. The cooperative has a day-care center especially built for their children so that they can be well looked after while they work under the hot sun. She's very happy about this. Some of the women don't want to send their children there, though, because they are worried they will be mistreated. But even these women provide produce for the day-care center to feed the children. The union also set up a consumer cooperative where members can buy goods cheaply, even clothes and capulanas. And the women took the initiative to branch out beyond food production into a brick-building cooperative. You see, she explained, men built the houses. But the houses were not really permanent, just reeds and mud. So, the women thought, why not bricks? The local clay was good. So they learned, with the help of voluntary organizations, to make bricks. "Now we will use them to build our own houses." The co-op is also planning to expand into small animal husbandry and to buy cattle for plowing. And again with funding from a voluntary organization, small, round cement dams were constructed to irrigate their crops. The dams have also improved the social conditions of the community. Locals are allowed to collect water from the dam, and while we were visiting a number of women arrived with large cans, scooped up the water, and retraced their steps back along the narrow paths to their homes.

Women are learning technical skills in the Tete cooperatives— these are no longer limited to men. Fernanda, the daughter of one of the co-op members, stood nearby. She has passed fifth grade and is being trained in more advanced skills that will enable her to help with technological problems for the coop and train others to improve their output.

"Now I feel I have a role in building my country," Carolina said.

"Before it was my husband who bought all the things we needed—soap, oil, and so forth. But now, it's me. He is unemployed. He's there at home, I'm here producing. I take home food that I have grown with my own hands. I also take home goods I buy out of my wages from the consumer cooperative of the union—shoes, sugar, clothes. This is why I am happy. All my husband does to help in the house is to collect wood. Everything else, everything, I do. These men, heh, they are lazy."

Namerie is also from Tete, from the district of Angonia. Along with most of the people of Angonia she had to flee when the bandit attacks became regular, and managed to find refuge in Malawi, near the border. Experiencing what many refugees were facing—lack of food in Malawi—she would walk back to tend her *machamba* and get food for her family. She had four children to feed, and she was pregnant with her fifth. It was not long before disaster struck: she ran into a group of bandits and was captured. They forced her to go with them, carrying all the food she had picked, and when they got to the camp they took it from her and ate it themselves. They kept her at a camp in Matenge and forced her to cook for them. But they didn't give any of the captives food. They would try to keep the skin of the beef to eat.

Sometimes the guards were inattentive, and one night she and a group managed to escape. She walked for many, many kilometers inside Mozambique trying to get to safety, wanting only to get back to her children. But instead she was recaptured and landed up in another *matsanga* encampment. To punish her, the bandits made her plow an entire field with her bare hands. And they sexually abused her, even though they knew she was pregnant. But undeterred, even though she was scared, she waited for an opportunity to escape yet again. And for the third time she ran into bandits. "They told me that we had come to 'liberated country.' But what I have seen, I know it is not liberated. I saw them kill so many people. They even killed their own bandits when they were wounded in combat or got sick. The bullet or the knife was their medicine for the sick."

In this third camp she was lucky. There she found a man whom she knew from Angonia. He was one of the *majubas*, who are the bandit police. Some of them are former collaborators with the Portuguese colonial regime who joined the MNR because they didn't like and feared the new government; some were disaffected Frelimo members; some were captives who were forced into this role and take it on for fear of punishment or because they want the better treatment they get.

Namerie and the *majuba* pretended not to recognize each other. It turned out that he had offered to join the MNR and be a *majuba* in the hopes of rescuing his captured family. And in his role of guiding captives from one camp to another, he had helped a number to escape. This brave man then helped Namerie. After a while, he asked the chief of the camp if he could have her as his wife. His request was agreed to—why shouldn't they trust him? He organized her escape. After five months, she finally returned to Malawi. But the bandits operated in Malawi and sometimes entered the refugee camps. People were known to be captured from there as well. Since she had been in three camps and was known to a lot of bandits, the camp leaders were afraid she would be kidnapped yet again. So she moved to the safety of Moatize, where we met her.

Namerie was hesitant about talking, nervous that the man who had saved her would be punished by the government, because he had been a *majuba*. He was now reunited with his family and no longer with the MNR. She never gave his name. We sat in the back of a closed-in jeep that had brought her from where she was staying in the further reaches of the camp. On her lap was the baby that was born shortly after she got to safety. About four months old, the chubby little girl never stopped smiling and grinning, a bundle of total happiness in the safety of her mother's lap.

Lina: educated, a writer, a leader, responsible for a district agricultural program, is pushing to extend Frelimo's commitment to equality, even as she exemplifies it. Eulalia and Carolina: barely literate, their lives transformed by their integration in production, are learning a new sense of self. It is they who are the breadwinners, the ones to go out each day, who purchase the goods that make a difference to their lives. They are providing their children with very different models of women, which are still within the framework of a peasant household. And Namerie: illiterate, resourceful, driven by her desire to care for and protect her children. Namerie's is the most tragic of the three lives, but made less personally tragic by her own qualities of exceptional courage.

The Linas, Eulalias, and Carolinas personify equality and development in Mozambique. But all the Nameries can personify is lack of peace, a lack that runs like a dangerous undertow throughout Mozambican life.

Yet in all the women, the struggle to survive is strong. In their accounts lies the profound and powerful story of women in Mozambique; the way they continue to build and rebuild against incredible odds and continue to hope for a better life. "We are not a nation sitting down to die, believe me," Lina said over and over again, trying to counter some of the images of a helpless and hopeless people. "I know. I see our strengths again and again."

And Salomé Moiane, OMM secretary-general, echoed this spirit after her visit to refugee camps in April 1988 when we met in New York a month later. She talked of how hard it was to look into faces of displaced women because the suffering she saw reflected there was so harsh. But her voice perked up when she described another impression: the way in which the women, with enormous courage and resilience, immediately set about cultivating crops. By resuming their work as the farmers in Mozambique, they are showing a deep will to survive: "Women are used to being strong. Despite the overwhelming problems they are facing, they remain strong. The women are not sitting in the camps listlessly waiting to die. They are fighting back by rebuilding their lives. The minds of women and the hearts of women are so big."

Notes

Prologue

1. Eduardo Mondlane, *The Struggle for Mozambique* (Harmondsworth: Penguin Books, 1969), p. 13 (reprint ed. London: Zed Books, 1983).
2. Quoted from George Houser and Herb Shore, *Mozambique: Dream the Size of Freedom* (New York: Africa Fund, 1975), p. 11.
3. Pruan Hassan, interviewed in Allen Isaacman and Barbara Isaacman, *Mozambique: From Colonialism to Revolution, 1900–1982* (Boulder: Westview Press, 1983).
4. In Margaret Dickinson, *When Bullets Begin to Flower* (Nairobi: East African Publishing House, 1972), p. 95.
5. Interview by Herb Shore, in Houser and Shore, *Mozambique*, p. 4.

Introduction: Equality, Development, Peace

1. Samora Machel, *Sowing the Seeds of the Revolution: Speeches of Samora Machel* (London: Committee for Freedom in Mozambique, Angola and Guinea-Bissau, 1973), p. 26.
2. Gita Sen and Caren Grown, *Development, Crises, and Alternative Visions* (New York: Monthly Review Press, 1984), p. 82.
3. Cited in Barbara Isaacman and June Stephen, *Mozambique: Women, the Law and Agrarian Reform* (Addis Ababa: United Nations, 1980), p. 71.

2: Village Under Siege

1. UNICEF, *Children on the Front Line: The Impact of Apartheid, Destabilization and Warfare on Children in Southern and South Africa* (New York: United Nations, 1987), pp. 14, 19.
2. Abdul Razak Noormahomed and Julie Cliff, *The Impact on Health in*

Mozambique of South African Destabilization (Maputo: Ministry of Health, 1987), p. 4.

3. Ibid., p. 1.
4. Cited in Barbara Isaacman and June Stephen, *Mozambique: Women, the Law and Agrarian Reform* (Addis Ababa: United Nations, 1980), p. 71.
5. Documents of the Third Party Congress, Maputo, 1977, cited in Isaacman and Stephen, *Mozambique*, p. 68.

3: Harvest of Bitterness

1. UNICEF, *Children on the Front Line: The Impact of Apartheid, Destablization and Warfare on Children in Southern and South Africa* (New York: United Nations, 1987), pp. 12–13.
2. Abdul Razak Noormahomed and Julie Cliff, *The Impact on Health in Mozambique of South African Destabilization* (Maputo: Ministry of Health, 1987), p. 4.
3. Ibid., p. 7.
4. Ruth Brandon Minter, "Mozambique's War of Terror," *Christianity and Crisis* 47, no. 12 (September 14, 1987), p. 285.
5. Quoted in "Africans Cite War's Toll on Children," *New York Times*, July 13, 1987.
6. Noormahomed and Cliff, *Impact on Health*, p. 23.
7. In Lucas Mhuti, ed., *Breakfast of Sjamboks* (Harare: Zimbabwe Publishing House, 1987), p. 70.
8. Lina Magaia, *Dumba Nengue: Run for Your Life: Peasant Tales of Tragedy in Mozambique* (Trenton: Africa World Press, 1988), p. 107.
9. Ibid., pp. 19–20.
10. Ibid., p. 44.
11. Frelimo Party Central Committee, Information Department, *The Children of War* (Maputo: Frelimo, 1987), p. 9.
12. Ibid., p. 11.
13. Ibid., pp. 11–12.
14. Quoted in Joseph Hanlon, *Beggar Your Neighbours: Apartheid Power in Southern Africa* (Bloomington: Indiana University Press, 1986), p. 29.
15. Ibid.

4: Rural Development Policy

1. Josina Machel, "The Role of Women in the Struggle," in Liberation Support Movement, *The Mozambique Women in Revolution* (Richmond, B.C., n.d.), p.5.
2. Ibid., p. 11.

3. Barbara Cornwall, *Bush Rebels* (New York: Holt, Rinehart and Winston, 1972).
4. Samora Machel, "The Liberation of Women is a Fundamental Necessity for the Revolution," in *Sowing the Seeds of Revolution: Speeches of Samora Machel* (London: Committee for Mozambique, Angola and Guinea, 1973), p. 26.
5. Samora Machel, Address to the Second Conference of the Organization of Mozambican Women, 1976. Unofficial translation.
6. Ibid.
7. Barbara Isaacman and June Stephen, *Mozambique: Women, the Law and Agrarian Reform* (Addis Ababa: United Nations, 1980), p. 79.
8. Signe Arnfred, informal report on women in Mozambique, photocopy, Maputo, 1981.
9. Ibid.
10. Cited in Joseph Hanlon, *Revolution Under Fire* (London: Zed Books, 1984), p. 110.

5: Transforming the Countryside

1. Nina Swaim, "Women and Water in Communal Village," Unpublished report for the Organization of Mozambican Women, Maputo, 1981.
2. Merle L. Bowen, "Women's Study in Lionde, Chokwe," Monap Project 7, Maputo, 1987, p. 13.
3. Swaim, "Women and Water."

6: Contradiction and Change

1. Cited in Otto Roesch, "Rural Mozambique Since the Frelimo Party Fourth Congress: The Situation in Baixo Limpopo," York University, Toronto, 1987, mimeo.
2. Merle L. Bowen, "Women's Study in Lionde, Chokwe," Monap Project 7, Maputo, 1987.
3. Cited in Signe Arnfred, "On Politics and Gender Struggle in Mozambique." Paper presented at the Review of African Political Economy Conference, Liverpool, September 1986.

7: Women in the Factories and at Home

1. Judith Marshall, "Literacy, State Formation and People's Power: Education in a Mozambican Factory," Ph.D. diss., University of Toronto, 1988, p. 253.

2. Samora Machel, "The Liberation of Women is a Fundamental Necessity for the Revolution," in *Sowing the Seeds of Revolution: Speeches of Samora Machel* (London: Committee for Mozambique, Angola and Guinea, 1973).
3. In Lucas Mhuti, ed., *Breakfast of Sjamboks* (Harare: Zimbabwe Publishing House, 1987), p.57.
4. Marshall, "Literacy," pp. 165ff.

8: Outside the New Family

1. Signe Arnfred, informal report on women in Mozambique, photocopy, Maputo, 1981.

10: Operation Production

1. Cited in Signe Arnfred, "On Politics and Gender Struggle in Mozambique." Paper presented at the Review of African Political Economy Conference, Liverpool, September 1986, p.35.
2. Ibid, p. 34.
3. Barbara Isaacman and June Stephen, *Mozambique: Women, the Law and Agrarian Reform* (Addis Ababa: United Nations, 1980), p.50.

11: Beyond the Family

1. Quoted in Barbara Isaacman and June Stephen, *Women, the Law and Agrarian Reform* (Addis Ababa: United Nations, 1980), p.101.
2. Both quoted in Judith Marshall, "Literacy, State Formation and People's Power: Education in a Mozambican Factory," Ph.D. diss., University of Toronto, 1988, p. 335. I have drawn heavily on this work (as well as conversations with Judith over the years), as indicated below.
3. Cited in Chris Searle, *Words Unchained: Language and Revolution in Grenada* (London: Zed Books, 1984).
4. Ibid., p. 122.
5. Second Conference of the Organization of Mozambican Women, "Full Text of Resolutions," *People's Power,* no.6, 1977.
6. Marshall, "Literacy," p. 143.
7. Ibid., p. 139.
9. Ibid., p. 341.
10. Ibid.

Selected Reading

Books and Articles

Egero, Bertil. 1987. *Mozambique: A Dream Undone. The Political Economy of Democracy, 1975–1984.* Uppsala: Nordiska afrikainstitutet.

First, Ruth. 1983. *Black Gold, The Mozambican Miner. Proletarian and Peasant.* Sussex: Harvester Press.

Gersony, Robert. 1988. "Summary of Mozambican Refugee Accounts of Principally Conflict-Related Experience in Mozambique." Mimeo. U.S. Department of State, Washington.

Hanlon, Joseph. 1986. *Apartheid's Second Front: South Africa's War Against Its Neighbours.* New York: Viking Penguin.

———. 1986. *Beggar Your Neighbours.* Bloomington: Indiana University Press.

———. 1984. *The Revolution Under Fire.* London: Zed Books.

Houser, George. 1988. *No One Can Stop The Rain: Glimpses of African Liberation.* New York: Pilgrim Press.

Isaacman, Allen and Barbara Isaacman. 1983. *Mozambique: From Colonialism to Revolution, 1900–1982.* Boulder: Westview Press.

Isaacman, Barbara and June Stephen. 1980. *Mozambique: Women, The Law and Agrarian Reform.* Addis Ababa: Economic Commission for Africa, United Nations.

Johnson, Phyllis and David Martin, eds., 1986. *Destructive Engagement: Southern Africa at War.* Harare: Zimbabwe Publishing House.

Knight, Derrick. *Mozambique: Caught in a Trap.* London: Christian Aid, 1988.

Kruks, Sonya and Ben Wisner. 1989. "Ambiguous Transformations: Women, Politics and Production in Mozambique," in Sonya Kruks, Rayna Rapp, and Marilyn Young, eds., *Promissory Notes: Women in the Transition to Socialism.* New York: Monthly Review Press.

Magaia, Lina. 1987. *Dumba Nengue, Run For Your Life: Peasant Tales of Tragedy in Mozambique.* Trenton: Africa World Press.

Minter, William. 1986. *King Solomon's Mines Revisited: Western Interests and the Burdened History of Southern Africa.* New York: Basic Books.

Mhuti, Lukas, ed., 1987. *Breakfast of Sjamboks*. Harare: Zimbabwe Publishing House.

Molyneux, Maxine. 1986. "Mobilization Without Emancipation? Women's Interests, State, and Revolution," in Richard Fagen, Carmen Diana Deere, and Jose Luis Coraggio, eds., *Transition and Development: Problems of Third World Socialism*. New York: Monthly Review Press.

Mondlane, Eduardo. 1983. *The Struggle for Mozambique*. London: Zed Books.

Munslow, Barry, ed. 1985. *Samora Machel, An African Revolutionary* London: Zed Books.

———. 1983. *Mozambique: The Revolution and Its Origins*. London: Longman.

Quan, Julian. 1987. *Mozambique, A Cry For Peace*. Oxford: Oxfam.

Roesch, Otto. 1987. "Rural Mozambique Since the Frelimo Party Congress: The Situation in the Baixo Limpopo." Mimeo, York University, Toronto. (To be published in an upcoming issue of *The Review of African Political Economy*.)

Saul, John, ed. 1985. *A Difficult Road: The Transition to Socialism in Mozambique*. New York: Monthly Review Press.

Searle, Chris. 1981. *We're Building the New School! Diary of a Teacher in Mozambique*. London: Zed Books.

Sen, Gita and Caren Grown. 1987. *Development, Crises, and Alternative Visions: Third World Women's Perspectives*. New York: Monthly Review Press.

UNICEF. *Children on the Front Line: The Impact of Apartheid, Destabilization and Warfare on Children in Southern and South Africa*. New York: United Nations Children's Fund.

Urdang, Stephanie. 1986. "Rural Transformation and Peasant Women in Mozambique." Geneva: International Labour Office. Working Paper.

———. 1985. "The Last Transition? Women and Development," in John Saul, ed., *A Difficult Road: The Transition to Socialism in Mozambique*. New York: Monthly Review Press.

———. 1979. *Fighting Two Colonialisms: Women in Guinea-Bissau*. New York: Monthly Review Press.

Walt, Gillian and Angela Melamed. 1983. *Changing Health Care in Mozambique*. London: Zed Books.

Periodicals

Africa News, P.O. Box 3851, Durham, NC 27702. Biweekly publication that regularly features articles on Mozambique.

AIM Bulletin, monthly news summary published in English by the Mozambique Information Agency, C.P. 896, Maputo.

Mozambique Support Network Newsletter, 343 Dearborn, Suite 601, Chicago, IL 60604.

Mozambique Update, Embassy of the People's Republic of Mozambique, 1990 M Street, N.W., Suite 570, Washington DC 20036

News Review, biweekly news summary published by the Mozambique Information Office, 7a Caledonian Road, London N1 9DX.

Southern Africa Review, bimonthly magazine that regularly features Mozambique and the frontline states. Toronto Committee for the Liberation of Southern Africa, 427 Bloor Street West, Toronto, Ont. M5S 1X7.

Solidarity and Material Aid Organizations

Africa Fund and the American Committee on Africa, 198 Broadway, New York, NY 10038 (212) 962-1210. Anti-apartheid organizations, focusing on education and support work for southern Africa. Periodic publications. Small material aid projects.

Mozambique Support Network, 343 Dearborn, Suite 601, Chicago, IL 60604. The network is made up of groups and individuals working on educational and material aid projects throughout the United States.

Washington Office on Africa, 110 Maryland Avenue, N.E., Washington, D.C. Publishes a regular newsletter, *Washington Notes on Africa*.

Index

Abandonment, 103, 105–6, 173, 179, 180–82, 203
African National Congress (ANC), 9, 39–40, 87
Agricultural cooperatives, 13, 50, 144–50, 188–99. *See also* Três de Fevereiro
Agriculture: in colonial Mozambique, 14–17; and equality of women, 25–27; and green zones, 144–50; impact of MNR attacks, 79–80, 109; OMM on collectivization of, 59; shift from state farms to family and private farming, 26–28; in Tete, 71, 79. *See also* Agricultural cooperatives; Communal villages; Rural development policies; State farms
Aleixo, Pedro, 77–78
Alexandria, Gloria, 192–93
Amati, Sarifa, 206
Angola, 17, 37, 68
Angonia district, 67, 75, 78
Arnfred, Signe, 105–6, 164–65
Atanasio, Andre, 75–76, 78, 83

Barata, Juliana, 163–64
Benjamin, Leonor, 231–32
Black market, 35, 81, 187
Boane district, 47, 48, 88
Botha, P. W., 38–39, 87
Bowen, Merle, 142–43
Brideprice. *See* Lobolo

Cabo Delgado province, 14, 15, 70, 105–6
Cabora Bassa, 67, 79
Cabral, Amilcar, 18, 215
Caetano, Juliana, 209–10
Caetano, Marcello, 37
Caju de Matola cashew processing factory, woman workers at, 175–78, 182, 184–85
Canals, 140–43
Che Guevara cooperative, 146–49
Child support, 181–82
Children, 40–41, 50, 52, 69, 72–73, 76–78, 83–86, 89, 238–39. *See also* Family life; Infant mortality rate
Chirime, Helena, 169
Chirore, Amelia Franice, 178–79, 180
Chissano, Joaquim, 40, 41–42, 134
Cliff, Dr. Julie, 57
Clothing, 73–74, 135, 136
Common-law marriage, 173, 184, 199
Communal villages, 30, 33, 56–62, 78–79, 88, 107–8, 114–19, 127–30, 142–50, 213–17
Companheiros, attitudes toward, 173–74, 176–77, 180
Companhia Industrial de Matola (CIM), women workers at, 159, 166–70, 173–75, 177, 222, 230–32
Cossa, Adelia, 180–81
Cossa, Amelia, 232
Cossa, Celina, 149
Cossa, Mariana, 201–2, 211–12
Cotton production, 14–15, 112
Courts, and child support, 181–82

Dance, 42–45, 112
Day-care centers, 34, 147–49, 157–58
Department of Natural Disasters and Calamities (DPCCN), 78–79, 80
Development programs, 23–24, 28–30, 57–58, 60–62, 71–72
Divorce, 31, 103, 165, 204. *See also* Single women
Domestic labor, 157–70, 174, 189–90, 197–98, 226–27, 231–32. *See also* Sexual division of labor

Dos Santos, Marcelino, 108
Drought, 67, 78–79, 136, 187, 188
Dumba Nenque (Magaia), 83–84, 238
Dumende, Antonio, 53–54

Eduardo Mondlane village, Boane, 47, 49–58, 61–62, 86, 116
Education, 105, 137, 152, 221–34, 236, 240
Elections, 115, 119–20
Emocha state farm, 100–4, 105
Ernesto, Eliza, 192
Estima, 67–70, 79, 86, 88
Extension agents, 142–43

Family farming, 26–27, 104, 107, 108, 142–43
Family Law, 183–84
Family relations, 58–60, 145–46, 173–75, 190. See also Gender conflict; Lobolo; Marriage; New family; Polygamy; Single women
Famine in Mozambique, 38, 72–73, 78
Fernando, Alda, 156
Filipe Magaia cooperative, 240–42
First, Ruth, 9, 39–40
Floods, 113–14, 140–43
Food supply, 34, 72, 80–81, 87, 136, 138, 147, 158–59, 169, 187–99
Forced labor, 13, 14–17, 101, 112
Forced marriage, 80–81, 196, 203, 205–6
Foreign currency, 34, 104, 115
Foreign exchange store, 148
Frelimo, 13–15, 17, 22, 26–28, 36, 39–40, 60–61, 69–71, 85, 91–109, 112–13, 114–16, 135, 160–65, 172, 183–84, 188–99, 202–19, 223–24
Front for the Liberation of Mozambique. See Frelimo
Fumo, Julieta, 173

Gaza, education in, 226–27
Gendenhuys, Deon, 87
Gender conflict, 24–25, 28, 31, 123–25, 134–35, 149–50, 157–70, 218–19. See also Family relations; Sexism
Gideon, Mavis, 49–52, 62–63
Grain mills, 116, 127–28
Gratification gifts, 207, 211–13
Green zones, 144–50, 239–40
Grupos dinamizadores, 112–13
Guebuza, Armando, 16, 190

Guimerães, Anastaçia, 101, 130, 137–39, 209
Gurue, 100–3, 109

Head, Judith, 103
Health care, 56–57, 61, 135. See also Rural clinics
Health workers, 53–54, 56, 57, 116
Hombé, Arminda, 160–61, 206–7
Household labor. See Domestic labor; Sexual division of labor

Illiteracy, 97, 221. See also Literacy campaigns
Industry, 71–72, 152–70
Infant mortality rate, 68
Investro Textile Factory, woman workers, 152–66, 174, 231
Irrigation, 106, 141–42, 146

Jaime, Regina, 194–96
Jonas, Salda, 173
José, Claudina, 65–67, 68–69, 74, 86, 89

Khan, Shafudine, 42
Kidnappings by MNR, 51–52, 53, 56, 57, 66, 84–85

Lace, Jose Augusto, 80
Lalu, Lucia, 164
Land distribution, 118–19, 140–43
Langa, Alda Abel, 179, 181–82, 185
Limpopo River, 113–14, 136, 140–43
Literacy campaigns, 31, 34, 105, 113, 178, 221–34
Lobolo, 93–94, 111, 117, 174, 179, 184, 195, 201–19
Lussanhande, 191–193

Machel, Graça, 39
Machel, Josina, 94–95, 96
Machel, Samora, 15, 17–18, 22, 39–40, 41, 44, 94, 96–97, 98, 162, 172, 217, 237
Macuana, Alicina, 222
Madonsela, Maria, 93–94, 99, 100, 104, 105
Mafumo, Felizmina, 177–78
Magaia, Lina, 44–45, 68, 69, 83–84, 133, 136, 140, 143, 179–80, 185, 236–39, 243, 244
Mahashane, Carlotta de Jesus, 178
Malawi, 38, 65, 71, 75, 79

Malnutrition, 50, 73, 77
Manhique, Isabel, 160, 163
Manhique, Leia (Mama Leia), 43–44, 111–30, 140, 163, 206, 208
Maputo, 33–35, 40–41, 47, 82, 187–89
Maria, Ilda, 166
Market women, 164–65
Marketing system, 142, 146–47
Marriage, 154, 176–77, 180–81, 184, 202. *See also* Family relations; Forced marriage; *Lobolo*; Polygamy; Weddings
Marshall, Judith, 10, 224, 225, 230–32
Masinga, Maria, 43
Massinga, Ricardina, 156–57
Matama, 194–96
Matama State Farm, Lichinga, 106–7
Mateos, Pauline, 95–96
Matsangaiza, Andre, 82
Matusi, Lisa, 211
Militia, 54, 88, 135–36
Ministry of Health, 68, 69
Minter, Ruth Brandon, 73–74
Moamba State Farm, 91–94, 99–100
Moatize, 71, 72–78, 79
Mohlanga, Gilda, 92–93, 99, 104, 105
Moiane, Salomé, 98–99, 244
Mondlane, Eduardo, 17, 113, 236
Mozambique National Resistance (MNR), 23, 37–40, 65, 71, 74–89, 132, 139, 240–43; attacks by, 28–30, 34, 40–41, 45, 47, 48, 49–59, 61–62, 65–67, 70, 75–76, 78–89, 109, 218, 229, 238–39
Mtevuye, Virginia, 210–11
Mueda massacre, 13, 17, 40
Mulengo, Adelaide, 231

Namerie, 242–43, 244
Nampula province, 100, 228–29
National People's Assembly, 119–20, 184
Ndabas family, 187–88
Ndimande, Rosalina, 91–92, 99–100
New family, 30
Ngoça, Sergio, 85
Niassa province, 70, 191–93, 195–99
Nkuna, Marta, 212

O'Meara, Dan, 71
Operation Production, 106, 187–99
Organization of Mozambican Women (OMM), 10, 43; campaign against polygamy and *lobolo*, 202, 204–7, 214–17; and day-care centers, 158; and educational centers for women, 228–29; Extraordinary Conference of, 99, 172–73, 213–17; and family relations, 207–9; founding conference, 22, 94, 96–97; Frelimo and, 26, 94, 98–99, 217; and gender bias of extension agents, 143; and gender conflict, 123–25, 160–66; and literacy campaigns, 135, 224–25; and Operation Production, 199; program for rural development, 26–27; role in communal villages, 23–24, 205–6; second conference, 59, 97–100, 103; and traditional cultural roles, 98; urban women in, 98; and UGC, 145; and wages, 168

Palace of Marriages, 172
Patriarchy, 28, 179, 189–90, 204
Penicela, Adelina, 221
Polygamy, 31, 105, 111, 117, 175, 182–83, 185, 201–19
Portugal: colonial rule in Mozambique, 14–17, 92–93, 101, 112, 137, 152, 153, 222, 223; abandonment of land after independence, 91, 101, 107; and coup of 1974, 37, 97, 112
Prostitutes, labeling of single women as, 173–74, 189, 193–94, 197, 198
Puala, Maria, 156

Rafael, Ruis, 48, 49, 53, 54
Rape, 14, 15, 57, 84, 197
Reagan, Ronald, 39
Rebecca, 47, 50, 52, 53, 54
Refugees, 73–89
Renamo. *See* Mozambique National Resistance
Rhodesia, 88; war with Mozambique, 23, 39, 45, 49, 71
Roesch, Otto, 141–42
Rural clinics, 53–54
Rural development policies, 91–109, 112–13, 140–43. *See also* Communal villages

Salazar, Antonio, 14
Samuel, Elena, 51–52, 54
Schools, 53, 56, 114, 135, 136, 159
Seco, Amelia, 157
Sexism, 91–92, 117, 126, 215–16
Sexual division of household labor, 23–25, 58–60, 129–30, 143, 154, 157–70

Single women, 31, 93–94, 103–4, 117, 156, 168–69, 173–77, 189–90
Sitoye, José, 210–11, 212
Slovo, Joe, 40
Smart, Teresa, 190–91, 192–98
Smith, Ian, 71, 88
Soccer team, women's, 154–55
South Africa, destabilization policies in Mozambique, 9, 23, 38–40, 19, 86–87
South African mines, 207, 211; Mozambicans working in, 82, 111–12, 117–18, 174, 178
Southern African Development and Coordination Conference (SADDC), 38–39, 42
State farms, 26–27, 30, 91–92, 106–9, 140–43, 188–99
Sumbane, Veronica, 167–68, 174–75
Swaim, Nina, 128, 129

Tea plantations, 100–4
Teachers, 54, 56, 66, 75–76, 148
Technology, introduction of, 127–30
Tembe, Marta, 152–53, 159
Tete, 65–68, 70–72, 74–89, 88;
Tomas, Viana, 156
Toys, 148–49
Tractor drivers, women as, 92–94, 100
Três de Fevereiro communal village, Gaza, 43–44, 111–30, 132–37, 140–44, 201, 205–6, 210, 227–28
Tsaquisse, Marcelina, 175–77
24 de Junho cooperative, 146, 214
U.S. National Council of Churches, 73–74
Umbeluzi River, 48–49, 50
União Geral das Cooperativas Agro-Pecurias de Maputo (UGC), 145–46, 149, 241
UNICEF, 68, 127, 147
United Nations, 41–42, 228; Decade for Women, 21–24, 27, 29–30, 61–62, 97

Vieira, Sergio, 223

Wages, 91–92, 104, 166–69, 174, 177

Water pumps, 114, 125–27, 136, 146
Water supply, 53, 56, 57, 115
Weddings, 172
Wife beating, 92, 93–94, 165, 179
Women's soccer team, first, 154–55
Women: abandoned by husbands, see Abandonment; during colonial period, 14; and educational campaigns, 226–27, 229–32; as elected officials, 120; and family agriculture, 59–60; in green zones, 144–50; and household labor as productive, 197–98; impact of polygamy on, 207–10; impact of revolution on, 22–30, 62–63, 65–67, 233–34; impact of war on, 86–89; in military, 95–96, 136, 237; as MNR prisoners, 242–43; new models of, 243–44; and rural development programs, 26; at state farms, 91–94, 100–6; and technical skills, 241; tractor drivers, 92–94; in Três de Fevereiro, see Três de Fevereiro; and UGC, 145–46. See also Women factory workers; Women's liberation
Women factory workers, 152–70
Women's Detachment, 95–96, 105–6
Women's liberation: and agricultural production, 25–27; and communal villages, 58–62; and destabilization, 23–24, 29–30; and Frelimo, 17, 22, 94–106; and gender bias of extension agents, 142–43; impact of war on, 18–19, 218; and independence, 184–85; and patriarchal attitudes, 28; and self-empowerment, 24; and sexual division of labor within household, 24–25; and Women's Detachment, 95–96
Working conditions, 91, 92–93, 101, 146–47, 167, 196

Xai-Xai, 132, 133, 139

Zambezia, 78; state farm in, 100
Zambia, 38, 65; refugees in, 79
Zeffenias, Rosa, 193, 198
Zimbabwe, 38, 39, 65, 79–80